RESPECT AND CRIMINAL JUSTICE

CLARENDON STUDIES IN CRIMINOLOGY

Published under the auspices of the Institute of Criminology, University of Cambridge; the Mannheim Centre for the Study of Criminology and Criminal Justice, London School of Economics, and the Centre for Criminology, University of Oxford.

RECENT TITLES IN THIS SERIES:

Respectable Citizens - Shady Practices: The Economic Morality of the Middle Classes
Farrall and Karstedt

Advocates of Humanity: Human Rights NGOs in International Criminal Justice
Lohne

Intimate Crimes: Kidnapping, Gangs, and Trust in Mexico City
Ochoa

Police Community Support Officers: Cultures and Identities within Pluralised Policing
O'Neill

Last Chance for Life: Clemency in Southeast Asian Death Penalty Cases
Pascoe

Police Unlimited: Policing, Migrants, and the Values of Bureaucracy
Mutsaers

Personalizing the State: An Anthropology of Law, Politics, and Welfare in Austerity Britain
Koch

Respect and Criminal Justice

GABRIELLE WATSON

OXFORD
UNIVERSITY PRESS

OXFORD
UNIVERSITY PRESS

Great Clarendon Street, Oxford, OX2 6DP,
United Kingdom

Oxford University Press is a department of the University of Oxford.
It furthers the University's objective of excellence in research, scholarship,
and education by publishing worldwide. Oxford is a registered trade mark of
Oxford University Press in the UK and in certain other countries

First Edition published in 2020

Published in the United States of America by Oxford University Press
198 Madison Avenue, New York, NY 10016, United States of America

British Library Cataloguing in Publication Data
Data available

Library of Congress Control Number: 2019946531

ISBN 978–0–19–883334–5

General Editors' Introduction

The *Clarendon Studies in Criminology* series aims to provide a forum for outstanding theoretical and empirical work in all aspects of criminology and criminal justice, broadly understood. The Editors welcome submissions from established scholars, as well as excellent PhD work. The Series was inaugurated in 1994, with Roger Hood as its first General Editor, following discussions between Oxford University Press and Oxford's Centre for Criminological Research. It is now edited under the auspices of three centres: the Institute of Criminology at the University of Cambridge, the Mannheim Centre for the Study of Criminology and Criminal Justice at the London School of Economics, and the Centre for Criminology at the University of Oxford. Each supplies members of the Editorial Board and, in turn, the Series General Editor or Editors.

This book is refreshing in its outlook and approach to the concept of 'respect' in criminal justice. Drawing on insights from philosophical and social scientific perspectives, Gabrielle Watson offers a deep exploration of 'respect' in the criminal justice context. As the author indicates, the book was prompted by a sense of curiosity as to why criminal justice agencies seemingly overlook or devalue a moral value as fundamental as respect. The focus on policing and imprisonment within the middle chapters of the book point to a 'respect deficit' and illuminate the different ways in which criminal justice practices are limited. The book also amounts to a strong critique of narrow instrumentalism that dominates some current approaches to criminal justice policy. The author also draws attention to some of the limitations of procedural justice without proper recourse to a normative and intrinsic view of 'respect'. The lucid arguments in the book thus take us further than discussions of 'dignity' and 'decency', which have become rather commonplace terms in criminal justice discourse and somewhat empty official words and 'administrative practices'. Indeed, the book makes a normative contribution to debate: it is about values and what matters, and how to 'create and sustain policing and imprisonment practices that are *characterised* – rather than merely *constrained* – by respect'. The concluding chapter addresses the issue of how best to embed respect in criminal justice practice, not in a utopian way, but in a modest and realistic way that makes it all seem possible. It is heartening to see the optimism and principled arguments within the book. We are writing this in the context of news from the current Prime Minister that sentencing is to get tougher and prison regimes harsher. This is somewhat removed from evidence-based policy that scholarship calls for, and at a distance from the author's insightful analysis which concludes that 'respect' in policing and in prisons can ultimately serve legitimacy and effective practice.

As General Editors, we recommend this book. It makes a significant contribution to the field of criminal justice. We have no doubt that this will become an indispensable reference for academics, and we hope that managers in various criminal justice contexts will read it too. The book also deserves wide readership amongst policymakers. We are enthusiastic in welcoming *Respect and Criminal Justice* to the *Clarendon Studies in Criminology* series.

Loraine Gelsthorpe and Kyle Treiber
Institute of Criminology, University of Cambridge
September 2019

Acknowledgements

In preparing this book for publication, I have incurred more debts of gratitude than I can reasonably acknowledge here. Nonetheless, I would like to extend my sincere thanks to those who have supported me with exceptional generosity.

First and foremost, I am deeply indebted to my academic mentors, Ian Loader and Lucia Zedner. They have held my work to exacting standards and offered the kind of written feedback on the manuscript—incisive, demanding, constructive, and thoughtful—one dreams of receiving. I am especially grateful to Ian for his encouragement when a book on 'respect' was little more than a tentative—and overly ambitious—idea, and to Lucia for her unparalleled support as I encountered the academic publication process for the first time.

Nicola Lacey examined the doctoral thesis on which this book is based. I am more grateful than I can say for this special privilege. Nicola encouraged me to be bold as a writer and a thinker, and the central argument of this book is richer and subtler as a direct result of her insights. Rachel Condry placed her faith in the project in its earliest formulation and, with characteristic kindness and generosity, supported it through to its completion. Julian V Roberts explored with me the practical challenges and benefits of embedding respect in criminal justice, and provided mentorship of a calibre one rarely encounters.

I am indebted to my former tutors at Edinburgh, Richard Sparks and Richard Jones, for introducing me to the discipline, nurturing my theoretical interests, and opening up the possibility of an academic career to me. In many ways, this book is the culmination of a process that began under their careful supervision several years ago.

The Economic and Social Research Council generously supported the research, and I completed the book during a blissful period as a Leverhulme Early Career Fellow in the Faculty of Law and Postdoctoral Research Fellow in Law at Christ Church, Oxford. I am incredibly thankful to the Leverhulme Trust and Christ Church for enabling me to hold these Fellowships concurrently and pursue academic work free from financial restrictions. At Christ Church, I had the privilege of testing and refining my ideas on respect with scholars from across the humanities and social sciences. These exchanges strengthened my view that there is much to be gained, personally and intellectually, if only one has the temerity to experiment at the margins of—and sometimes move beyond—one's own disciplinary terrain.

I offer my warm thanks to my students in Criminal Law, Jurisprudence, and the Philosophy of Punishment at Oxford. In bringing fresh perspectives to bear on enduring legal and philosophical issues, they have enriched me, and taught me just as much as I have taught them.

I have presented this research—at various stages of its development—in Oxford, Cambridge, and Berlin. I thank all attendees for their time and willingness to engage both charitably and critically with my work. I am grateful too to the General Editors, Loraine Gelsthorpe and Kyle Treiber, for the opportunity to publish in the Clarendon series; the anonymous reviewers at Oxford University Press for perceptive commentary and critique, and Amy Baker, Kathryn Plunkett, Arokia Anthuvan Rani, and Rebecca Olley for handling the production and marketing of the book.

Jacqueline Thalmann, Curator at the Christ Church Picture Gallery; Sarah Simblet, Fine Artist at Christ Church and The Ruskin School of Art; and Ros Holmes, Historian of Art at Christ Church and Manchester, made numerous suggestions for a cover image, and offered invaluable advice on my final selection.[1]

Four family members—my mother, Bronwen; my sister, Natasha; my late father, George, and my late grandmother, Arma—provided unwavering support, and instilled in me a deep understanding of respect that could not have been gleaned from academic study alone. With love and gratitude, I dedicate this book to them.

Gabrielle Watson
Christ Church, Oxford
August 2019

[1] *Justitia*, the personification of justice within Roman mythology, appears on the cover for two reasons. In standard interpretations, the blindfold is a positive attribute, signifying fairness and impartiality in law. In this book, I claim that when 'respect' is compromised, so too are these legal values. More subtly, the Latin origin of the word 'respect'—*respicere*—is 'to look back at' or 'to look again'. With this etymological consideration in mind, *Justitia* appears on the cover wearing the blindfold (in some depictions—notably, at the Old Bailey—it is left out altogether). The purpose of so doing is to hint at the momentous disregard—even sightlessness—of criminal justice institutions where respect is concerned.

Contents

Table of Cases xi
Table of Legislation xiii
List of Abbreviations xv

Introduction 1

1. In Search of Respect in Criminal Justice 7
   A. Defining Respect 10
   B. Situating Respect 26

Part I On Respect, Policing, and Procedural Justice

2. Procedural Justice and Narrow Instrumentalism 43
   A. Why Respect? 44
   B. The Instrumental Case 46
   C. The Intrinsic Case 60

3. Stop and Search as a Respectful Encounter 68
   A. Critique 70
   B. Beyond Critique 85

Part II On Respect and Prison Life

4. Penal Policies and Institutional Sociologies 97
   A. Institutional Sociologies of the Prison 99
   B. The *Woolf* Report 103
   C. The Shaping of Modern Imprisonment 108
   D. Prisons after *Woolf* 126

5. Respect at Prison Mealtime 132
   A. Historical Context 135
   B. Preparation 139
   C. Consumption 148
   D. Resistance 156

6. Realising Respect 165
A. The Elusive Promise 169
B. Institutional Design 181

Bibliography 193
Index 225

Table of Cases

UNITED KINGDOM CASE LAW

R (Roberts) v Comr of Police of the Metropolis
[2015] UKSC 79. . . . . 75–76 n29, 165 n1, 172–73 n23

UNITED STATES CASE LAW

Borden v Hofmann 974 A2d 1249 (Vt 2009) 138 n31
Prude v Clarke 675 F3d 732 (7th Cir 2012). 138 n31

Table of Legislation

UNITED KINGDOM

Criminal Justice and Public Order Act 1994, s 60 . . 75–76, 75–76 n29, 165
Mental Capacity Act 2005 159
Police and Criminal Evidence Act 1984, Code A (2009), s 3.1 . . . . .165 n1
Police and Criminal Evidence Act 1984, Code A (2014)
s 1—2.11 . . . . 88–89 n82
s 1.1 . . . . 75–76 n31
s 1.4 . . . . 71 n12
s 3.1 . . . . 70–71 n8
s 3.2 . . . . 83 n59
Police and Criminal Evidence Act 1984, Code C (2018), s 1.0 . . . . 44–45 n6
Poor Law Amendment Act 1834 . . . . 135–36 n17
Prisoners (Temporary Discharge for Ill-Health) Act 1913 . . . . 137–38 n24
The Prison Rules 1999, Rule 24(2) 139–40 n34
The Prison Rules 1999, Rule 24(3) 141–42 n45
Vagrancy Act 1824 . . . . 73 n23

List of Abbreviations

BME	Black and minority ethnic
HMP	Her Majesty's Prison
HMYOI	Her Majesty's Young Offender Institution
MQPL	Measuring the Quality of Prison Life
NOMS	National Offender Management Service
PSI	Prison Service Instruction
PSO	Prison Service Order
SQL	Staff Quality of Life

Introduction

Nothing is good ... without respect.

Portia, *The Merchant of Venice* (5.1.2556)

Respect is a value whose importance in contemporary criminal justice many would endorse in principle. It is well established that every person, by virtue of his humanity, has a claim to respect that need not be negotiated and cannot be forfeited. As a means by which to recognise a person's intrinsic worth, respect is attitudinal but also requires a degree of expressive action.[1] Rich and ongoing debates about respect beyond criminal justice—notably, in philosophy and elsewhere in the social sciences—indicate that scholarly interest in respect surpasses disciplinary boundaries, that it is of considerable explanatory and normative scope, and that it matters.[2] It is curious, then, that despite academic reflection on the 'democratic design' of penal institutions in recent decades,[3] respect is more akin to a slogan than a foundational value of criminal justice practice.

[1] See Robin S Dillon, 'Respect' in Edward N Zalta (ed), *The Stanford Encyclopedia of Philosophy* (Stanford University 2018) <http://plato.stanford.edu/entries/respect/> accessed 1 August 2019 (hereafter Dillon, *Stanford Encyclopedia of Philosophy*). See also Thomas E Hill Jr, *Respect, Pluralism, and Justice: Kantian Perspectives* (OUP 2000) and Carla Bagnoli, 'Respect and Membership in the Moral Community' (2007) 10(2) Ethical Theory and Moral Practice 113 (hereafter Bagnoli, 'Respect'). On respect and expressive action, see Richard Sennett, *Respect: The Formation of Character in an Age of Inequality* (Penguin 2004) (hereafter Sennett, *Respect*).

[2] Dillon, *Stanford Encyclopedia of Philosophy* (n 1); Hill, *Respect, Pluralism, and Justice* (n 1); Bagnoli, 'Respect'; Sennett, *Respect* (n 1); and Philippe Bourgois, *In Search of Respect: Selling Crack in El Barrio* (CUP 1995) (hereafter Bourgois, *Respect*).

[3] See, eg, Nicola Lacey, *The Prisoners' Dilemma: Political Economy and Punishment in Contemporary Democracies* (CUP 2008) 13–14 (hereafter Lacey, *Prisoners' Dilemma*).

Respect and Criminal Justice. Gabrielle Watson, Oxford University Press (2020). © Gabrielle Watson.
DOI: 10.1093/oso/9780198833345.001.0001

This book was prompted by an enduring sense of curiosity as to why criminal justice institutions—whether by neglect or intent—collectively overlook or devalue a moral value as fundamental as respect. A good deal of evidence has accumulated to suggest that institutional understandings of respect are reductive, and its role and value are taken for granted. It is notable too that a reductive approach to respect is, on occasion, evident in the academy.[4] The implication is that respect is not an easily accessible object of study because explicit appeals to the idea are—in research and practice—opaque and gestural. But it is precisely because this is so that respect has a strong claim to our attention.

A study of this length cannot provide full coverage of every aspect of the criminal process and its relationship to respect, but it can identify and explore some strong, recurring themes in relation to two—perhaps the most emotionally charged, morally contested, and politically sensitive—of those institutions. The core claim is that, in policing and imprisonment, there is an overwhelming preoccupation with instrumental outcomes, with the result that respect is understood, at best, as a weak side-constraint on the pursuit of those outcomes.[5] The aim is not to discredit the various functions—crime control and order maintenance, for example—that these institutions purport to perform. It is simply to suggest that these instrumental concerns are held in their proper place. At present, a clear orientation towards outcomes—and the means used to achieve those outcomes—erodes respect, and narrows its range and significance.

The book is organised as follows. Chapter 1 attends to the deceptively simple question: what is respect? This entails a detailed examination of the literature on respect in philosophy and elsewhere in the social sciences. Having explored what respect means in general terms—though this is hotly contested—the

[4] See, in particular, chs 2 and 4.

[5] The term 'side-constraint' is attributed to Nozick in Robert Nozick, *Anarchy, State, and Utopia* (Basic Books 1974) 28–29. On side-constraints in criminal justice, see RA Duff and Sandra Marshall, 'Benefits, Burdens and Responsibilities: Some Ethical Dimensions of Situational Crime Prevention' in Andrew von Hirsch, David Garland, and Alison Wakefield (eds), *Ethical and Social Perspectives on Situational Crime Prevention* (Hart 2000) 19–21 and John Braithwaite and Philip Pettit, *Not Just Deserts: A Republican Theory of Criminal Justice* (Clarendon Press 1990) 26–36.

chapter sketches and filters the most prominent classic and contemporary works into an understanding of respect for criminal justice.[6] It then delineates the limits of respect and clarifies its relationship to a cluster of related values, namely, dignity, esteem, recognition, decency, and status. There are distinctions that can and should usefully be made between these values but, as will soon become clear, they are used interchangeably—and ill-advisedly—in academic research and official discourse and even, on occasion, in order to promote a weak approximation of respect.[7]

The next task is to situate respect in criminal justice in contextual and methodological terms. Much of this work must be justificatory both of respect and of my own methodological choices. Having explained what respect means and why it has been selected for examination, the chapter considers why policing and imprisonment have been selected as contexts for that examination and how an interpretive approach offers a means by which to conduct that examination.[8] But the intention behind this chapter is not only to establish that the study is feasible at all. It is also to anticipate the challenges involved in a study that aims to move criminal justice scholarship into a new and largely unexplored terrain.

Chapters 2, 3, 4, and 5 critically examine what I term the 'respect deficit' in policing and imprisonment. Respect shows great flexibility as a concept of critical enquiry for criminal justice. It has a striking capacity to sharpen our critique of a diverse range of theories, policies, and practices, in this book, with reference to procedural justice (chapter 2), stop and search (chapter 3),

[6] See, eg, n 1 and n 2.

[7] In policing, see, eg, College of Policing, *Code of Ethics: A Code of Practice for the Principles and Standards of Professional Behaviour for the Policing Profession of England and Wales* (College of Policing 2014) . See, in particular, s 2.1 Policing principles. *Respect*. 'You treat everyone with respect' and s 3.1.2 Standards of professional behaviour, *Authority, respect and courtesy*. Police officers must 'act with self-control and tolerance, treating members of the public with respect and courtesy' and police officers must 'remain composed and respectful.' In prisons, see, eg, National Offender Management Service, *Annual Report and Accounts 2016–2017* (National Offender Management Service 2017) 3, 'In delivering offender management services, we will … treat offenders with decency and respect.'

[8] See, eg, Peregrine Schwartz-Shea and Dvora Yanow, *Interpretive Research Design: Concepts and Processes* (Routledge 2012) and Michael Walzer, *Interpretation and Social Criticism* (Harvard University Press 1993).

penal policies and institutional sociologies (chapter 4), and prison mealtime (chapter 5).[9] It swiftly emerges that these practices are merely *constrained* and not *characterised* by respect. Respect is understood only in terms of its basic capacity to set weak ethical constraints on instrumental outcomes, and there is some resistance towards framing respect in more robust terms, whereby it could infuse the very foundational values on which these practices are based.

When an institution treats respect as a weak side-constraint on instrumental outcomes, its practices must be organised according to—and be shown to be minimally consistent with—the value. But the strategy adopted by both institutions for achieving minimal consistency with respect leaves much to be desired. Both institutions appeal to the word 'respect'—relying on its inclusive ethos in official discourse when it is expedient to do so—but rarely and only superficially address the prior question of *what it is* to respect and be respected.[10] And so respect is reduced to the status of a keyword or slogan. As with keywords and slogans more generally, the aim is not only to make a declarative statement or cultivate a shared purpose within an institution but also to provide a shortcut through the challenge of communicating a complex idea. In this way, such empty appeals to respect can distort as much as they communicate.[11] When there is a lack of specificity in understanding and giving effect to respect, it does much to magnify the status inequalities that have come to define policing and imprisonment. It also shows scant regard for the fact that respect—or lack thereof—tends to be felt more keenly by ethnic minority groups

[9] The four substantive chapters on policing and imprisonment are organised thematically and symmetrically. On both occasions, the critique of respect shifts from the general to the particular; from an examination of a large body of literature to the isolation of a discrete institutional practice (procedural justice to stop and search; institutional sociologies of the prison to prison mealtime).

[10] See, eg, n 7.

[11] On keywords, see Raymond Williams, *Keywords: A Vocabulary of Culture and Society* (Fontana 1976) and Tony Bennett, Lawrence Grossberg, and Meaghan Morris (eds), *New Keywords: A Revised Vocabulary of Culture and Society* (Blackwell 2005). On slogans, see Ira Sharkansky, 'Slogan as Policy' (2002) 4(1) Journal of Comparative Policy Analysis: Research and Practice 75 and Robert E Denton Jr, 'The Rhetorical Functions of Slogans: Classifications and Characteristics' (1980) 28(2) Communication Quarterly 10.

and those whose sense of belonging and social possibility in society are precarious.[12]

The principal objective of the book—extending through chapters 1 to 5—is to foreground respect, easily approved yet scarcely examined within policing and imprisonment, refine it, and then redirect it in such a way that prompts deeper reflection about the manner in which these practices are conducted.[13] Crewe has observed that the 'changed texture' of modern imprisonment demands a new conceptual vocabulary to make sense of it.[14] An analogous argument could be advanced in relation to the changed texture of modern policing, and I hope to show that respect has much to offer.

While respect is clearly of analytic value, it is also a matter of material significance with immediate implications for policing and imprisonment reform. Both institutions would be well advised to prioritise respect as a means by which to confer value upon others, and reflect seriously on its meaning, possibilities, and limits. In prisons, there might even be scope to give expression to the 'democratic intuition' of reintegrative and inclusionary punishment that Lacey envisages.[15]

How can these institutions give effect to respect? It is a precious commodity to be carefully cultivated. The dominant institutional approach to respect would prove difficult to correct, sustained as it is by superficial understandings, convenient fictions, and a preoccupation with outcomes. One such convenient fiction is to be found in the Code of Ethics published by the College of Policing. 'Courtesy and respect' are delineated as key standards of professional behaviour and respecting a citizen's legal rights is proposed as a means by which to maintain this standard. However, this act is distinct from respect *per se*. Respect for a citizen's legal rights

[12] See Bourgois, *Respect* (n 2). On ontological security, see Ian Loader and Neil Walker, *Civilizing Security* (CUP 2007).

[13] Lacey engages in a comparable interpretive project: Lacey, *Prisoners' Dilemma* (n 3).

[14] Ben Crewe, 'Depth, Weight, Tightness: Revisiting the Pains of Imprisonment' (2011) 13(5) Punishment & Society 509, 510.

[15] Lacey, *Prisoners' Dilemma* (n 3) 16–17. On the importance of criminal punishment as a means by which to take individuals seriously and to attest to their being basically respected, see Avishai Margalit, *The Decent Society* (Harvard University Press 1996). See, in particular, ch 2, 'Justifying respect' and ch 4, 'Putting Social Institutions to the Test'.

could easily have been phrased as upholding or enforcing their rights, in which case it would have very little to do with respect.[16]

It is important not to overstate the reformative potential of respect or inflate expectations of what criminal justice institutions can realistically accomplish. Nonetheless, subject to political and economic constraints, there is scope to re-evaluate respect in practice. Respect need not be utopian. It simply requires a degree of mutual understanding when it is owed to, called for, deserved, elicited, or claimed by another.[17] The concluding chapter addresses the issue of how best to embed respect in criminal justice practice. With a sense of modest realism, it sets out those challenges in detail—and envisages the advances that could be made—in inscribing respectful relations between state and subject.[18]

[16] College of Policing, *Code of Ethics* (n 7).

[17] On the reciprocal nature of respect, see, eg, Sennett, *Respect* (n 1).

[18] On the state and its citizens as 'respecting agents', see Peter Balint, 'Respect Relationships in Diverse Societies' (2006) 12(1) Res Publica 35. The usual caveats apply in relation to the relevance of intellectual thought to criminal justice policy reform: see Roger Hood, 'Criminology and Penal Change: A Case Study of the Nature and Impact of Some Recent Advice to Governments' in Roger Hood (ed), *Crime, Criminology and Public Policy: Essays in Honour of Sir Leon Radzinowicz* (Heinemann Educational 1974); David Garland and Richard Sparks, 'Criminology, Social Theory and the Challenge of our Times' in David Garland and Richard Sparks (eds), *Criminology and Social Theory* (Clarendon Press 2000); Lucia Zedner, 'Useful Knowledge? Debating the Role of Criminology in Post-war Britain' in Lucia Zedner and Andrew Ashworth (eds), *The Criminological Foundations of Penal Policy: Essays in Honour of Roger Hood* (OUP 2003); Kevin D Haggerty, 'Displaced Expertise: Three Constraints on the Policy-relevance of Criminological Thought' (2004) 8(2) Theoretical Criminology 211; and Ian Loader and Richard Sparks, *Public Criminology?* (Routledge 2010).

1

In Search of Respect in Criminal Justice

In criminal justice—as in many academic disciplines—some ideas are deemed worthier of critical reflection than others. Some ideas are absorbed and brought into focus, while others remain implicit and unelaborated. These ideas do not necessarily remain implicit by reason of their complexity, irrelevance, or incompatibility with the criminal justice agendas of the day. Instead, the process can be passive, whereby some ideas are simply treated as self-evident. On this view, it is easy to imagine how a value such as respect can come to inform a diverse range of theories, policies, and practices but for there to be long and sustained periods of silence on its precise meaning and significance.[1]

One compelling example of this passive process—described by Polanyi as 'tacit knowing'—is the manner in which respect has remained on the periphery of criminal justice theory, policy, and practice, drifting in and out of sight.[2] A good deal of evidence has accumulated to suggest that at two defining stages in the criminal process—policing and imprisonment—understandings of respect are reductive and its role and value are taken for granted.[3] And

[1] On the passive process of 'backgrounding' knowledge, see Mary Douglas, *Implicit Meanings: Selected Essays in Anthropology* (Routledge 1975).

[2] On 'tacit knowing', see Michael Polanyi, *The Tacit Dimension* (Doubleday 1966) ch 1.

[3] In policing, see, eg, College of Policing, *Code of Ethics: A Code of Practice for the Principles and Standards of Professional Behaviour for the Policing Profession of England and Wales* (College of Policing 2014). See, in particular, s 2.1 Policing principles. *Respect*. 'You treat everyone with respect' and s 3.1.2 Standards of professional behaviour, *Authority, respect and courtesy*. Police officers must 'act with self-control and tolerance, treating members of the public with respect and courtesy' and police officers must 'remain composed and respectful'. In prisons, see, eg, National Offender Management Service, *Annual Report and Accounts*

Respect and Criminal Justice. Gabrielle Watson, Oxford University Press (2020). © Gabrielle Watson.
DOI: 10.1093/oso/9780198833345.001.0001

while the tendency to consign respect to the background is primarily evident in criminal justice practice, on occasion, it is also reflected in academic discourse.[4]

There is a notable exception to this tendency to overlook respect. Over a decade ago, the word 'respect'—if not a fully developed idea of what it might entail—came to occupy the political foreground in the form of the Respect Agenda advanced by Blair's Labour government.[5] The agenda linked anti-social behaviour and incivility to a weakened sense of community. It was envisaged that a model of active social democratic citizenship—informed by greater respect for and between citizens—would effectively correct these behaviours. Less well documented, however, is that the government approached the task of cultivating respect between state and citizen with cavalier detachment. The agenda did not adequately define respect. Instead, it claimed that respect—in forming part of our everyday social relations—is 'an expression of something people intuitively understand'.[6] In other words, respect was posited as a kind of code or 'lay morality' to which citizens had already subscribed. It was also unclear as to whether—according to the agenda—respect was to be 'earned' or extended to all citizens solely by virtue of their humanity. And despite a convenient gloss on the idea of respect itself, the government's rhetoric of 'conform or face the consequences' ensured that the liberal vocabulary of respect was used divisively.[7] In this way, the

2016–2017 (National Offender Management Service 2017) 3, 'In delivering offender management services, we will … treat offenders with decency and respect.'

[4] On criminal justice in the 'academic world' and the 'applied domain', see Stanley Cohen, *Against Criminology* (Transaction Publishers 1988) 67.

[5] See, eg, Home Office (Respect Task Force), *Respect Action Plan* (Home Office/The National Archives 2006) (hereafter Home Office, *Respect Action Plan*). For academic commentary on the agenda, see Elizabeth Burney, *Making People Behave: Anti-Social Behaviour, Politics and Policy* (Willan 2005) and Andrew Millie (ed), *Securing Respect: Behavioural Expectations and Anti-Social Behaviour in the UK* (Policy Press 2009) (hereafter Millie (ed), *Securing Respect*).

[6] Home Office, *Respect Action Plan* (n 5) 5. On respect as a form of 'lay morality', see Andrew Sayer, 'Class, Moral Worth and Recognition' (2005) 39(4) Sociology 947. On the primacy of respect, and the search for standards that allow us to justify our conduct to each other, see Thomas M Scanlon, *What We Owe to Each Other* (Belknap Press of Harvard University Press 1998) (hereafter Scanlon, *What We Owe to Each Other*).

[7] On the role of language in promoting punitive sentiments in criminal justice, see Michael J Coyle, *Talking Criminal Justice: Language and the Just Society* (Routledge 2013). On counterproductive efforts to 'enforce' respect during this

agenda was concerned less with the meaning of respect and more with the subtler political and social control tasks that the word itself could perform.

While the agenda drew inspiration from the work of Richard Sennett, Sennett maintained that its vision was far from progressive, despite its appropriation of—and *prima facie* commitment to—respect. For Sennett, the political focus should have been directed away from the low-grade disorder of a minority and towards the redesign of public institutions which serve all citizens.[8] Instead, the agenda was defined by a clear preoccupation with the 'worth' of citizens at a time when some citizens were made to feel worth less than others.[9]

This book offers the first sustained examination of respect and criminal justice, extending a handful of shorter contributions on this theme.[10] Its principal aim is to examine the merits of respect as an intellectual resource and, in particular, as a means by which to sharpen our critique of policing and imprisonment. This is an

period, see Jon Bannister, Nick Fyfe, and Ade Kearns, 'Respectable or Respectful? (In)civility and the City' (2006) 43(5/6) Urban Studies 919. On respect as a rhetorical device in political discourse, see Sune Lægaard, 'What Does "Respect for Difference" Mean?' in Peter Balint and Sophie Guérard de Latour (eds), *Liberal Multiculturalism and the Fair Terms of Integration* (Palgrave Macmillan 2013) (hereafter Lægaard, 'Respect for Difference').

[8] Richard Sennett, 'Views on Respect' BBC News (9 January 2006) <http://news.bbc.co.uk/1/hi/uk/4589616.stm> accessed 1 August 2019.
See also Petersilia, reviewing Gottschalk, on 'tired, liberal arguments' about changing conditions rather than changing the system that reacts to those conditions: Joan Petersilia, 'Review of Marie Gottschalk, *Caught: The Prison State and the Lockdown of American Politics* (2015)' (2017) 19(5) Punishment & Society 625, 630.

[9] See, eg, Peter Squires, '"You lookin' at me?" Discourses of Respect and Disrespect, Identity and Violence' in Millie (ed), *Securing Respect* (n 5).

[10] See Susie Hulley, Alison Liebling, and Ben Crewe, 'Respect in Prisons: Prisoners' Experiences of Respect in Public and Private Sector Prisons' (2012) 12(1) Criminology & Criminal Justice 3 (hereafter Hulley et al, 'Respect in Prisons'); Michelle Butler and Deborah H Drake, 'Reconsidering Respect: Its Role in Her Majesty's Prison Service' (2007) 46(2) The Howard Journal of Criminal Justice 115; Michelle Butler, 'What are you Looking at? Prisoner Confrontations and the Search for Respect' (2008) 48(6) The British Journal of Criminology 856; Andrew Millie, *Philosophical Criminology* (Policy Press 2016) ch 7, 'Respect', and Lindsay Farmer, 'Disgust, Respect, and the Criminalization of the Offence' in Rowan Cruft, Matthew H Kramer, and Mark R Reiff (eds), *Crime, Punishment, and Responsibility: The Jurisprudence of Antony Duff* (OUP 2011).

ambitious task, not least because it involves a challenge to the definitional self-evidence of respect to which criminal justice scholars and practitioners routinely subscribe.[11]

This chapter pursues three distinct lines of enquiry and reflection. What is respect? The first task is to attend to this deceptively simple question. In so doing, the chapter assembles materials on respect from philosophy and elsewhere in the social sciences. Second, having explored what respect means in general terms—though this is hotly contested—the chapter sketches and filters the most prominent classic and contemporary works into an understanding of respect for criminal justice. By initiating a dialogue with related disciplines in this way, the aim is to build a strong conceptual platform from which to engage with the substantive material on policing and imprisonment in subsequent chapters. Third, the chapter situates respect in criminal justice in contextual and methodological terms. Much of this work must be justificatory both of respect and of my own methodological choices. Having explained in some detail what respect means and why it has been selected for examination, the chapter considers why policing and imprisonment have been selected as contexts for that examination, and how an interpretive approach offers a means by which to conduct that examination.[12]

A. Defining Respect

1. The concept in cognate disciplines

Respect is an open-textured and continually shifting notion. While philosophers and social scientists have been highly attuned to its role, value, and significance, these scholars have routinely posed diverse questions of respect. It is notable too that members of the same discipline have perceived respect differently and pursued markedly different lines of enquiry.[13] This ambivalence—most

[11] There is a precedent for work of this kind in political theory: see Robert L Oprisko, *Honor: A Phenomenology* (Routledge 2012).

[12] See, eg, Peregrine Schwartz-Shea and Dvora Yanow, *Interpretive Research Design: Concepts and Processes* (Routledge 2012) (hereafter Schwartz-Shea and Yanow, *Interpretive Research Design*) and Michael Walzer, *Interpretation and Social Criticism* (Harvard University Press 1993).

[13] Robin S Dillon, 'Respect' in Edward N Zalta (ed), *The Stanford Encyclopedia of Philosophy* (Stanford University 2018) <http://plato.stanford.edu/entries/respect/> accessed 1 August 2019 (hereafter Dillon, 'Respect'). See also Carla

easily discernible in philosophy—produces divergent understandings of the constitutive elements and qualities of respect as well as conflicting answers to fundamental questions such as when and on what grounds we owe and are entitled to respect. In this way, respect is a striking example of a word that has 'a core of settled meaning' and 'a penumbra of non-focal meaning over which there is disagreement'.[14]

That said, it is possible to attribute a broad set of research interests to philosophers and social scientists respectively. Philosophers have been concerned primarily to analyse the conceptual structure of respect and set out the standards by which it is to be afforded, experienced, or evaluated. They have also demonstrated a sustained interest in the relationship between respect and a cluster of related concepts, namely, dignity, esteem, recognition, decency, and status.[15] Meanwhile, social scientists have investigated and framed respect in terms of subjective beliefs and experiences having been prompted, we might assume, by a shared methodological interest in ethnography and participant observation.[16]

Bagnoli, 'Respect and Membership in the Moral Community' (2007) 10(2) Ethical Theory and Moral Practice 113 and Stephen D Hudson, 'The Nature of Respect' (1980) 6(1) Social Theory and Practice 69.

[14] Nicola Lacey, *The Prisoners' Dilemma: Political Economy and Punishment in Contemporary Democracies* (CUP 2008) 6 (hereafter Lacey, *Prisoners' Dilemma*).

[15] See, eg, Dillon, 'Respect' (n 13); Richard Stith, 'The Priority of Respect: How Our Common Humanity Can Ground Our Individual Dignity' (2004) 44(2) International Philosophical Quarterly 165; Jan Narveson, 'Race, Social Identity, Human Dignity: Respect for Individuals' (2000) 16 Social Philosophy Today 159; Allen W Wood, 'Respect and Recognition' in John Skorupski (ed), *The Routledge Companion to Ethics* (Routledge 2010) (hereafter Wood, 'Respect and Recognition'); Charles Taylor, 'The Politics of Recognition' in Amy Gutmann (ed), *Multiculturalism: Examining the Politics of Recognition* (Princeton University Press 1992) (hereafter Taylor, 'Politics of Recognition'); James W Boettcher, 'Respect, Recognition, and Public Reason' (2007) 33(2) Social Theory and Practice 223; and Colin Bird, 'Status, Identity, and Respect' (2004) 32(2) Political Theory 207 (hereafter, Bird, 'Status, Identity, and Respect').

[16] Richard Sennett, *Respect: The Formation of Character in an Age of Inequality* (Penguin 2004) (hereafter Sennett, *Respect*) and Philippe Bourgois, *In Search of Respect: Selling Crack in El Barrio* (CUP 1995) (hereafter Bourgois, *Respect*).

2. Respect and philosophy

The fluidity and complexity of respect might go some way to explaining why criminal justice scholars and practitioners—often pragmatic, empirically motivated, or reformist in their approaches—have traditionally resisted it.[17] This ambivalence, however, is no reason to direct our attention away from philosophical work on respect. Scholars including Ashworth and Zedner have referred to the 'obvious relevance' of philosophy, insisting that its normative arguments can and should flow seamlessly into criminal justice debates.[18]

The Kantian notion of respect for persons provides an important starting point for philosophical discussions of respect.[19] Much contemporary philosophical work focuses either on working out Kantian answers to issues concerning the grounds and scope of respect for persons or on critiquing the account and developing alternatives.[20] The two most prominent social scientific accounts of respect are also informed by Kantian reasoning, even if they only implicitly acknowledge its foundational importance.[21]

The essence of Kant's account is that all persons are worthy of respect by virtue of their autonomy and rationality. Respect,

[17] On the reception of criminological knowledge, see Ian Loader and Richard Sparks, *Public Criminology?* (Routledge 2010) 120.

[18] Lucia Zedner, 'Pre-Crime or Post-Criminology?' (2007) 11(2) Theoretical Criminology 261, 273 and Andrew Ashworth, 'Criminal Justice, Not Criminology?' in Mary Bosworth and Carolyn Hoyle (eds), *What Is Criminology?* (OUP 2011). See also Richard Quinney, 'Criminology as Moral Philosophy, Criminologist as Witness' in Darnell F Hawkins, Samuel L Myers Jr, and Randolph N Stone (eds), *Crime Control and Social Justice: The Delicate Balance* (Praeger 2003).

[19] Mary J Gregor and Jens Timmermann (eds), Immanuel Kant, *Groundwork of the Metaphysics of Morals* (CUP 2012) published originally as Immanuel Kant, *Grundlegung zur Metaphysik der Sitten* (Johann Friedrich Hartknoch 1785) (hereafter Kant, *Groundwork*) and Mary J Gregor (ed), Immanuel Kant, *The Metaphysics of Morals* (CUP 2017) published originally as Immanuel Kant, *Die Metaphysik der Sitten* (Friedrich Nicolovius 1798–1803) (hereafter Kant, *Metaphysics of Morals*).

[20] See, eg, Thomas E Hill Jr, *Respect, Pluralism, and Justice: Kantian Perspectives* (OUP 2000) (hereafter Hill, *Respect, Pluralism, and Justice*); Dillon, 'Respect' (n 13) s 2.2 *Kant's Account of Respect for Persons* and Robin S Dillon, 'Respect: A Philosophical Perspective' (2007) 38(2) Gruppendynamik und Organisationsberatung 201, 208 (hereafter Dillon, 'Respect: A Philosophical Perspective').

[21] Sennett, *Respect* (n 16) and Bourgois, *Respect* (n 16).

in this sense, is a moral right that includes an obligation not to treat others instrumentally or 'as a means'.[22] Kant holds that all and only persons are 'ends in themselves', which is to say that they have an intrinsic and incomparable moral worth called dignity. Respect is considered to be the only suitable acknowledgement of an individual's dignity. As such, we have an absolutely binding moral obligation to respect each other and ensure that it is evidenced in both our attitudes and conduct. In recent decades, philosophers have identified this form of respect as 'moral recognition respect'.[23]

There are two clear implications of the Kantian account of moral recognition respect. First, when all individuals are equal in dignity and moral status, each not only has a right to respect but a duty to respect themselves. Second, the respect-worthiness of individuals is not conditional on how well or badly those capacities are exercised or whether they act morally or have morally good characters. Dignity implies absolute worth. It cannot be diminished or lost through wrong actions or bad character, nor can it be increased through virtue or morally right action. Moral recognition respect is not something that we earn or fail to earn but something that we are owed unreservedly as rational human beings.[24]

Notwithstanding its dominance within Liberalism, the Kantian account has attracted considerable commentary and critique. Is rational autonomy what gives individuals the unconditional claim to moral recognition respect? Some philosophers suggest that this is too thin a view of what matters to individuals because it overlooks the moral importance of individual qualities and attributes.[25] Rather than disregarding what distinguishes one person from another, some commentators argue that respect should involve attending to each person *as an individual*. In other words, respect should involve valuing difference as well as sameness and interdependence as well as independence.[26] Others defend the

[22] Hill, *Respect, Pluralism, and Justice* (n 20) and Dillon, 'Respect' (n 13) s 2.2 *Kant's Account of Respect for Persons*.

[23] See, eg, Dillon, 'Respect' (n 13).

[24] ibid.

[25] See, eg, Robin S Dillon, 'Respect and Care: Toward Moral Integration' (1992) 22(1) Canadian Journal of Philosophy 105.

[26] Hill, *Respect, Pluralism, and Justice* (n 20) and Taylor, 'Politics of Recognition' (n 15).

Kantian account by noting that while difference and identity are appropriate objects of other forms of consideration, showing respect for these attributes would inevitably introduce an element of hierarchical discrimination that is antithetical to the equality among persons that Kant's idea of respect for persons is supposed to express.[27]

Furthermore, some contemporary—and decidedly less liberal—accounts have questioned the Kantian notion that all persons are owed respect regardless of their conduct or the character traits that they display. On this view, moral recognition respect should be forfeitable. Some scholars contend, for example, that those who commit crimes remorselessly warrant less—or no—respect.[28] To borrow Margalit's terms, the claim is that these criminals have 'desecrated their humanity': the very nature that was to serve as a source of respect in the first place.[29] Other accounts remain consistent with pure Kantian reasoning in insisting that respect cannot be surrendered. Duff claims, for example, that convicted offenders remain both humans and citizens worthy of respect, and must, in punishment, be treated as such.[30] An important implication of this view is that excessively harsh forms of punishment are automatically ruled out on moral grounds.[31]

Philosophers credit Darwall with developing the leading contemporary philosophical account of respect. Extending and modifying the Kantian perspective, he proposes two kinds of respect, which he terms 'appraisal respect' and 'recognition respect'.[32]

[27] Bird, 'Status, Identity, and Respect' (n 15).

[28] On the merits and limits of this argument, see David Middleton, 'Introduction' Special Issue on Respect (2006) 12(1) Res Publica 1 and Hill, *Respect, Pluralism, and Justice* (n 20) ch 4.

[29] Avishai Margalit, *The Decent Society* (Harvard University Press 1996) 64 (hereafter Margalit, *Decent Society*).

[30] RA Duff, 'A Criminal Law for Citizens' (2010) 14(3) Theoretical Criminology 293 and RA Duff, 'Citizens (Even) in Prison' (2014) 43(1) Netherlands Journal of Legal Philosophy 3 (hereafter Duff, 'Citizens'). See also Bottoms and Tankebe, for whom 'right relationships are those that … respect the prisoner as a human being, take account of his welfare needs, and so on, yet at the same time uphold and maintain the societal norms under which it was deemed necessary to require the individual to serve a prison sentence': Anthony Bottoms and Justice Tankebe, 'Beyond Procedural Justice: A Dialogic Approach to Legitimacy in Criminal Justice' (2012) 102(1) The Journal of Criminal Law and Criminology 119, 156.

[31] Dillon, 'Respect: A Philosophical Perspective' (n 20).

[32] Stephen L Darwall, 'Two Kinds of Respect' (1977) 88(1) Ethics 36 (hereafter Darwall, 'Two Kinds of Respect').

Appraisal respect is a positive evaluation of a person's character or conduct. Notably, this form of respect is a matter of degree: we can respect someone more or less highly and respect one person more highly than another. The implication is that appraisal respect can result in a negative assessment of an individual or his traits: we can respect a person's talents, for example, yet regard him as far from a moral exemplar.[33] Originally, Darwall distinguished appraisal respect from esteem, describing esteem as another attitude of positive assessment whose wider basis includes any features in virtue of which we can think well of someone, though commentators tended to treat them as synonymous. Darwall later conceded this point and identified appraisal respect as a form of esteem.[34]

Recognition respect, by contrast, requires us to pay close attention to questions of standing and authority. We show recognition respect when we give due regard to some fact about an object and regulate both our attitudes and conduct on the basis of—or by constraints derived from—that fact. Worthy objects of recognition respect include laws, social institutions, someone's feelings, the personas individuals adopt in different contexts, and persons as such.[35]

There is scope, of course, to question the sharpness of Darwall's analytic distinction since, for some commentators, appraisal respect *presupposes* recognition respect. It involves recognising that a person, for example, has a certain kind of standing and authority and then appraises that person or his qualities as good or bad in relation to that standing and authority.[36]

In *Taking Rights Seriously*, Dworkin defends the view that society owes its members equal resources and, in so doing, develops a leading perspective on respect.[37] In objecting to the commonly

[33] Dillon, 'Respect' (n 13).

[34] Stephen L Darwall, 'Respect and the Second-Person Standpoint' (2004) 78(2) Proceedings and Addresses of the American Philosophical Association 43.

[35] Darwall, 'Two Kinds of Respect' (n 32).

[36] See, eg, Bennett W Helm, *Communities of Respect: Grounding Responsibility, Authority, and Dignity* (Oxford University Press 2017) (hereafter Helm, *Communities of Respect*).

[37] Ronald Dworkin, *Taking Rights Seriously* (Duckworth 1977) (hereafter Dworkin, *Taking Rights Seriously*). See also Uwe Steinhoff (ed), *Do All Persons Have Equal Moral Worth? On 'Basic Equality' and Equal Respect and Concern* (OUP 2015) (hereafter Steinhoff, *Equal Moral Worth*) and Jan Narveson (ed), *Respecting Persons in Theory and Practice: Essays on Moral and Political Philosophy* (Rowman & Littlefield 2002) 59–60. On the relevance of Dworkin's

held belief that liberty and equality are fundamentally opposed to one another, he suggests that rights to various liberties are themselves derived from a form of a right to equality, which he calls the 'right to equal concern and respect'. To treat people with concern is to treat them as 'capable of suffering and frustration' and to treat them with respect is to treat them 'as capable of forming ... intelligent conceptions' of how to act.[38] Dworkin elaborates further by suggesting that the abstract right to equal concern and respect can refer either to the right to be treated as an equal or the right to equal treatment. The former is 'the right to equal concern and respect in the political decision about how goods, opportunities, [and liberties] are to be distributed',[39] while the latter is a right to the same distribution of goods, opportunities, or liberties as anyone else. The former is primary and only sometimes implies the latter.

For Dworkin, the right to equal concern and respect is 'axiomatic'.[40] It is also of a fundamentally different character from other rights, in part, because it is possible to derive a collective goal from that axiomatic basic right.[41] Dworkin describes the method by which individual rights are derived from the basic right. Individuals have a basic right that institutions responsible for making political decisions treat them fairly and equally. Institutions are justified if they promote this basic right. However, these institutions might not be self-correcting and so individual rights are required in order to rectify any strong tendencies to distribute goods, liberties, and opportunities in such a way that violates the basic right. In other words, individual rights function as a corrective to those collective goals which are considered defective—for example, because they are not egalitarian or fair—thus preserving equal concern and respect.[42]

right to equal concern and respect to criminal justice, and especially to debates about mass incarceration, see Albert W Dzur, Ian Loader, and Richard Sparks (eds), *Democratic Theory and Mass Incarceration* (OUP 2016) (hereafter Dzur et al, *Democratic Theory and Mass Incarceration*).

[38] Dworkin, *Taking Rights Seriously* (n 37) 272.

[39] ibid 237.

[40] ibid xii.

[41] ibid, Introduction.

[42] Dworkin, *Taking Rights Seriously* (n 37).

Aside from the celebrated accounts of respect developed by Kant, Darwall, and Dworkin, it is possible to extrapolate some recurring themes from the broader philosophical literature on respect. First, there is a broad consensus among philosophers that respect has both a behavioural and an attitudinal component.[43] Respect can inhere, for example, in the act of obeying, praising, or emulating others, not violating or interfering with them, assisting them, protecting them, leaving them alone, talking about them only in ways that reflect their worth or status, and objecting to others' disrespectful talk. However, it is routinely—and mistakenly—assumed by those outside of philosophy that respect is exhausted by reference to the kinds of acts it requires or prescribes.[44] Respect is also—and perhaps more centrally—about having or expressing a certain attitude towards the object of respect. As an attitude, respect has both cognitive and affective dimensions. It can involve certain beliefs, perceptions, and judgements but it can also prompt emotional responses, feelings, and ways of experiencing.[45] In this way, respect can be more or less rational.[46]

Second, as its Latin root, *respicere*—'to look back at' or 'to look again'—indicates, respect is responsive and relational.[47] We experience the object of respect as constraining our attitudes and actions and we respond by acknowledging its claim to our attention.[48] Most philosophers agree that to respect another is to value his intrinsic worth as independent of our antecedent interests and perhaps even in conflict with them. In this way, it is possible to respect someone's opinion on a given matter

[43] See, eg, Dillon, 'Respect' (n 13).

[44] ibid.

[45] Sarah Buss, 'Respect for Persons' (1999) 29(4) Canadian Journal of Philosophy 517.

[46] See, however, the philosophical literature on rationality and the emotions, in particular, de Sousa's work which questions the widespread assumption that rationality and emotion are opposed. Instead, he makes the case that emotions are a special kind of perception and that they have an important role to play in rational beliefs and decision-making processes: Ronald de Sousa, *The Rationality of Emotion* (MIT Press 1987).

[47] The prefix 're', while referring to the act of *returning the look* of another, could also be treated as an intensifier, implying prolongation or persistence of attention: Wood, 'Respect and Recognition' (n 15).

[48] See, eg, Wood, 'Respect and Recognition' (n 15) and Stephen L Darwall, *The Second-Person Standpoint: Morality, Respect, and Accountability* (Harvard University Press 2006).

without necessarily approving of or agreeing with it.[49] By contrast, to ignore, disregard, or be oblivious to something, to dismiss it lightly or carelessly, or to misinterpret it negligently is to disrespect it.[50]

Third—as discussed in relation to Kant and Darwall—a reading of the broader literature reveals that the grounds on which respect is owed is a recurring—though contested—issue. For scholars committed to traditional Kantian reasoning, respect is a fundamental moral right and thus owed to everyone indiscriminately.[51] For those inclined towards a contemporary reworking of the Kantian account, respect is afforded on a selective basis and there is scope for it to be earned or lost.[52]

These ideas provide a point of entry into the ongoing debate on respect and equality. Philosophers debate what it means to recognise another as equal—or what equal respect demands—and, in so doing, draw a distinction between *respect of sameness* and *respect of difference*.[53] *Respect of sameness* is a conventional notion—considered vital for a just society—with a powerful pedigree from Kant onwards. As will now be clear, it denotes that all individuals are owed respect—or have equal moral standing—solely by virtue of their personhood.[54] A key question to arise, however, is whether treating others with respect must *always* entail equal treatment on this basis. For some philosophers, personhood is not the only or even the most important general category and there is scope to supplement it with a form of respect for—as opposed to mere toleration or dismissal of—difference, diversity, and individual or group identities.[55] In some cases, the argument is a bolder one, namely, that it makes no sense to ground respect in a general—even 'empty'—category such as personhood and that

[49] Dillon, 'Respect' (n 13).

[50] ibid.

[51] Hill, *Respect, Pluralism, and Justice* (n 20).

[52] Dillon, 'Respect: A Philosophical Perspective' (n 20) 208 and Robert L Arrington, 'On Respect' (1978) 12(1) The Journal of Value Inquiry 1.

[53] Steinhoff, *Equal Moral Worth* (n 37); Lægaard, 'Respect for Difference' (n 7), and Peter Balint, 'Respect Relationships in Diverse Societies' (2006) 12(1) Res Publica 35 (hereafter Balint, 'Respect Relationships').

[54] Steinhoff, *Equal Moral Worth* (n 37) and Lægaard, 'Respect for Difference' (n 7). See also Margalit, *Decent Society* (n 29) 44.

[55] Balint, 'Respect Relationships' (n 53).

any substantive notion of respect can *only* be tied to individual or collective differences. On this view, *respect of sameness*—in failing to deal justly with the real and important characteristics that distinguish individuals from one another—might even manifest as an insult. Which differences deserve respect and why is a matter of some debate, but philosophers routinely place emphasis on the cultural or religious aspects of group identities. Kymlicka, for example, argues that minority groups—routinely neglected or demeaned by the dominant value system of society—require respect in order for their members' autonomy to be fulfilled.[56] Meanwhile, Fraser proposes that we change the institutionalised value patterns that deny some differences equal social status, so that differences can be seen to be worthy of respect.[57]

Sceptics claim that difference and identity do not easily admit of an egalitarian interpretation and to aspire to 'equal' respect of these characteristics is to commit a category mistake.[58] For these scholars, *respect of difference* makes sense only at the cost of egalitarianism because it necessitates a 'grading' of certain traits and risks arbitrarily privileging certain individuals or groups. And since accounts of difference and identity can be marked by 'historical contingency and cultural incommensurability', it is difficult to imagine how best to go about 'equalizing' the recognition of these characteristics.[59]

(a) Distinguishing respect

The philosophical literature is instructive in delineating the limits of respect and clarifying its relationship to a cluster of related values, namely, dignity, esteem, recognition, decency, and status. Why clarify respect in this way? First, there is the idea that respect is not a 'sharp' construct with clear boundaries, and so its

[56] Will Kymlicka, *Multicultural Citizenship: A Liberal Theory of Minority Rights* (Clarendon Press 1995). See also John Tomasi, 'Kymlicka, Liberalism, and Respect for Cultural Minorities' (1995) 105(3) Ethics 580.

[57] Nancy Fraser, 'Rethinking Recognition' (2000) 3 New Left Review 107.

[58] See, eg, Mattias Iser, 'Recognition' in Edward N Zalta (ed), *The Stanford Encyclopedia of Philosophy* (Stanford University 2019) <http://plato.stanford.edu/entries/recognition/> accessed 1 August 2019 (hereafter Iser, 'Recognition'). See also Bird, 'Status, Identity, and Respect' (n 15) and Margalit, *Decent Society* (n 29) 62.

[59] Bird, 'Status, Identity, and Respect' (n 15) 223.

capacity to be associated with a wider vocabulary of terms allows us to make better sense of it.[60] Second, there are distinctions that can and should usefully be made between these values but, as will become clear in subsequent chapters, they are used interchangeably—and ill-advisedly—in academic research and official discourse and even, on occasion, in order to promote a weak approximation of respect.[61]

This chapter has already clarified the relationship of respect to dignity, where respect is understood as the only suitable acknowledgement of an individual's dignity (or intrinsic moral worth).[62] It has also clarified the relationship of respect to esteem, where—according to Darwall and other contemporary commentators—appraisal respect is understood as a form of esteem.[63]

The relationship between respect and recognition is less clear-cut, since the word 'recognition' has made its way into philosophical commentaries on respect in various ways, for example, as a shorthand for the form of respect articulated in Kant's account (as in moral recognition respect) and as a means by which to give something—such as a legal rule—standing or authority in Darwall's account (as in recognition respect).[64] Elsewhere, philosophers have described the assigning of equal respect as the 'central dimension' of recognition.[65] Scanlon, for example, considers respect to express the foundation of morality. He continues:

> The contractualist ideal of acting in accord with principles that others (similarly motivated) could not reasonably reject is meant to characterise the relation with others the value and appeal of which underlies our reasons to do what morality requires. This relation … might be called a relation of mutual recognition.[66]

[60] Hulley et al, 'Respect in Prisons' (n 10).

[61] See, eg, n 3.

[62] See, eg, Hill, *Respect, Pluralism, and Justice* (n 20) and Dillon, 'Respect' (n 13).

[63] See, eg, Darwall, 'Two Kinds of Respect' (n 32) and Helm, *Communities of Respect* (n 36).

[64] Kant, *Groundwork* (n 19); Kant, *The Metaphysics of Morals* (n 19); and Darwall, 'Two Kinds of Respect' (n 32).

[65] Iser, 'Recognition' (n 58) s 2.2.

[66] Scanlon, *What We Owe to Each Other* (n 6) 162. On mutual recognition and the 'exchange' of respect, see also Peter Somerville, '"The Feeling's Mutual:" Respect as the Basis for Cooperative Interaction' in Millie (ed), *Securing Respect* (n 5) 140 (hereafter Somerville, 'Respect as the Basis for Cooperative Interaction').

By contrast, other theorists of recognition have focused on its relationship to the negative experience of disrespect.[67] For these philosophers, the normative expectation of being treated with respect is most obvious when we consider extreme forms of humiliation in which individuals are symbolically and materially excluded from humanity, for example, when they are treated as mere objects.[68] This approach accords with a study conducted by Hulley et al, in which prisoners approached respect in binary terms and were at greater ease describing disrespect than respect. It also accords with work by Margalit, for whom the issue has to do with cognition: it is easier to detect and analyse wrongs or negative experiences than positive ones.[69] In response to extreme forms of humiliation, misrecognition, and disrespect, Margalit has concluded that our primary political aim should be to strive for a decent society instead of a fully just one.[70]

This leads to the relationship of respect to decency. Minimal decency, according to Kantian thought, denotes a basic ethical obligation of kindness.[71] Any acts which move beyond the minimum threshold of decency are classed as supererogatory acts: morally good, but more than is strictly necessary. For Kant, the role of the state should be to enact laws that require behaviour that is conducive with the minimum standard of decency.[72] Margalit, by contrast, analyses the role and value of decency in social institutions in negative terms. According to Margalit, a society is decent when its institutions do not humiliate citizens.[73] He frames this idea in various ways. A decent society is 'one that fights conditions which constitute a justification for its dependents to consider themselves

[67] See, eg, Axel Honneth, *Disrespect: The Normative Foundations of Critical Theory* (Polity 2007).

[68] Iser, 'Recognition' (n 58).

[69] Hulley et al, 'Respect in Prisons' (n 10) and Margalit, *Decent Society* (n 29) 4–5.

[70] Margalit, *Decent Society* (n 29) 271–91.

[71] Kant, *Groundwork* (n 19); Kant, *The Metaphysics of Morals* (n 19); and Hill, *Respect, Pluralism, and Justice* (n 20).

[72] Kant, *Groundwork* (n 19); Kant, *The Metaphysics of Morals* (n 19); and Hill, *Respect, Pluralism, and Justice* (n 20). See also David Heyd, 'Supererogation' in Edward N Zalta (ed), *The Stanford Encyclopedia of Philosophy* (Stanford University 2016) <http://plato.stanford.edu/entries/supererogation/> accessed 1 August 2019.

[73] Margalit, *Decent Society* (n 29) 1.

humiliated',[74] 'one that does not violate the rights of people dependent on it',[75] 'a non-humiliating [society]',[76] and 'one whose institutions do not violate the dignity of people in its orbit'.[77]

It might be said that decency—as articulated by both Kant and Margalit—posits a modest approach to social relations. Respect is distinct from decency in at least two ways. First, respect is inherently more aspirational in that it prescribes behaviour that moves beyond a minimum standard or baseline condition and which is often—though not exclusively—framed in positive terms. Second, as we have seen, respect requires both attitude and action, while assessments of decency in an institution or society are made primarily with reference to the latter.

While respect—which refers to the assigning of intrinsic moral worth—is clearly distinct from status—which refers to a person's relative social position or standing—the two concepts are routinely discussed in relation to each other and it is worth clarifying the nature of that discussion. It has been proposed that a respectful interaction allows individuals to assert claims about their status vis-à-vis each other. To respect someone's status, the argument goes, is to avoid the ambiguity inherent in any attempt to respect his identity.[78] This is why it makes sense for Kantians to talk of an individual's dignity (which is, of course, a status) as commanding attitudes of respect.[79]

Arguments about the compatibility of respect and status—over respect and identity—often point to greater coherence and clarity. It has been argued, for example, that when an individual enjoys a certain status, it generates an automatic expectation about how he is to be treated.[80] On this view, status easily admits of comparison, since the treatment one person can expect to command on the basis of his status can be assessed against that which others can expect to command. This is arguably not true of difference and identity. These characteristics do not generate automatic expectations about how a person is to be treated. Deliberative interaction

[74] ibid 10.
[75] ibid 28.
[76] ibid 41.
[77] ibid 51.
[78] Bird, 'Status, Identity, and Respect' (n 15).
[79] See, eg, Hill, *Respect, Pluralism, and Justice* (n 20) and Helm, *Communities of Respect* (n 36).
[80] Bird, 'Status, Identity, and Respect' (n 15).

with features of another person's identity is inevitably more fluid and open-ended and, by extension, less open to comparison.[81]

3. Respect and the social sciences

There are very few notable social scientific studies of respect. Sennett explores the scarcity of mutual respect in conditions of inequality, the necessary conditions for its generation, and the forces that contribute to its erosion in modern society.[82] In a manner that is suggestive of philosophical work on respect, Sennett ascribes significance to its relational and dialogic character. In particular, he views respect as involving a form of mutuality that 'requires expressive work', where mutual respect must be 'enacted' or 'performed'.[83] For Sennett, then, respect is not a passive state or intrinsic quality—like dignity, for example[84]—but, rather, a form of positive consideration and a practice that requires a degree of active participation.[85]

Sennett eschews the traditional Kantian view of respect based on simple egalitarianism (we should treat others with respect *because* we are of equal status) and suggests an alternative form of respect that is readily adaptable to modern society (we should treat others with respect *despite* the fact that we are of unequal status).[86] In short, his claim is that respect can—and should—be cultivated and expressed in conditions of structured status inequality.[87] For true mutuality, this action—or performance—must be reciprocated by others. In this way, respect provides a good guide for cooperative interaction.[88]

Bourgois presents a compelling real-world examination of respect as a central organising dynamic of street culture. This forms part of his ethnography of social marginalisation, ethnic segregation, and street-level drug dealing in East Harlem (El Barrio). Bourgois describes the myriad ways in which respect is sought

[81] ibid.
[82] Sennett, *Respect* (n 16).
[83] ibid 59.
[84] See, eg, Dillon, 'Respect' (n 13).
[85] ibid. See also Hulley et al, 'Respect in Prisons' (n 10).
[86] Hill, *Respect, Pluralism, and Justice* (n 20).
[87] Sennett, *Respect* (n 16). See also Nira Yuval-Davis, Kalpana Kannabiran, and Ulrike Vieten (eds), *The Situated Politics of Belonging* (SAGE 2006).
[88] Millie (ed), *Securing Respect* (n 5).

and realised in the urban ghetto, where the key marker of—and means by which to obtain—respect is a willingness to engage in violent behaviour and where criminal sanction is, by implication, an omnipresent threat.[89]

An obvious strength of this work is its insight into the thought processes of those involved in the underground drug economy of El Barrio. Bourgois' liberal use of transcripts of conversations with drug dealers relates the ways in which these individuals understand and interpret their circumstances. His combination of the 'organic intellect' of the drug dealers—as told in their own words—with an analysis of the broader socio-economic context is valuable in drawing attention to the interface between structural constraints and individual action. For Bourgois, the actions of El Barrio's drug dealers are best understood as an alternative means by which to gain respect, power, and a sense of 'autonomous personal dignity' denied to them by mainstream culture.[90]

Despite Bourgois' emphasis on the prevalence of addiction, substance abuse, and violence in El Barrio, one of the most insightful chapters is that which contains fewest incidents of violence. Bourgois focuses instead on a different challenge faced by the inhabitants of El Barrio, namely, the experience of being disrespected and demeaned in their encounters with the 'mainstream'. Unfamiliar with the impersonality of the bureaucratic world, their encounters often result in their humiliation and withdrawal from the labour market, and this is exacerbated by the vast socio-economic distance between the residents of El Barrio and members of mainstream society.[91]

In evaluating Bourgois' contribution, we might refer to Hudson on the three broad classes of meaning conveyed by individual words and phrases. The first is its referential meaning (roughly, what the word or phrase refers to), the second is its social meaning (the context in which the word or phrase is articulated and understood), and the third is its emotive meaning

[89] Bourgois, *Respect* (n 16). See also Philippe Bourgois, 'In Search of Masculinity: Violence, Respect and Sexuality among Puerto Rican Crack Dealers in East Harlem' (1996) 36(3) The British Journal of Criminology 412.

[90] Bourgois, *Respect* (n 16) 8.

[91] ibid. On respect and social inequality, see also Somerville, 'Respect as the Basis for Cooperative Interaction' (n 66).

(the irreducibly affective implications of the word or phrase).[92] Bourgois is only implicitly concerned with the referential meaning of respect and related terms. He conveys, for example, the popularity of the slang term 'diss' among the participants of the study, which refers primarily to disrespectful talk but also to the separate act of criticising another. In this way, he prompts us to reflect on the continual possibility of semantic modification of the word 'respect' itself and the manner in which it continues to evolve in our own moral vocabulary.[93] His principal contribution, however, is in exposing and subjecting to scrutiny the more nuanced social and emotive meanings of respect.[94]

It might be said that both social scientific studies of respect are at once in conflict and in agreement with each other. On the one hand, both Sennett and Bourgois move away from pure Kantian reasoning on respect, whereby respect is due to an individual by virtue of his humanity and his status as a rational agent.[95] Rather, both Sennett and Bourgois describe a situation—that is certainly not new in social scientific research—whereby a so-called 'rational agent' is caught up in overbearing social structures that constrain his individual autonomy and over which he has little or no control. Despite—or perhaps because of—these conditions, both Sennett and Bourgois view respect as a kind of social currency. Respect can provide structure to social relations and it can be plausibly established in conditions of structured status inequality. On the other hand, the studies contrast sharply on the issue of how best to cultivate respect in practice. For Sennett, we are respectful when we relate to others with a sense of mutual understanding. For Bourgois, respect—in the urban ghetto, at least—is a matter of physical intimidation and violence, obtained through a display of 'masculine' behaviour that is directly antithetical to that envisaged by Sennett. This is not to suggest that one explication of respect is 'right' and the other is misguided or 'wrong'. Sennett and Bourgois simply provide alternative interpretations

[92] Richard A Hudson, *Language Networks: The New Word Grammar* (OUP 2007).

[93] Bourgois, *Respect* (n 16). See also Bryan A Garner, *The Oxford Dictionary of American Usage and Style* (OUP 2000) see 'dis' (also 'diss').

[94] Bourgois, *Respect* (n 16).

[95] Kant, *Groundwork* (n 19); Kant, *The Metaphysics of Morals* (n 19); and Hill, *Respect, Pluralism, and Justice* (n 20).

of the same elusive concept, both of which are highly instructive where criminal justice is concerned.

B. Situating Respect

Having mapped salient aspects of the intellectual terrain of respect in cognate disciplines, the chapter now offers a preliminary sketch of the role and value of respect in criminal justice. The aim is to render respect plausible, defensible, and sufficiently well connected to some significant criminal justice issues in advance of a critical examination of policing and imprisonment in subsequent chapters.

The task is to identify which constitutive elements and qualities of respect are especially relevant in the complex moral context of criminal justice. The philosophical literature on respect—which, as we have seen, is routinely concerned with the conceptual structure or 'anatomy' of respect—is especially instructive here.[96] The chapter proceeds with the important caveat that these qualities are not fixed. It will be necessary, of course, to subject them to further examination in subsequent chapters.

While the philosophical and social scientific literatures provide an important grounding in respect *per se*, they are less helpful in considering how respect operates in criminal justice. It will be necessary, then, to supplement this scholarship with the literatures on intrinsic and extrinsic value, and on side-constraints.[97] In so

[96] See, eg, Hill, *Respect, Pluralism, and Justice* (n 20); Dillon, 'Respect' (n 13); and Helm, *Communities of Respect* (n 36).

[97] On intrinsic and extrinsic value, see, eg, Michael J Zimmerman, 'Intrinsic vs. Extrinsic Value' in Edward N Zalta (ed), *The Stanford Encyclopedia of Philosophy* (Stanford University 2019) <http://plato.stanford.edu/entries/value-intrinsic-extrinsic/> accessed 1 August 2019 (hereafter Zimmerman, 'Intrinsic vs. Extrinsic Value'). On side-constraints, see Nozick in Robert Nozick, *Anarchy, State, and Utopia* (Basic Books 1974) 28–29; Daniel Nolan, 'Consequentialism and Side Constraints' (2009) 6(1) Journal of Moral Philosophy 5; and Theresa Lopez, Jennifer Zamzow, Michael Gill, and Shaun Nichols, 'Side Constraints and the Structure of Commonsense Ethics' (2009) 23(1) Philosophical Perspectives 305. On side-constraints in criminal justice, see RA Duff and Sandra Marshall, 'Benefits, Burdens and Responsibilities: Some Ethical Dimensions of Situational Crime Prevention' in Andrew von Hirsch, David Garland, and Alison Wakefield (eds), *Ethical and Social Perspectives on Situational Crime Prevention* (Hart 2000) 19–21 and John Braithwaite and Philip Pettit, *Not Just Deserts: A Republican Theory of Criminal Justice* (Clarendon Press 1990) 26–36 (hereafter Braithwaite and Pettit, *Not Just Deserts*).

doing, I develop the argument that policing and imprisonment currently suffer from a respect deficit, since they treat respect as a weak side-constraint on the pursuit of instrumental outcomes and not as a value that is built into the very purposes and rationale of the practices themselves. The implications of this view are significant given Dillon's claim that we must view the presence or deficiency of respect in an institution as one indicator among many that it is just or unjust.[98]

More generally, the discussion that follows is receptive to research by Hulley et al in which they call for a more 'nuanced understanding' of respect and the conditions under which it is experienced.[99] It is similarly receptive to Duff's comments on the scope for a more searching description or 'carefully nuanced analysis' of respect in criminal justice, and his call for an adequate normative account of its significance.[100]

1. Constitutive elements and qualities of respect

(a) Act and attitude

A prominent idea to emerge from the literature is that of respect as both an act and attitude.[101] We can glean from both philosophy and social science that the act of respect is relational or dialogic, involving an iterative process of claim and response. As relational, respect is deeply social: it is object-generated rather than wholly subject-generated, something that is owed to, called for, deserved, elicited, or claimed by another.[102] This conception of respect appears to be easily translatable to policing and imprisonment and especially to the power-holders and their audiences who must somehow attempt to relate to each other. By contrast, Sennett's notion that respect must be 'enacted' or 'performed' seems less germane to criminal justice. His language of performance implies an element of superficiality that is at odds with the well-established idea that respect is signified as much in a person's attitude as it is in his actions. To respect an individual is not only to rehearse a set

[98] Dillon, 'Respect: A Philosophical Perspective' (n 20).

[99] Hulley et al, 'Respect in Prisons' (n 10) 4.

[100] RA Duff, 'Punishment, Dignity and Degradation' (2005) 25(1) Oxford Journal of Legal Studies 141, 149..

[101] See, eg, Dillon, 'Respect' (n 13).

[102] ibid.

of actions but to *believe* that he has a legitimate claim to desirable treatment.[103] If a police officer, for example, 'performs' respect or gives the appearance of valuing a citizen—and does so only cynically, while lacking the appropriate conviction—the question arises as to whether respect is truly in evidence at all.

(b) Respect of similarities and of differences

As described in detail earlier, a key distinction in the philosophical literature is that made between respect of similarities and of differences. The distinction resonates particularly well in the context of policing and imprisonment, given that both institutions drift—however inadvertently—between both forms of respect. Both institutions have made public their commitment to demonstrating respect for cultural differences in certain circumstances—the provision of ethnic meals in prison is a prime example—without giving up the conviction—in official discourse, at least—that those we police and imprison also deserve a basic form of respect on the basis of their personhood alone.[104] Subsequent chapters explore whether and, if so, how this distinction manifests itself in policing and imprisonment. The decision to move forward with reference to both forms of respect—rather than endorse one and dismiss the other—is a deliberate attempt to think about respect 'representatively' in a manner that Arendt envisages: to depict the experience of respect from a range of potentially competing perspectives and interpretational possibilities.[105]

The idea that we must respect—or, at least, acknowledge—difference seems to be especially relevant in policing and imprisonment, given current levels of racial tension and the challenges encountered by the authorities in negotiating and attempting to assuage that tension.[106] The work by Bourgois is instructive here

[103] See, eg, Theodore M Benditt, 'Why Respect Matters' (2008) 42(4) The Journal of Value Inquiry 487.

[104] National Offender Management Service, *Catering: Meals for Prisoners* (PSI 44/2010, National Offender Management Service 2010) and n 3.

[105] Hannah Arendt, *The Human Condition* (University of Chicago Press 1958) (hereafter Arendt, *Human Condition*).

[106] David Lammy, *The Lammy Review: An Independent Review into the Treatment of, and Outcomes for, Black, Asian and Minority Ethnic Individuals in the Criminal Justice System* (Ministry of Justice 2017) and David Lammy, *Open Letter to the Prime Minister* (7 September 2017) <https://assets.publishing.service.gov.uk/government/uploads/system/uploads/attachment_data/file/643002/david-lammy-open-letter-to-prime-minister.pdf> accessed 1 August 2019.

in showing that forms of racism and racial stereotypes can fundamentally exclude entire groups from being able to obtain respect. He describes, for example, how the Puerto Rican men of his research—who saw their drug dealing as a means of acting out their roles as 'men'—tended to have that role interpreted through a racialised prism when arrested.[107]

(c) Respect, status, and power

As we have seen, another recurring theme in the literature is the relationship of respect to notions of status and power. The question arises as to whether—in policing and imprisonment—it is possible to generate respect despite the structured status or power inequalities between the actors concerned. According to Sennett, respect can mitigate status inequalities or even obscure them entirely.[108] Elsewhere, it has been suggested that respect has the potential to alleviate status asymmetries but not power asymmetries: 'Status is grounded and influenced by feelings of respect. Power, by contrast, is based on one's structural position and is therefore less open to challenge.'[109]

If this is true, then it is notable that the terms are often used interchangeably and without adequate differentiation in the policing and imprisonment literatures, for example, to denote stratified social relationships or the relative positioning of individuals in an interaction.[110] Perhaps the complexity lies in the fact that status and power often align: status can be maintained through restraint in the use of power and power can also be used to gain status.[111] The implications of such a claim for respect in the context of criminal justice must be left open at this stage and will be subject to close examination in subsequent chapters.

[107] Bourgois, *Respect* (n 16). See also Sara Ahmed, *On Being Included: Racism and Diversity in Institutional Life* (Duke University Press 2012) (hereafter Ahmed, *On Being Included*).

[108] Sennett, *Respect* (n 16).

[109] Jeffrey W Lucas and Amy R Baxter, 'Power, Influence, and Diversity in Organisations' (2012) 639(1) *The ANNALS of the American Academy of Political and Social Science* 49 (hereafter Lucas and Baxter, 'Power, Influence, and Diversity').

[110] See further chs 2, 3, 4, and 5.

[111] Lucas and Baxter, 'Power, Influence, and Diversity' (n 109).

(d) Respect at the individual and institutional level

The scholarship on respect by Margalit and Dworkin is helpful in drawing attention to the role and value of respect not only at the individual but also at the institutional level.[112] To borrow Ahmed's term, respect appears to have an 'institutional life' in policing and imprisonment—as it appears in policy statements, mission statements, and other official discourse—that is worthy of sustained reflection.[113]

The appeal to respect in official discourse gives the *appearance* of respect and intrinsic valuing between state and citizen but provides no guarantee that respect is actually achieved in practice. If those in authority speak of—and make a public commitment to—respect, then an institutional culture is likely to be generated around the word.[114] For Ahmed, when a particular word is given institutional approval, it accrues value as the 'right' or most desirable way to speak about certain practices; generating a set of unannounced rules about what can and cannot be said.[115] There is a distinct possibility that, in criminal justice, respect has become less about the quality of social relations and has taken on a new role as an official word, a keyword—or even a slogan—in official documentation. But saying 'respect' does not make it so, and if the institutional commitment to respect does not translate into practice, then its only function is to reaffirm the authority of the institution that announces it.[116] This is a cynical view, certainly, but it has been confirmed by Ahmed in relation to the word 'diversity' in institutions.[117] At this stage, the question remains open as to whether there is an analogous approach to respect in the context of policing and imprisonment.

[112] Margalit, *Decent Society* (n 29) and Dworkin, *Taking Rights Seriously* (n 37).

[113] Ahmed, *On Being Included* (n 107) ch 2.

[114] ibid 59.

[115] Ahmed, *On Being Included* (n 107).

[116] JO Urmson and Marina Sbisà (eds), John L Austin, *How to Do Things with Words* (2nd edn, Harvard University Press 1975) 7–11 'Can Saying Make it So?' On official documents that express a commitment to an ideal—in this case, diversity—and the superficial approach to such ideals in practice, see Sara Ahmed, '"You End up Doing the Document Rather than Doing the Doing": Diversity, Race Equality and the Politics of Documentation' (2007) 30(4) Ethnic and Racial Studies 590.

[117] Ahmed, *On Being Included* (n 107).

2. Instrumental outcomes, side-constraints, and foundational values

In this section, I offer an interpretation of how respect currently operates in the context of policing and imprisonment, which I intend to trace through subsequent chapters. The literatures on intrinsic and extrinsic value, and on side-constraints are instructive here.[118]

(a) Intrinsic and extrinsic value

Philosophers routinely make a distinction between intrinsic and extrinsic value. Both have become philosophical terms of art, providing labels for concepts which feature in common sense or everyday thought. When we attend to the *intrinsic* value of something, we value it 'in itself', 'for its own sake', 'as such', or 'in its own right'.[119] Some philosophers have proposed the 'isolation test' as a means by which to determine intrinsic value. If the concept existed *in isolation*, would we value it? On the basis of this test, as well as the celebrated Kantian account of respect, we can be sure that respect has intrinsic value; that it is non-instrumentally good.[120] By contrast, were we to treat respect—somewhat mistakenly—as having *extrinsic* value, we would consider it to be valuable *only* for the sake of something else to which it is related in some way.[121] This distinction is abstract but it matters for the purposes of the next section, which sets out the role and value of respect in policing and imprisonment in more concrete terms.

(b) Respect as a weak side-constraint on the pursuit of instrumental outcomes

We might view criminal justice as characterised by—and proceeding with reference to—two central considerations: instrumental outcomes and moral values. The preoccupation of

[118] For some key contributions, see n 97.

[119] Zimmerman, 'Intrinsic vs. Extrinsic Value' (n 97) s 2. For an early expression of intrinsic value, see George E Moore, *Principia Ethica* (CUP 1903). See also Eva Bodansky and Earl Conee, 'Isolating Intrinsic Value' (1981) 41(1) Analysis 51; Shelly Kagan, 'Rethinking Intrinsic Value' (1998) 2(4) The Journal of Ethics 277; and Toni Rønnow-Rasmussen and Michael J Zimmerman (eds), *Recent Work on Intrinsic Value* (Springer 2005).

[120] Zimmerman, 'Intrinsic vs. Extrinsic Value' (n 97) s 4.

[121] ibid s 6. See also Ben Bradley, 'Extrinsic Value' (1998) 91(2) Philosophical Studies 109.

criminal justice institutions with instrumental outcomes is well documented. For Garland, when 'social practices and institutions become more instrumentally effective … they become less compelling or meaningful for their human agents'.[122] But the question of precisely how instrumental outcomes and moral values interrelate—or enter into criminal justice institutions and the deliberations of their actors—has only occasionally been subject to examination.[123] Are moral values such as respect viewed as intrinsically valuable such that they might override the institutional preoccupation with instrumental outcomes? Alternatively, is the weight attached to moral values reducible to their capacity to achieve instrumental outcomes?

This book explores the latter question and suggests that respect is treated, at best, as a weak side-constraint on the pursuit of the instrumental outcomes of policing and imprisonment such as crime control, order maintenance, and managerialism. Yet it is worth noting that side-constraints are not inherently weak or liable to be overwhelmed by instrumental considerations.[124] If a side-constraint is strong—like a Dworkinian trump right—then it is, in fact, a very powerful limit on the pursuit of other goals.[125] If side-constraints are framed in adequately robust terms, we might even argue that they infuse the very foundational values on which criminal justice practices are based. At present, however, respect is far from being treated as a foundational value to be built into the purposes and rationale of criminal justice practices, and there is a need for a deeper understanding of the conceptual contours of respect if it is to be 'maximally realised'.[126] There is a good deal of evidence to suggest that only a surface understanding of respect

[122] David Garland, *Punishment and Modern Society* (Clarendon Press 1990) 179. See also Arie Freiberg, 'Affective Versus Effective Justice: Instrumentalism and Emotionalism in Criminal Justice' (2001) 3(2) Punishment & Society 265.

[123] See, eg, Ben Crewe and Alison Liebling, 'Are Liberal-Humanitarian Penal Values and Practices Exceptional?' in Thomas Ugelvik and Jane Dullum (eds), *Penal Exceptionalism? Nordic Prison Policy and Practice* (Routledge 2011).

[124] See, eg, Mill on the harm principle or Hart's approach to incorporating the principle of distributive fairness into his otherwise instrumental theory of punishment: John Stuart Mill, *On Liberty* (JW Parker and Son 1859) and HLA Hart, *Punishment and Responsibility: Essays in the Philosophy of Law* (Clarendon Press 1968).

[125] Side-constraints might even forbid certain types of unjust action irrespective of what instrumental benefits that action might produce.

[126] Braithwaite and Pettit, *Not Just Deserts* (n 97) 28.

has been attained, and there is also some resistance towards the idea that we can legitimately pursue instrumental outcomes only insofar as they themselves preserve and value respect.

3. Contexts

The practices of policing and imprisonment have been selected to form the structural basis of this book as they are among the most emotionally charged, morally contested, and politically sensitive in the criminal process. They are also, for Ristroph, too rarely juxtaposed in academic discussion.[127] Less well documented, however, is that for those we seek to police and punish, respect is routinely among the core values at stake.[128]

It is an obvious—though not insignificant—point that both practices involve a considerable degree of state-sanctioned coercion.[129] Liebling insists that coercive practices and displays of power—especially in conditions of confinement—must be handled in such a way that fosters and maintains civic virtues.[130] But when the asymmetries of power between the power holder and the recipient of that power become especially pronounced, it inevitably results in the heightened vulnerability of the latter. Respect, then, is more likely to be rendered fragile or even non-existent, thus undermining what we would typically expect of a respectful interaction, namely, a form of intrinsic valuing based on mutual cooperation and understanding.[131]

127 See, eg, Lucia Zedner, *Criminal Justice* (OUP 2004) and Jonathan Jacobs and Jonathan Jackson (eds), *The Routledge Handbook of Criminal Justice Ethics* (Routledge 2016). On the centrality of policing to criminal justice scholarship, Ristroph writes: 'We may overlook the harms of the criminal law, or confuse its purported aspirations with its actual achievements, if we locate the law wholly in substantive prohibitions.' Alice Ristroph, 'The Thin Blue Line from Crime to Punishment' (2018) 108(2) The Journal of Criminal Law and Criminology 305, 333.

128 For important exceptions, see Albert W Dzur, Ian Loader, and Richard Sparks, 'Punishment and Democratic Theory: Resources for a Better Penal Politics' in Dzur et al, *Democratic Theory and Mass Incarceration* (n 37); Duff, *Citizens* (n 30); and Hulley et al, 'Respect in Prisons' (n 10).

129 Lacey, *Prisoners' Dilemma* (n 14).

130 Alison Liebling, *Prisons and their Moral Performance: A Study of Values, Quality, and Prison Life* (OUP 2004). See also Ian Loader, 'For Penal Moderation: Notes Towards a Public Philosophy of Punishment' (2010) 14(3) Theoretical Criminology 349.

131 See, eg, Dillon, 'Respect' (n 13).

It follows that respect—or lack thereof—is not a solely abstract concern. When there is a lack of specificity in understanding and giving effect to respect, it is likely to affect the concrete experiences of policing and imprisonment and magnify the status inequalities not only between state and citizen, but also between citizens. A reductive approach to respect, for example, shows scant regard for the fact that respect—or lack thereof—tends to be felt more keenly by ethnic minority groups and those whose sense of belonging and social possibility in society are precarious; isolating yet further those who are already disenfranchised.[132]

It is more than a little ironic, then, that respect is posited as a core value of the police and HM Prison Service and figures prominently in the policy statements and official discourse of both institutions.[133] Subsequent chapters explore just how far policing and imprisonment practices are from genuine—as opposed to superficial—displays of respect, despite the public commitment of both institutions to the value.

(a) Context, jurisdiction, and the assumed universality of respect

A note on the assumed universality of respect is in order. Respect is routinely posited as transcending the particularities of cultures and moral traditions. We need only look to the *Human Rights Standards and Practice for the Police* to find calls for police officers to treat suspects 'respectfully' or the *Standard Minimum Rules for the Treatment of Prisoners* to find calls for prison officers to 'command the respect of prisoners' and reaffirm their self-respect, both of which extend to 193 member states.[134] Terms

[132] Bourgois, *Respect* (n 16). This process is also suggestive of the celebrated essay by Garfinkel: Harold Garfinkel, 'Conditions of Successful Degradation Ceremonies' (1956) 61(5) American Journal of Sociology 420.

[133] See, eg, n 3.

[134] Office of the United Nations High Commissioner for Human Rights, *Human Rights Standards and Practice for the Police (Expanded Pocket Book on Human Rights for the Police)* Professional Training Series No.5/Add.3 (United Nations 2004) and United Nations Office on Drugs and Crime, *The United Nations Standard Minimum Rules for the Treatment of Prisoners (The Nelson Mandela Rules)* (UNODC 2015). On the global reach of respect, see Martha C Nussbaum, *Beyond the Social Contract: Toward Global Justice*, The Tanner Lectures on Human Values delivered at the Australian National University and Clare Hall, University of Cambridge (Tanner Humanities Center, University of Utah 2002 and 2003). Self-respect is widely considered to be a discrete concept and is beyond the scope of this book: see, eg, Dillon, 'Respect' (n 13) s 4 'Self-Respect'.

such as humanity, inhumanity, and degradation seem to express a similar aspiration. There is a prevailing sense that—for all the differences between individuals—there are universal standards that define the ways in which we should—or should not—treat and relate to each other.[135]

However, it is possible that the standards invoked by respect are not necessarily commonly held by all and that respect depends instead on the ethnic, religious, cultural, national, and ideological commitments of the society in which it is expressed. On this view, while respect is a common feature of most contexts and jurisdictions—and while that idea is no doubt oriented in a universalistic direction—it is subject to interpretation and has a marked context-sensitivity that stands in need of further reflection.[136] If respect is shaped decisively by its context, it will not be enough to examine the practices of policing and imprisonment *in general*. Rather, a dual focus on policing and imprisonment in England and Wales—while drawing comparisons with practices in other jurisdictions when it is valuable to do so—will go some way towards investigating this more nuanced claim.

4. Approach

On the assumption that criminal justice practices are open to interpretation—and that my interpretation of respect as a weak side-constraint on the pursuit of instrumental outcomes is but one plausible interpretation—this book adopts an interpretive approach that views policing and imprisonment as contextualised social interactions for the production of meaning.[137] While

[135] Jeremy Waldron, '*The Coxford Lecture*. Inhuman and Degrading Treatment: The Words Themselves' (2010) 23(2) Canadian Journal of Law & Jurisprudence 269 and Lægaard, 'Respect for Difference' (n 7). On the presumption that certain norms of conduct are genuinely cross-cultural or universally valid, see further Cécile Fabre and David Miller, 'Justice and Culture: Rawls, Sen, Nussbaum and O'Neill' (2003) 1(1) Political Studies Review 4.

[136] On the context-sensitivity of respect, see Joseph Raz, 'On Respect, Authority, and Neutrality: A Response' (2010) 120(2) Ethics 279. cf Green's position that 'respect for persons is mandatory, not optional, and though its requirements and expression are shaped by culture and history, it is not dependent for its ultimate binding force on such contingencies.' Leslie Green, 'Two Worries about Respect for Persons' (2010) 120(2) Ethics 212.

[137] On interpretation, see, eg, Schwartz-Shea and Yanow, *Interpretive Research Design* (n 12).

an interpretive approach is, for the most part, extremely well suited to a study of respect, it is important too to acknowledge its limits. It is possible to point to an interpretive tension, for example, which is especially pronounced where respect is concerned. In view of this tension, I propose a modification to the classic interpretive approach, informed by the work of Gadamer.[138]

An interpretive approach has a distinctive orientation towards knowledge and its development, and places 'contextuality' at the centre of its logic. It is concerned with the ways in which that contextual sensibility might, first, condition our conceptual understanding and, second, be maximised to construct and deconstruct meaning. The idea is that knowledge can be sought, by means of *in situ* concept formation and development, about how we make individual and collective sense of the contexts that we inhabit.[139] Contextuality thus provides a direct rationale for the 'thick description' that Geertz describes.[140] Thick description refers to the ways in which we might embed meaning in context and is considered to be an essential characteristic of interpretive analysis.[141]

An interpretive approach is characterised by an iterative process of hermeneutic 'sense-making' that cannot be specified fully *a priori,* not least because of what Schwartz-Shea and Yanow observe as its 'unfolding' character.[142] In this way, interpretation can be distinguished sharply from a positivist design, where formal 'hypothesis testing' figures centrally and conceptual definitions are precise and abstracted from their contexts. Viewed from an interpretivist perspective, the positivist orientation towards the 'general' obscures the intimacy and inseparability of the meaning-context link.

[138] Hans-Georg Gadamer, *Truth and Method* (2nd rev edn, Continuum 2004) (hereafter Gadamer, *Truth and Method*). See also Jeff Malpas, 'Hans-Georg Gadamer' in Edward N Zalta (ed), *The Stanford Encyclopedia of Philosophy* (Stanford University 2018) <http://plato.stanford.edu/entries/gadamer/> accessed 1 August 2019 (hereafter Malpas, 'Gadamer').

[139] Schwartz-Shea and Yanow, *Interpretive Research Design* (n 12). See also Jerome S Bruner, *Acts of Meaning* (Harvard University Press 1990) and Paul Rabinow and William M Sullivan (eds), *Interpretive Social Science: A Second Look* (University of California Press 1987).

[140] Clifford Geertz, *The Interpretation of Cultures* (Basic Books 1973) ch 1.

[141] ibid.

[142] Schwartz-Shea and Yanow, *Interpretive Research Design* (n 12) 53.

For interpretivists, the task of constructing 'meaning', though ambiguous, is viewed in positive terms, since it creates the scope for multiple interpretational possibilities (of, in this case, what it means to cultivate respect in criminal justice). In creating a multiplicity of potential meanings and the particular forms that they might take, the connection to context is integral to both the design of interpretive research and its conduct.[143] Epistemologically, this is the reason for attempting to make sense of the contexts that individuals inhabit and, ontologically, in attending to their use of language as a means by which to construct their contexts. For White, interpretive research 'takes language seriously' given that language is considered to be at the nexus of meaning, context, and action.[144]

More generally, an interpretive approach is sensitive to what Arendt has described as the practice of 'thinking [about] what we do',[145] that is, a style of attentiveness to reality that aims to clarify some basic truths about the practices in which criminal justice actors are actively—and routinely—engaged. In this way, the practice of interpretation can be viewed as an ameliorative exercise insofar as it renders respect more 'researchable' for the criminal justice scholar.

(a) An interpretive tension

Notwithstanding the merits of the interpretive approach, it is important to approach it with a degree of scepticism. In particular, one of its foundational principles merits further reflection. Strict interpretivists privilege 'concept development' over positivist '*a priori* concept formation'. On this view, knowledge and meaning must 'emerge' out of the analysis and by no means inform it in the first place.[146] There is scope, however, to question this aspect of the interpretivist approach on phenomenological grounds.

[143] See, eg, Fred R Dallmayr and Thomas A McCarthy (eds), *Understanding and Social Inquiry* (University of Notre Dame Press 1977).

[144] Jay D White, *Taking Language Seriously: The Narrative Foundations of Public Administration Research* (Georgetown University Press 2001) ch 2.

[145] Arendt, *The Human Condition* (n 105) 5. For an application of Arendt's principle to criminal justice, see Robert P Burns, *A Theory of the Trial* (Princeton University Press 1999) and Robert P Burns, 'The Distinctiveness of Trial Narrative' in RA Duff, Lindsay Farmer, Sandra Marshall, and Victor Tadros (eds), *The Trial on Trial (Volume 1): Truth and Due Process* (Hart 2004).

[146] Schwartz-Shea and Yanow, *Interpretive Research Design* (n 12).

The idea of concept development involves 'bracketing off' prior knowledge entirely but it seems neither possible nor desirable to do so. Rather, it seems inevitable that some form of—albeit loose and potentially disparate—conceptual knowledge of respect would precede the analysis and thereafter serve to guide the interpretive process. In essence, the issue is one of causal order, which is especially pertinent given my core assumptions about respect and criminal justice, articulated in full in the previous section. According to strict interpretivists, this commentary is at odds with the interpretivist claim to 'theory-neutral' concept development and the idea that concepts 'emerge' from their contexts.[147]

A better description of the practice of interpretation might be to say that our conceptual understandings commonly derive from a tension or dialogue between the expectations that we bring to the analysis—based on our prior knowledge—and what we observe there. In subscribing to this view, the approach I adopt in this book is interpretive while nonetheless being open to adaptation in view of positivist concerns.

Gadamer's 'positive' conception of prejudicial understanding is instructive in this regard.[148] For Gadamer, the practice of interpretation—in his hermeneutic philosophy, a text, and equally for the purposes of analysing literature and official documentation in criminal justice—is necessarily 'pre-judgemental'.[149] On this view, the articulation of some core assumptions on respect need not be viewed as exercising a problematic or distorting influence on the research process. This is especially so since, for Gadamer, prior knowledge can become the focus of interrogative questioning in its own right and, by extension, is open to revision. The advantage of prior knowledge is in 'opening up' the discussion and facilitating the research process by creating scope to enter into a dialogue with the matter at issue.[150]

[147] ibid.

[148] Gadamer, *Truth and Method* (n 138). Developed initially within the tradition of philosophical hermeneutics, Gadamer's work has had influence in sociology and legal theory: William N Eskridge Jr, 'Gadamer/Statutory Interpretation' (1990) 90(3) Columbia Law Review 609.

[149] Malpas, 'Gadamer' (n 138).

[150] Gadamer, *Truth and Method* (n 138). See also Derek Layder, *New Strategies in Social Research: An Introduction and Guide* (Polity 1993) and Derek Layder, *Sociological Practice: Linking Theory and Social Research* (SAGE 1998) (hereafter Layder, *Sociological Practice*).

In sum, an interpretive approach provides a promising means by which to examine and critique a concept as indeterminate as respect. Its emphasis on context allows me to develop a particular—rather than all-purpose—account of respect that is sensitive to the complex moral contexts of policing and imprisonment. That said, it is important not to gloss over the implications of the interpretivist commitment to 'theory-neutral' concept development.[151] There appears to be scope for a more moderate approach that privileges a degree of prior knowledge, informed by Gadamer's work on 'pre-understanding' and the 'functionality' of preconceived ideas.[152]

(b) The interpretive approach in practice

Having established that respect is open to interpretation, the question arises as to how to give effect to the principles of interpretation in practice.[153] This book offers a close reading of the role and value of respect in the theoretical and empirical literatures on policing and imprisonment alongside a wide range of policy documents, mission statements, principles of professional conduct, inspection reports, and Freedom of Information requests. In this way, it is possible to prioritise—as interpretivists envisage—a contextual understanding of respect over a purely abstract one.[154]

While commitments to and endorsements of respect are widely diffused in official discourse, it swiftly emerges that such discourse is merely *constrained* and not *characterised* by respect. While respect is considered relevant to the pursuit of instrumental aims—recent inspection reports, for example, attribute 'respect scores' to prisons on a scale of one to four—these reports provide little to no elaboration on the prior question of what respect *actually* involves.[155] The advantage of the hermeneutic method is that

[151] Anthony Bottoms, 'The Relationship Between Theory and Empirical Observations in Criminology' in Roy D King and Emma Wincup (eds), *Doing Research on Crime and Justice* (2nd edn, Oxford University Press 2007).

[152] Gadamer, *Truth and Method* (n 138).

[153] See further Layder, *Sociological Practice* (n 150) and Susan J Brison, 'The Theoretical Importance of Practice' in Ian Shapiro and Judith Wagner DeCew (eds), *Theory and Practice: NOMOS XXXVII*. Yearbook of The American Society for Political and Legal Philosophy (New York University Press 1995).

[154] Gadamer, *Truth and Method* (n 138).

[155] Her Majesty's Chief Inspector of Prisons for England and Wales, *Annual Report 2017–18* (The Stationery Office 2018) Appendix 2, 107–08.

it provides the freedom to suggest, at this stage, that superficial appeals to respect are damaging—with implications that go far beyond the document in question—without having to remain committed to such a view, should it transpire that this is not the case. In subsequent chapters, it will be possible to develop a richer understanding of respect inductively out of this speculative claim. More detail will be required, for example, on whether and, if so, how a reductive approach to respect at the level of official discourse translates into a reductive approach to respect in practice.

The immanent capacity of respect to function as a concept of critical enquiry for criminal justice, while notable, must not be overstated. Criminal justice practice is defined by a plurality of values, which are not ordered in a fixed or definite way and are not derivable from a single fundamental value.[156] As such, it would be naïve to propose respect as an overarching analytic category and suggest that we can critique policing and imprisonment practices exclusively in these terms. Nonetheless, there is much to be gained by foregrounding respect, easily approved yet scarcely examined within policing and imprisonment, refining it, and then redirecting it in such a way that prompts deeper reflection about the manner in which these practices are conducted. In so doing, I hope to show that respect is much more than a marginal concern where matters of criminal justice, or injustice, are at stake.

[156] See further Jonathan Jacobs, 'Criminal Justice and the Liberal Polity' (2011) 30(2) Criminal Justice Ethics 173 and Lucia Zedner, 'Reparation and Retribution: Are They Reconcilable?' (1994) 57(2) The Modern Law Review 228.

PART I

On Respect, Policing, and Procedural Justice

2

Procedural Justice and Narrow Instrumentalism

One persistent aspect of accounts of procedural justice relates to the role and value of 'respect' in citizens' encounters with the police. In privileging procedures over outcomes, procedural justice—as standardly conceived—provides an optimistic view of the capacity of the police to bridge differences, interests, and values through respectful practices and decision-making.[1] This chapter reflects on that familiar narrative and proposes that respectful relations have become—however unintentionally—a subsidiary concern of policing scholars and practitioners alike. Crime control outcomes increasingly occupy a central place on the intellectual agenda and, in practice, there is evidence of procedural justice being pursued on largely pragmatic 'law and order' grounds.[2] When these instrumental concerns are not held in their proper place, we risk the erosion not only of respect but also of a range of other intrinsic values—transparency, neutrality, fairness, recognition, voice—that, taken together, comprise the very idea of procedural justice itself.

The chapter proceeds as follows. First, it offers some preliminary comments on respect, and makes the case for prioritising it as a value that is of both analytic interest and material significance in policing and procedural justice. Second, it critiques the current approach to procedural justice in research and practice.

[1] John W Thibaut and Laurens Walker, *Procedural Justice: A Psychological Analysis* (Wiley 1975) (hereafter Thibaut and Walker, *Procedural Justice*) and Tom R Tyler, *Why People Obey the Law* (Yale University Press 1990) (hereafter Tyler, *Why People Obey the Law*).

[2] On assessing the validity of an idea by its success in the active solution of a problem, see, eg, P Kyle Stanford, 'Instrumentalism' in Sahotra Sarkar and Jessica Pfeifer (eds), *The Philosophy of Science: An Encyclopedia* (Routledge 2005).

Respect and Criminal Justice. Gabrielle Watson, Oxford University Press (2020).
DOI: 10.1093/oso/9780198833345.001.0001

In developing that critique, it is not the aim to discredit the pursuit of instrumental outcomes *per se*. It is simply to suggest that we pursue them only insofar as they preserve the core intrinsic values at play. Third, it develops a non-instrumental account of procedural justice in which respect is posited as the unifying value at stake. The account signifies a departure from established patterns of working in procedural justice research and practice, where the real value and potential of respect as a critical and regulative ideal has been diminished by the tendency to construct it as a weak side-constraint on dominant instrumental concerns, and the failure to develop it in intrinsic terms.

A. Why Respect?

The issue of respect in police-public relations is not new, having first been raised by the 1929 Royal Commission on the Police and again by its counterpart in 1962. Encouragingly, the 1962 report confirms that 'no less than 83 per cent of those interviewed professed great respect for the police'.[3] Oral histories endorse these findings, giving the impression of a 'well-respected' police force, albeit operating in a period that was not free from tension.[4] Increasingly, however, concerns arose about a lack of—or inability to cultivate—respect in police-public relations; an issue that was presumably exacerbated by the relatively low levels of confidence in the police reported in the Crime Survey for England and Wales and elsewhere.[5] Police forces across England and Wales responded by positing respect as one of their core values and, in 2013, the College of Policing also published

[3] Royal Commission on the Police, *Report of the Royal Commission on Police Powers and Procedure* (The Stationery Office 1929) and Royal Commission on the Police, *Final Report* (The Stationery Office 1962) 103.

[4] Barbara Weinberger, *The Best Police in the World: An Oral History of English Policing from the 1930s to the 1960s* (Scolar Press 1995) and Jonathan Jackson and Ben Bradford, *Police Legitimacy: A Conceptual Review* (National Policing Improvement Agency 2010) 5.

[5] On increasingly fractious police-public relations over the issue of respect, see Howard S Cohen and Michael Feldberg, *Power and Restraint: The Moral Dimension of Police Work* (Praeger 1991). On declining confidence in the police, see Ben Bradford, 'Voice, Neutrality and Respect: Use of Victim Support Services, Procedural Fairness and Confidence in the Criminal Justice System' (2011) 11(4) Criminology & Criminal Justice 345 (hereafter Bradford, 'Voice, Neutrality and Respect').

a Code of Ethics which proposed respect as an ethical basis for—and a standard by which to evaluate—police work.[6] Despite these commitments to respect at the level of official discourse, the public still perceive a lack of—and call for more—respect, and are now doing so more and more audibly.[7]

Ideally, the police would cultivate respectful relations with citizens—recognise their moral standing, accord them a baseline moral status, or include them within the scope of their moral concern—in a manner that reaffirms that there are non-instrumental reasons to protect or support them. But when the success of policing is increasingly conceived in terms of—and measured by—its results, it follows that respect will operate, at best, as a weak side-constraint on the pursuit of those results. To treat respect in this way is to gloss over its depth, scope, and purchase and overlook the prior question of *what it is* for officials and citizens to respect and be respected.

The key motivation behind making respect central to a non-instrumental account of procedural justice is as follows. To treat procedural justice as a means by which to control crime is to render its values hostage to the empirical question of whether or not it is successful in achieving this outcome. If it were to transpire that procedural justice is not instrumentally effective, we would have less reason to value respect. The intrinsic case for respect, by contrast, is that it is to be valued irrespective of whether it is implicated in the pursuit of a certain outcome because it builds into policing an

[6] Home Office, *Revised Code of Practice for the Detention, Treatment and Questioning of Persons by Police Officers: Police and Criminal Evidence Act 1984 Code C* (The Stationery Office 2018) 1.0 and Her Majesty's Inspectorate of Prisons for England and Wales and Her Majesty's Inspectorate of Constabulary, *Expectations for Police Custody: Criteria for Assessing the Treatment of and Conditions for Detainees in Police Custody* (Her Majesty's Inspectorate of Prisons for England and Wales and Her Majesty's Inspectorate of Constabulary 2016) s 3: 'Respect and treatment'. See also College of Policing, *Code of Ethics: A Code of Practice for the Principles and Standards of Professional Behaviour for the Policing Profession in England and Wales* (College of Policing 2014) (hereafter College of Policing, *Code of Ethics*) s 2.1 Policing principles. *Respect*. 'You treat everyone with respect' and s 3.1 Standards of professional behaviour 2. *Authority, respect and courtesy*. Police officers must 'act with self-control and tolerance, treating members of the public with respect and courtesy' and police officers must 'remain composed and respectful'.

[7] Martyn Johnson, as told to Sam Rowe, 'No One has Any Respect for Police Officers Anymore' *The Telegraph* (19 November 2014).

ethical sensitivity that we value in a liberal democracy. In this way, respect speaks to the idea—articulated by Loader—that it matters *how* we control crime and not just that we do so.[8]

B. The Instrumental Case

The original intention behind procedural justice was to resolve the tension between due process and crime control models of policing by elevating professional standards and the consolidation of institutional legitimacy above short-term concerns about crime control.[9] In recent years, however, it has been narrowly construed, such that justice—insofar as we might call it justice—is in the crime control outcome, and the procedure is considered a good one to the extent that it generates that outcome.

This instrumentalism takes on two distinct but interacting forms, both of which have gone unremarked. The first relates to academic research, where we have seen a proliferation of outcome-oriented accounts of procedural justice. These accounts assume a fundamental split between means and ends which, when over-emphasised, risk the erosion of a range of intrinsic values, including respect. The second relates to policing practice. It is possible to point to a relatively narrow attitude held by many police officers tasked with giving effect to procedural justice, for whom the paradigm is principally of pragmatic benefit. In this way, procedural justice—as conceived by some scholars in the academy and enacted in practice—serves less to create scope for the cultivation of intrinsic values than to marginalise or displace them.

1. Instrumentalism in policing research

A systematic search has revealed over twenty thousand articles pertaining to procedural justice and the related issue of legitimacy.[10]

[8] Ian Loader, 'Policing, Recognition, and Belonging' (2006) 605(1) The ANNALS of the American Academy of Political and Social Science 201 (hereafter Loader, 'Recognition and Belonging').

[9] See, eg, Mike Hough, 'Procedural Justice and Professional Policing in Times of Austerity' (2013) 13(2) Criminology & Criminal Justice 181 (hereafter Hough, 'Procedural Justice and Professional Policing').

[10] Lorraine Mazerolle, Sarah Bennett, Jacqueline Davis, Elise Sargeant, and Matthew Manning, *Legitimacy in Policing: A Systematic Review* (The Campbell Collaboration 2013).

Much of this work is framed in terms of instrumental effectiveness, and we can infer from it a great deal about the professional orientations of a growing contingent of scholars. With few exceptions, procedural justice research is presented as having the capacity to promote change and inform policy rather than assuming an analytic or interpretive—and rather less 'functional'—approach to the governance of crime.[11]

That said, an inclination towards the instrumental is not new. This is especially true when we locate procedural justice within a broader set of theories of normative compliance, which can be traced back to Durkheimian and Weberian thinking on the roots of social order.[12] Some decades later, McBarnett—in arguing that due process is *for* crime control—was among the first to prioritise instrumental considerations within criminological thinking,[13] though Shklar had earlier made the point that the ideological rhetoric of legalism served the instrumental purposes of the legal process.[14] While McBarnett's insight exerted considerable influence on the scholarship that followed,[15] it appears to have been taken up more enthusiastically by policing scholars than by criminologists and criminal justice scholars writing on the justice process and due process. Campbell, Ashworth, and Redmayne in *The Criminal Process*, Sanders, Young, and Burton in *Criminal Justice*,

[11] See further Lucia Zedner, 'Useful Knowledge? Debating the Role of Criminology in Post-war Britain' in Lucia Zedner and Andrew Ashworth (eds), *The Criminological Foundations of Penal Policy: Essays in Honour of Roger Hood* (OUP 2003) (hereafter Zedner, 'Useful Knowledge?')

[12] Émile Durkheim, *The Rules of Sociological Method* (1st American edn, Free Press 1982) and Max Weber, *Economy and Society: An Outline of Interpretive Sociology* (Bedminster Press 1968) (hereafter Weber, *Economy and Society*).

[13] Doreen J McBarnett, *Conviction: Law, the State and the Construction of Justice* (Macmillan 1981).

[14] Judith N Shklar, *Legalism: Law, Morals, and Political Trials* (Harvard University Press 1964).

[15] See, eg, Uglow's argument that the function of the police in a liberal society is not only to shape morality but to 'fight crime' and 'maintain order' and Banks' argument that 'when the police treat people with courtesy and respect, police legitimacy is enhanced, and this treatment promotes compliance with police commands': Steve Uglow, *Policing Liberal Society* (OUP 1988) and Cyndi Banks, *Criminal Justice Ethics: Theory and Practice* (5th edn, SAGE 2019) 88–89.

and Zedner in *Criminal Justice*, for example, appear to be greatly interested in non-instrumental questions of procedural justice.[16]

There appear to be two kinds of instrumental account of procedural justice in circulation. There are those accounts that directly instrumentalise procedural justice and do so unambiguously, the most obvious being those studies that test a set of hypotheses derived from procedural justice theory in pursuit of specific behavioural or crime control outcomes.[17] Then there are those accounts that do so indirectly. These accounts are not unconcerned with the intrinsic values of procedural justice, but they are ultimately consigned to the margins and, in some studies, even appear to cut against a vision of the practice as pragmatically appealing.[18] In the latter case, there is a continued concern with the evaluation of procedural justice in terms of its consequences. Intrinsic values, including respect, are undermined because they are secondary to the outcomes achieved, rather than being inherent in what is meant by just policing.

Early work on procedural justice, in particular that of Thibaut and Walker, presented a directly instrumental interpretation of procedural justice findings.[19] For Thibaut and Walker, citizens defined fair procedures as those which allowed them to state their case and present their evidence prior to a decision being made. The authors' interpretation of this finding was that citizens were primarily concerned to ensure a fair outcome and thus achieve distributive fairness. On this view, the aim of a fair procedure was to produce a fair outcome.

Tyler's extensive work in this area is notable in that it is comprised of accounts that are both directly and indirectly instrumental

[16] Liz Campbell, Andrew Ashworth, and Mike Redmayne, *The Criminal Process* (5th edn, OUP 2019); Andrew Sanders, Richard Young, and Mandy Burton, *Criminal Justice* (4th edn, OUP 2010); and Lucia Zedner, *Criminal Justice* (OUP 2004).

[17] See, eg, Mike Hough, Jonathan Jackson, Ben Bradford, Andy Myhill, and Paul Quinton, 'Procedural Justice, Trust, and Institutional Legitimacy' (2010) 4(3) Policing 203 (hereafter Hough et al, 'Procedural Justice') and Lyn Hynds and Kristina Murphy, 'Public Satisfaction with Police: Using Procedural Justice to Improve Police Legitimacy' (2007) 40(1) Australian & New Zealand Journal of Criminology 27.

[18] See, eg, Tom R Tyler, 'Enhancing Police Legitimacy' (2004) 593(1) The ANNALS of the American Academy of Political and Social Science 84 (hereafter Tyler, 'Police Legitimacy').

[19] Thibaut and Walker, *Procedural Justice* (n 1).

in nature. On occasions when Tyler's work has subscribed to a directly instrumental approach, the line of argument pursued is that procedural justice is valuable because it enhances citizens' willingness to comply with police officials and other legal authorities.[20] One of Tyler's most prominent works is directly instrumental in that it is concerned to explore, in empirical terms, the question of why people comply with the law and how their compliance is achieved.[21] The study, conducted in Chicago, confirms that two factors—the degree of legitimacy citizens accord to legal authorities and their compliance with those authorities—are causally related to the manner and quality of treatment that they receive. An earlier study by Tyler, in which he interviews a random sample of citizens regarding their encounters with the police and the courts, pursues a similarly instrumental line of argument.[22] Of the 652 citizens who had encountered these authorities, Tyler finds that the procedurally just or unjust features of their encounters had substantial effects on their evaluations of the authorities involved and their views about the legitimacy of those authorities. For Tyler, identification of these features was instructive because they were found to affect citizens' acceptance of police decisions as well as their compliance with the law more generally. Tyler has since conducted a number of survey-based studies that confirm these early findings and strengthen his case for the instrumental value of procedural justice.[23]

In his work more generally, Tyler appears to be deeply supportive of the view that the ability of the police to secure and maintain orderly social relations—in essence, their ability to be authoritative—is a key indicator of their viability as an institution and, conversely, that the ability of the police to manage non-compliant populations can function as a kind of 'performance

[20] See, eg, Tyler, *Why People Obey the Law* (n 1).

[21] ibid.

[22] Tom R Tyler, 'Conditions Leading to Value-Expressive Effects in Judgments of Procedural Justice: A Test of Four Models' (1987) 52(2) Journal of Personality and Social Psychology 333. See also E Allan Lind and Tom R Tyler, *The Social Psychology of Procedural Justice* (Plenum 1988).

[23] Tom R Tyler and Yuen J Huo, *Trust in the Law: Encouraging Public Cooperation with the Police and Courts* (Russell Sage Foundation 2002) and Jason Sunshine and Tom R Tyler, 'The Role of Procedural Justice and Legitimacy in Shaping Public Support for Policing' (2003) 37(3) Law & Society Review 513 (hereafter Sunshine and Tyler, 'Procedural Justice and Legitimacy').

litmus test'.[24] According to Tyler, then, the act of securing citizens' voluntary compliance should not be underestimated, primarily for the purpose of maintaining safe, orderly communities but also because it functions as a self-legitimation activity for the police. Tyler and Blader explore this precise issue. Their study examines how forms of voluntary cooperation can be generated and maintained by the police, the instrumental value of which is, again, self-evident.[25]

While Tyler attends, on occasion, to the intrinsic features of legitimate policing, he ultimately defends the practice as one with considerable instrumental appeal.[26] We can only speculate as to why Tyler elects to defend procedural justice in this way. On the one hand, he may simply hold strong views regarding the merits of an instrumental approach to procedural justice. On the other hand, it is possible that his reasons for advocating this approach are strategic. Given that the US is heavily reliant on managerialist and repressive crime control strategies, it may be necessary to defend procedural justice in accessible language—and promote its instrumental benefits—in order to ensure that the ideas have some purchase in American criminal justice.[27] Analytic work on the idea of procedural justice itself may be of little relevance unless it is accompanied by a persuasive case for its effectiveness, in particular, in relation to crime control and the maintenance of order.

While the claim that procedural justice has been instrumentalised is not uncontroversial—especially given the dichotomous treatment of due process and crime control set out in Packer's landmark analysis[28]—a number of other procedural justice scholars have, in recent decades, shaped their research projects in such a way that

[24] Stephen D Mastrofski, Jeffrey B Snipes, and Anne E Supina, 'Compliance on Demand: The Public's Response to Specific Police Requests' (1996) 33(3) Journal of Research in Crime and Delinquency 269.

[25] See, eg, Tom R Tyler and Steven L Blader, *Cooperation in Groups: Procedural Justice, Social Identity, and Behavioral Engagement* (Psychology Press 2000) (hereafter Tyler and Blader, *Cooperation in Groups*).

[26] Tyler, 'Police Legitimacy' (n 18).

[27] Nicola Lacey, *The Prisoners' Dilemma: Political Economy and Punishment in Contemporary Democracies* (CUP 2008) 22–23 and David Garland, *The Culture of Control: Crime and Social Order in Contemporary Society* (OUP 2001) (hereafter Garland, *Culture of Control*).

[28] Herbert L Packer, 'Two Models of the Criminal Process' (1964) 113(1) University of Pennsylvania Law Review 1.

lends credence to this charge. The literature is replete with studies that emphasise the instrumental benefits of procedural justice in promoting self-regulatory behaviour and in allowing the authorities to shape the behaviour of people within the communities they police. Many of these studies subscribe to an approach that is either directly or indirectly instrumental in nature.

A directly instrumental approach is evident, for example, in work by Saarikkomäki that purports to 'use' the idea of procedural justice in order to improve police legitimacy,[29] as well as in a series of survey-based studies by Tyler, Sunshine and Tyler, and Bradford et al that have sought, in various ways, to operationalise trust and legitimacy as 'compliance with the law' or 'cooperation with the police'.[30] Jackson et al pursue an analogous line of enquiry in exploring why trust between citizens and the criminal justice system is important for instrumental reasons.[31] Their principal finding was that perceptions of unfair and disrespectful treatment have implications for citizens' compliance with the law, inciting non-cooperation and generating a heightened sense of conflict in police-public interactions.

Some studies are broader in scope, suggesting, for example, that citizens place considerable importance on a variety of non-instrumental criteria. These have been labelled 'relational criteria' since they provide citizens with feedback about the quality of their treatment by authorities and institutions.[32] Respect is routinely nominated as one such relational criterion, together with the trustworthiness of the authorities, the neutrality of their decision-making processes, and opportunities for citizens to participate.[33]

[29] Elsa Saarikkomäki, 'Perceptions of Procedural Justice Among Young People: Narratives of Fair Treatment in Young People's Stories of Police and Security Guard Interventions' (2016) 56(6) The British Journal of Criminology 1253 (hereafter Saarikkomäki, 'Perceptions of Procedural Justice').

[30] Tom R Tyler, 'Multiculturalism and the Willingness of Citizens to Defer to Law and Legal Authorities' (2000) 25(4) Law & Social Inquiry 983; Sunshine and Tyler, 'Procedural Justice and Legitimacy' (n 23); and Ben Bradford, Jonathan Jackson, and Elizabeth A Stanko, 'Contact and Confidence: Revisiting the Impact of Public Encounters with the Police' (2009) 19(1) Policing and Society 20.

[31] Jonathan Jackson, Ben Bradford, Mike Hough, Andy Myhill, Paul Quinton, and Tom R Tyler, 'Why do People Comply with the Law? Legitimacy and the Influence of Legal Institutions' (2012) 52(6) The British Journal of Criminology 1051 (hereafter Jackson et al, 'Why Do People Comply with the Law?')

[32] Tom R Tyler and E Allan Lind, 'A Relational Model of Authority in Groups' (1992) 25 Advances in Experimental Social Psychology 115.

[33] See, eg, Tyler, *Why People Obey the Law* (n 1).

Yet, while research strongly supports the argument that an important aspect of procedural justice involves relational criteria, in procedural justice scholarship, it continues to be explored in an instrumental way.

A recent article by Bottoms and Tankebe adopts an indirectly instrumental approach.[34] Its primary aim is to explore the content of the concept of legitimacy—in particular, its dual and relational character—in the context of policing and prisons and with detailed reference to the political science literature. Drawing on Weber's scholarship on this theme,[35] Bottoms and Tankebe explore which factors create and sustain legitimacy and why legitimacy is desirable within a social system. This is an important theoretical contribution, but it is not to overlook the authors' interest in the empirical tasks of measuring 'power-holder legitimacy' and 'audience legitimacy' with a view to enhancing the perceived effectiveness of the authorities in instrumental terms.[36]

In another contribution, Tankebe analyses the relative merits of both instrumental and non-instrumental approaches to legitimacy and procedural justice.[37] He calls for the prioritisation of careful empirical analysis in policing studies and outlines the need for further work on the operationalization of police legitimacy, especially power-holder legitimacy.[38] He also highlights the scope for non-instrumental research projects—his suggestions include the development of a richer understanding of the concept of legitimacy as well as normative work on the 'moral validity' of police power—because 'answers to these questions are interesting for their own sake, and can illuminate our understanding of legitimacy in different socio-cultural contexts'.[39] Comments of this nature are notable not only for their relative infrequency in the literature but also because they express normative views about the

[34] Anthony Bottoms and Justice Tankebe, 'Beyond Procedural Justice: A Dialogic Approach to Legitimacy in Criminal Justice' (2012) 102(1) The Journal of Criminal Law and Criminology 119 (hereafter Bottoms and Tankebe, 'Beyond Procedural Justice').

[35] Weber, *Economy and Society* (n 12).

[36] Bottoms and Tankebe, 'Beyond Procedural Justice' (n 34) 160–70.

[37] Justice Tankebe, 'Police Legitimacy' in Michael D Reisig and Robert J Kane (eds), *The Oxford Handbook of Police and Policing* (OUP 2014) (hereafter Tankebe, 'Police Legitimacy').

[38] ibid 253.

[39] ibid 254.

principles that should guide policing studies. It is encouraging that Tankebe attributes value to non-instrumental forms of enquiry.

2. Constrained, not characterised, by respect

Respect, as a self-proclaimed value and feature of the official discourse of the police, is already a resource internal to policing practice and, therefore, it might be assumed, intrinsically valuable to everyday police work. An important implication of a narrowly instrumentalist approach, however, is that procedural justice comes to be merely *constrained* and not *characterised* by respect.[40] Too often respect is treated—by policing scholars and police officers alike—as a weak side-constraint on the pursuit of crime control outcomes rather than a value that is centrally implicated in the idea of procedural justice itself.

This tendency can be detected in research by van Stokkom, which explores individual emotional responses to procedurally just treatment.[41] Van Stokkom situates his analysis in relation to a series of contentious and highly emotional police-public interactions that took place in Amsterdam, following the introduction of a zero-tolerance policy towards minor legal infringements and anti-social behaviour. In exploring these interactions from the perspectives of both the police and the policed, he considers cases where citizens had insulted the police as well as complaints made to the police by citizens claiming inappropriate treatment.

Van Stokkom poses the rhetorical question: 'Why is it that exercising authority and conferring respect cause so much trouble

[40] For some opaque references to the importance of mutual respect in policing, see Michael J Palmiotto and N Prabha Unnithan, *Policing and Society: A Global Approach* (Delmar Cengage Learning 2011) 171; Frank Leishman, Barry Loveday, and Stephen P Savage, *Core Issues in Policing* (2nd edn, Longman 2000) 84; and Saarikkomäki, 'Perceptions of Procedural Justice' (n 29). Even those studies which move beyond a strictly instrumental discussion of procedural justice contain vague references to respect. See, eg, Tom R Tyler and Robert J Bies, 'Beyond Formal Procedures: The Interpersonal Context of Procedural Justice' in John S Carroll (ed), *Applied Social Psychology and Organizational Settings* (Psychology Press 2015).

[41] Bas van Stokkom, 'Dealing with Defiant Citizens: Building Emotional Intelligence into Police Work' in Susanne Karstedt, Ian Loader, and Heather Strang (eds), *Emotions, Crime and Justice* (Hart 2011) (hereafter van Stokkom, 'Emotional Intelligence').

these days?'[42] He goes on to observe in citizens an increased 'status sensitivity' in their encounters with the police. Certainly, policing can feel coercive, but it also depends at almost every level on forms of cooperation and consensus.[43] Van Stokkom appears to be sensitive to this view, arguing that overt displays of police power must be handled in such a way that fosters and maintains moral values. Citizens expect persuasion from the authorities—rather than strict orders—and to be treated with respect.

Van Stokkom's treatment of respect is nuanced, for example, in his observation that ethnic minority groups may experience respectful treatment differently, not least because their sense of belonging and social possibility in society are often precarious. Elsewhere, his treatment of respect is less than satisfying, especially when he neglects to offer a definition of respect and leaves open the question as to whether the 'status sensitivity' he perceives is a question of—or even depends upon—respect.[44] Certainly, respect has the potential to mitigate—if not fully solve—the conditions of structured status inequality that characterise the police-public interaction. But when respect is understood reductively by the police, it creates symbolic boundaries between those of differing status, often constituting the citizen as inferior, wholly 'other', or simply invisible. Lack of respect, in short, means status subordination, and a serious violation of justice to which procedural *justice* aspires.

What initially looks like procedural justice may look like procedural injustice on a second reading. Van Stokkom's proposal, for example, that 'police officers have to develop more personal forms of respect capable of building citizen compliance' demonstrates a *prima facie* interest in enhancing respectful relations in practice.[45] Yet we are left wondering what might constitute a 'more personal' form of respect. The appeal to respect, then, provides an ethical tone to an otherwise pragmatic—if extremely

[42] ibid 242.

[43] Nicola Lacey, 'Introduction: Making Sense of Criminal Justice' in Nicola Lacey (ed), *A Reader on Criminal Justice* (OUP 1994) 5.

[44] See, eg, in political theory, Colin Bird, 'Status, Identity, and Respect' (2004) 32(2) Political Theory 207 (hereafter Bird, 'Status, Identity, and Respect') and, in anthropology, Philippe Bourgois, *In Search of Respect: Selling Crack in El Barrio* (CUP 1995) (hereafter Bourgois, *Respect*).

[45] van Stokkom, 'Emotional Intelligence' (n 41) 251.

compelling—argument for the incorporation of 'emotional intelligence' into police work, ranging from emotional awareness to the 'strategic expression' of emotions by the police.[46] Furthermore, van Stokkom's interest in the emotions is partially undermined when he neglects to acknowledge the affective basis of respect itself. Instead, we are given the false impression that respect is emotionally flat or incapable of producing an emotional response.[47] This is an especially striking omission given that the earliest conceptualisations of respect were in affective terms.[48]

If a moral value as distinctive as respect—prioritised by some scholars as a 'fundamental moral right'[49]—cannot be shown to be a foundational value of procedural justice, then the paradigm would appear to be flawed in a significant way. Van Stokkom's study provides one illustrative example of the reluctance of policing scholars to explore the precise meaning and scope of respect and its implications for procedural justice. A marked enthusiasm for the instrumental benefits of procedural justice means that respect is treated, at best, as a weak side-constraint on the pursuit of those instrumental benefits.

Importantly, the issue is not that instrumental outcomes are pursued at all. These concerns must simply be held in their proper place. It would have been perfectly acceptable for van Stokkom to have constructed a *post hoc* account of the incidental instrumental benefits of respect, provided that those anticipated benefits did not motivate the display of respect in the first place. Insofar as respect continues to be treated as a means by which to secure instrumental outcomes, it becomes increasingly difficult to subscribe to the version of procedural justice that he seeks to advance.

[46] ibid 250.

[47] For research in social psychology that confirms that respect produces an emotional response, see Naomi Ellemers, Bertjan Doosje, and Russell Spears, 'Sources of Respect: The Effects of Being Liked by Ingroups and Outgroups' (2004) 34(2) European Journal of Social Psychology 155.

[48] See, eg, John J Drummond, 'Respect as a Moral Emotion: A Phenomenological Approach' (2006) 22(1) Husserl Studies 1 and Thomas E Hill Jr, *Respect, Pluralism, and Justice: Kantian Perspectives* (OUP 2000).

[49] See, eg, Carla Bagnoli, 'Respect and Membership in the Moral Community' (2007) 10(2) Ethical Theory and Moral Practice 113 (hereafter Bagnoli, 'Respect') and OH Green, 'Introduction' Special Issue on Respect for Persons (1982) 31 Tulane Studies in Philosophy 1.

3. *Instrumentalism in policing practice*

Police reform has been defined in recent years by an increased awareness and implementation of policies of procedural justice.[50] It would appear, however, that the same instrumentalism that has shaped the framework through which procedural justice is understood by policing scholars also underlies the attitudes of police officers tasked with giving effect to procedural justice in practice. Notably, there has been some experimentation with the use of both standardised and personalised scripts for police officers, which aim to bring about procedural justice through the recitation of a particular form of words. These scripts typify an instrumental approach and make clear that pragmatic concerns have shaped—and continue to shape—policing practice.[51]

The arguments in favour of personalised scripted language for procedural justice tend to be framed in terms of increased accuracy and efficiency. The Queensland Community Engagement Trial—a study of random roadside breath tests—was the first of its kind to operationalise a 'legitimacy script' and a supporting checklist reflecting four key components of procedural justice: neutrality, citizen participation, respect, and trustworthy motives. In that study, police officers were provided with a script but were encouraged to adapt the wording and delivery in order to accommodate stylistic preferences and cultivate a 'fluid and mutually engaging' police-public encounter. The tension between achieving a level of competency in the articulation of the dialogue and allowing for a

[50] See, eg, Police Executive Research Forum, *Legitimacy and Procedural Justice: A New Element of Police Leadership* (Bureau of Justice Assistance, US Department of Justice 2014) and Hough, 'Procedural Justice and Professional Policing' (n 9).

[51] See, eg, Lorraine Mazerolle, Sarah Bennett, Emma Antrobus, and Elizabeth Eggins, 'Procedural Justice, Routine Encounters and Perceptions of Police: Main Findings from the Queensland Community Engagement Trial (QCET)' (2012) 8(4) Journal of Experimental Criminology 343 (hereafter Mazerolle et al, 'Procedural Justice'); Dennis Rosenbaum and Daniel Lawrence, *Teaching Respectful Police-Citizen Encounters and Good Decision-Making: Results of a Randomized Control Trial with Police Recruits* (Institute for Public Policy and Social Research, Michigan State University 2011) (hereafter Rosenbaum and Lawrence, *Teaching Respectful Police-Citizen Encounters*); and Levin Wheller, Paul Quinton, Alistair Fildes, and Andy Mills, *The Greater Manchester Police Procedural Justice Training Experiment: The Impact of Communication Skills Training on Officers and Victims of Crime* (College of Policing 2013) (hereafter Wheller et al, *Procedural Justice Training Experiment*).

more flexible interpretation of that dialogue was described by one police officer in the following way:

> The message had to get across—it had to *look like* or *sound like* it was the officer personally taking an interest in the individuals … unfortunately for the entire duration of the six months I recall one particular officer just simply putting the card in his hand [in reference to the procedural justice script] and reading it straight to them. I didn't intervene with that … I said … if you feel you're getting the message across to the people you're talking to, do whatever suits you … Other officers were very, very good; they never looked at it once.[52]

Since reading the script verbatim can minimise the intended importance of its message, the results of this pilot led to additional refinements in terms of the language used and the sequence of verbal delivery.[53]

Just as a genuine expression of respect must be accompanied by the appropriate attitude or intent, Rosenbaum and Lawrence—in their experimentation with procedural justice scripts—queried whether a police officer's verbal statements must be accompanied by an internal commitment to procedural justice or 'whether it is sufficient that the victim [or] complainant hears the statements'.[54] In so doing, the authors acknowledge—if only implicitly—that the words we utter can enhance and intensify our sense of responsibility for the sentiments expressed. Notwithstanding the authors' reservations about 'automated dialogue', the results of the study were consistent with the Queensland Community Engagement Trial in indicating that procedural justice behaviours can be scripted and taught to police officers and, by implication, that such scripts provide a plausible means by which to formulate an ethical response in a complex moral terrain.[55]

It is nonetheless ironic that policing organisations have experimented with procedural justice scripts, given the emphasis in

[52] Lorraine Mazerolle, Elise Sargeant, Adrian Cherney, Sarah Bennett, Kristina Murphy, Emma Antrobus, and Peter Martin, *Procedural Justice and Legitimacy in Policing* (Springer 2014) 51.

[53] ibid and Mazerolle et al, 'Procedural Justice' (n 51).

[54] Rosenbaum and Lawrence, *Teaching Respectful Police-Citizen Encounters* (n 51) 19.

[55] ibid. On automated dialogue, see Lorraine Mazerolle and William Terrill, 'Making Every Police-Citizen Interaction Count: The Challenges of Building a Better Cop' (2018) 17(1) Criminology & Public Policy 89.

procedural justice theory on the 'social connection' between the police and the communities they serve.[56] Procedural justice scripts are vulnerable to criticism for their inauthenticity alone, for they assume that procedural justice can be rehearsed and recited, when it is best achieved through free-flowing conversation and mutual understanding. But this instrumental approach is not only operationally constraining. The scripts also invite a broader critique of the police as concerned primarily with producing certain patterns of behaviour in citizens, especially those that align with state-directed standards. Insofar as this is the case, procedural justice scripts are more likely to be an instance of 'responsibilization' than be viewed as a genuine attempt to cultivate respect.[57]

So understood, procedural justice scripts have the potential to complicate the very interactions that they are supposed to mediate. Goffman's concept of 'facework'—the presentations of self that we make for various audiences—is instructive here.[58] According to Goffman, we routinely engage in a series of 'performances' in order to appear competent as we move from audience to audience. When we adopt a performative notion of procedural justice, it makes little sense to reflect on whether police officers are genuinely respectful. It makes more sense to reflect on which audiences they are performing for and in which contexts.

A UK-based procedural justice training experiment led by Wheller et al implicitly adopted this position and rejected the use of procedural justice scripts altogether.[59] It was anticipated that the time and effort required to prepare a procedural justice script would outweigh its instrumental or non-instrumental benefits, not least because a diverse repertoire of verbal statements would have to be developed for use in different situations. It was also anticipated that experienced police officers would resist scripted language and display a degree of scepticism as to whether it would prescribe meaningful ethical guidelines for policing practice. Police officers might prefer instead to rely on their own 'moral

[56] See, eg, Ben Bradford and Jonathan Jackson, 'Enabling and Constraining Police Power: On the Moral Regulation of Policing' Jonathan Jacobs and Jonathan Jackson (eds), *The Routledge Handbook of Criminal Justice Ethics* (Routledge 2016).

[57] Garland, *Culture of Control* (n 27).

[58] Erving Goffman, *The Presentation of Self in Everyday Life* (Social Sciences Research Centre, University of Edinburgh 1956).

[59] Wheller et al, *Procedural Justice Training Experiment* (n 51).

literacy' or empathetic expertise. The understandable concern was that a procedural justice script would restrict or place limits on the real 'craft' of policing.[60]

The linguistic philosopher, Austin, proposed that in order to make sense of a particular utterance we must locate that utterance within a 'total speech situation'.[61] There are strong reasons to believe that the 'total speech situation' has been left unexplored in these experiments, especially when we consider the identities of minority communities. Respect is relational and highly contextual.[62] When it is taken for granted that a script can be recited to all citizens in the same way—that it is universally applicable—we risk undermining the identities of ethnic minority groups who often have radically different understandings of respect and diverse subjective responses to its expression. Scripted language considered respectful by a police officer might be viewed as suspect or even disrespectful by a citizen to whom it is expressed, especially if that citizen considers the police officer to represent a social group to which they do not belong. In this way, procedural justice scripts, in posing a risk to a citizen's ontological security, can result in the very antithesis of respect for an individual's identity as well as his group identity.[63]

In short, the relationship between procedural justice scripts, respect, and ethnicity would appear to be more complex and

[60] See further, eg, Hough, 'Procedural Justice and Professional Policing' (n 9) 194 and Barbara Herman, *Moral Literacy* (Harvard University Press 2007).

[61] JO Urmson and Marina Sbisà (eds), John L Austin, *How to Do Things with Words* (2nd edn, Harvard University Press 1975).

[62] See, eg, Robin S Dillon, 'Respect' in Edward N Zalta (ed), *The Stanford Encyclopedia of Philosophy* (Stanford University 2018) <http://plato.stanford.edu/entries/respect/> accessed 1 August 2019.

[63] On the profound effects of discriminatory policing on minority communities, see Bourgois, *Respect* (n 44). On injurious language, see Judith Butler, *Excitable Speech: A Politics of the Performative* (Routledge 1997). On recognition and belonging, see Loader, 'Recognition and Belonging' (n 8). On ontological security, see Ian Loader and Neil Walker, *Civilizing Security* (CUP 2007). On respect, see Richard Sennett, *Respect: The Formation of Character in an Age of Inequality* (Penguin 2004); Sune Lægaard, 'What Does "Respect for Difference" Mean?' in Peter Balint and Sophie Guérard de Latour (eds), *Liberal Multiculturalism and the Fair Terms of Integration* (Palgrave Macmillan 2013); and Peter Balint, 'Respect Relationships in Diverse Societies' (2006) 12(1) Res Publica 35. On procedural justice and diversity, see Tom R Tyler, 'Governing amid Diversity: The Effect of Fair Decision-making Procedures on the Legitimacy of Government' (1994) 28(4) Law & Society Review 809.

nuanced than has been assumed. While policing organisations are seen to be reforming through experimentation with, and incorporation of, procedural justice policies, respect for all citizens, and ethnic minority groups in particular, continues to be understood as a weak side-constraint on instrumental outcomes.

C. The Intrinsic Case

The flexibility of respect is such that it provides a means by which to advance a critique of the current approach to procedural justice, as well as a means by which to reimagine it. Certainly, procedural justice has considerable practical appeal, offering a credible language by which to deliver effective crime control and reform the practice of policing. But it must not be viewed in narrowly instrumental terms.

In developing an intrinsic case for procedural justice, the aim is not to dispense with instrumental concerns entirely but simply to make space for non-instrumental concerns—especially those which pertain to respect—and provide an alternative means by which to understand and approach the practice. Why respect? Respect inheres, sometimes intangibly but no less influentially, in a number of key procedural justice indicators, namely, neutrality, transparency, fairness, recognition, and voice.[64] If adequately understood and enacted, respect could function not as a weak side-constraint on the pursuit of instrumental outcomes but as the unifying value at stake in the very idea of procedural justice itself.

Not least because of its prominence within the literature, I adopt the Bottoms and Tankebe distinction between *the quality of decision-making* (neutrality, transparency) and *the quality of treatment* (fairness, recognition, and voice) here.[65] However, while this dichotomy can perform a useful classificatory function, it is less helpful in achieving a deeper understanding of the content of procedural justice itself. Bottoms and Tankebe observe, for example, that the two sets of indicators 'tend to have rather different

[64] This list of procedural justice 'indicators' is drawn from the work of Raymond Paternoster, Robert Brame, Ronet Bachman, and Lawrence W Sherman, 'Do Fair Procedures Matter? The Effect of Procedural Justice on Spouse Assault' (1997) 31(1) Law & Society Review 163 and Tyler and Blader, *Cooperation in Groups* (n 25).

[65] Bottoms and Tankebe, 'Beyond Procedural Justice' (n 34).

emotional connotations' and, for this reason, they pursue distinct lines of argument in relation to each set. For the authors, 'quality of decision-making' embraces a range of concerns that might be categorised according to the principles of natural justice, while 'quality of treatment' is 'personal'.[66] The advantage of focusing on respect is that it allows us to evaluate all of the indicators, while simultaneously speaking to their varied affective implications. In other words, when the indicators are viewed through the prism of respect, it becomes clear that, for reasons other than classification, there is no need to separate them.

1. Neutrality

The idea of neutrality is essential to the perceived quality and fairness of decision-making in procedural justice and respect is certainly implicated.[67] It is well established, for example, that citizens conceptualise procedurally just decision-making as impartial and based on objective indicators, rather than subjective views. Given that most citizens—though not most offenders who have repeated interactions with the police—lack criminal justice expertise and may not be in an informed position as to the most appropriate outcome, they are attentive instead to the decision-making process and the extent to which the outcome demonstrates evidence of neutrality. In this way, citizens depend heavily on the inferences that they make about officials' intentions during the decision-making process. To the extent that those inferences are positive ones and there is a clear commitment to neutrality, the citizen is offered—at the very least—a procedural form of respect.

2. Transparency

The idea of transparency is similarly fundamental to the quality of decision-making and is routinely classed as a key feature of the procedurally just encounter. As with neutrality, in an interaction that promotes transparency, respect is more than a mere abstraction. Rather, it is evident when officials explain the decision-making

[66] ibid 145.

[67] See, eg, David de Cremer and Steven L Blader, 'Why do People Care About Procedural Fairness? The Importance of Belongingness in Responding and Attending to Procedures' (2006) 36(2) European Journal of Social Psychology 211.

process as well as the decision itself to citizens, who can then systematically process and analyse the information to the degree that they desire.[68] Respect for citizens is also promoted within and through the interaction when, in pursuit of transparency, officers modify their conduct in order to give an appropriate level of attention to individual needs and concerns. In this way, respect provides an important ethical basis for the practice of transparent decision-making.

3. Fairness

Loader appeals to the non-instrumental value of policing in proposing that 'the police must treat all those with whom they come in to contact with fairness and respect'.[69] For Loader, these principles offer a means by which to evaluate police work and are also regulative ideals in guiding our aspirations for what policing can be. Furthermore, his work provides an important hint that—in the context of procedural justice, at least—the egalitarian notions of fairness and respect are closely related.[70]

The preoccupations of other policing scholars with the joint role of fairness and respect in securing instrumental outcomes has meant that the precise nature of their conceptual relationship has been left unarticulated.[71] An obvious challenge is that beyond the intuitive notion of fairness—the act of attributing to each his due—there are several plausible conceptions of the idea. They point in different directions. One prominent conception is that fairness requires a reciprocal interaction. Another prominent

[68] ibid.

[69] Ian Loader, 'In Search of Civic Policing: Recasting the "Peelian" Principles' (2016) 10(3) Criminal Law and Philosophy 427, 434 (hereafter Loader, 'In Search of Civic Policing'). On distributive fairness, procedural fairness, and respect, see also Independent Police Commission, *Policing for a Better Britain* (Independent Police Commission 2013).

[70] Loader, 'In Search of Civic Policing' (n 69). See also Andrew Millie and Karen Bullock, 'Policing in a Time of Contraction and Constraint: Re-imagining the Role and Function of Contemporary Policing' (2013) 13(2) Criminology & Criminal Justice 133.

[71] For two contrasting views on the relationship between fairness and respect in political philosophy, see Jonathan Wolff, 'Fairness, Respect, and the Egalitarian Ethos' (1998) 27(2) Philosophy & Public Affairs 97 and Timothy Hinton, 'Must Egalitarians Choose Between Fairness and Respect?' (2001) 30(1) Philosophy & Public Affairs 72.

idea is that fairness is responsive to need; that those in greatest need of fairness should have first claim to it. Then, of course, there is the distinguished Rawlsian notion of 'justice as fairness', which considers, from a normative standpoint, the social institutions that would be created as a result of a hypothetical contract made under conditions that ensured that all the contractors treat one another fairly.[72]

It would appear that procedural justice is organised—if only implicitly—according to the first view of fairness as involving reciprocity, given that procedural justice requires social interaction. According to proponents of procedural justice, fairness extends both to citizens (who demonstrate positive responses to officials when they regard their encounters with them as procedurally fair) and officials (where fairness can inform the internal organisation of police forces).[73] In this way, fairness extends both to vertical relationships between officials and citizens and horizontal relationships between officials.

When Bradford asserts that fairness in procedural justice promotes 'a sense of inclusion and value', while unfairness 'communicates denigration and exclusion' he is, we might assume, alluding to the relevance of respect in shaping the experience of procedural fairness.[74] Precisely *how* respect is implicated in procedural fairness or the sustaining of fair interactions between individuals is a more complex issue. One possible explanation is that when a police officer prioritises fair treatment as part of a procedurally just interaction, he communicates the regard with which he holds the citizen and offers him respect. However, to the extent that his commitment to a fair interaction is prompted only or, in part, by a Code of Ethics—for example, the policing principle of 'fairness' proposed by the College of Policing[75]—he might be said to have shown a strictly procedural form of respect.

[72] John Rawls, *A Theory of Justice* (Belknap Press of Harvard University Press 1971) and John Rawls, *Justice as Fairness: A Restatement* (Harvard University Press 2001).

[73] The receptiveness of citizens to fair treatment is otherwise known as the 'fair process' effect. See, eg, Ben Bradford, 'Police and Social Identity: Procedural Justice, Inclusion and Cooperation between Police and Public' (2014) 24(1) Policing and Society 22.

[74] ibid 22.

[75] College of Policing, *Code of Ethics* (n 6).

4. Recognition

When Tyler and Smith conceive of respect in procedural justice as the quality of treatment that individuals receive, they accurately observe that respect is implicated in the interaction itself, but gloss over the intricacies of that interaction.[76] *Prima facie*, recognition—as a form of interpersonal treatment—is not dissimilar to respect. As with respect, it is firmly established that mutuality is the explanatory and normative core of recognition. To recognise another is a genuinely interpersonal endeavour, which presupposes a subject and object of recognition.[77] In this way, appeals to recognition and respect in procedural justice must be finely differentiated. In the research literature to date, their similarities and differences have received scant analytic attention.

It is widely accepted among philosophers that the assigning of respect is a central dimension of recognition. In two contemporary contributions, Bagnoli subscribes precisely to this view, while Honneth proposes a tripartite model of recognition as 'love', 'respect', and 'esteem' in which respect is posited as one of three distinct modes of recognition.[78] As we saw in chapter 1, even its derivation from the Latin *respicere*, meaning 'to look back at' or 'to look again', implies that respect is a particular mode of recognising another.[79]

It would be relatively uncontroversial, then, to posit respect as implicated in the process of recognition that characterises procedural justice. The question of precisely *how* respect is implicated is more complex. The dominant understanding of respect as a mode of recognition, to which both Bagnoli and Honneth subscribe, involves respecting a citizen as an equal.[80] This flat form

[76] Tom R Tyler and Heather J Smith, 'Justice, Social Identity, and Group Processes' in Tom R Tyler, Roderick M Kramer, and Oliver P John (eds), *The Psychology of the Social Self* (Erlbaum 1999).

[77] Mattias Iser, 'Recognition' in Edward N Zalta (ed), *The Stanford Encyclopedia of Philosophy* (Stanford University 2019) <http://plato.stanford.edu/entries/recognition/> accessed 1 August 2019.

[78] Bagnoli, 'Respect' (n 49) and Axel Honneth, *The Struggle for Recognition: The Moral Grammar of Social Conflicts* (Polity 1995) (hereafter Honneth, *Recognition*).

[79] Allen W Wood, 'Respect and Recognition' in John Skorupski (ed), *The Routledge Companion to Ethics* (Routledge 2010) (hereafter Wood, 'Respect and Recognition') and Stephen L Darwall, *The Second-Person Standpoint: Morality, Respect, and Accountability* (Harvard University Press 2006).

[80] Bagnoli, 'Respect' (n 49) and Honneth, *Recognition* (n 78).

of recognition respect for the humanity of a person can be distinguished from another common usage of respect, namely, an evaluative form of respect for the moral qualities of an individual's character or conduct. In the former case, a citizen is respected solely by virtue of the fact that he is a human being capable of autonomous agency, while in the latter case, an individual's moral character or conduct are valued.[81]

With that distinction in mind, it is worth drawing attention to Hegtvedt's empirical observation that adequate recognition in procedural justice can prompt internalised responses such as feelings of self-worth and valued membership of a group.[82] By contrast, when recognition is lacking, Jackson et al observe that 'the police's message [to citizens] is stark: [they] are not valued by society'.[83] Yet the dominant understanding of recognition—based on simple egalitarianism—fails to value individual attributes and functions in a way that is apparently mechanical and emotionally flat. This raises an intriguing terminological question. Might it be that the proponents of procedural justice are relying mistakenly on recognition as opposed to respect? Respect is the richer concept here, in that it can move beyond a basic recognition of autonomous agency and exhibits an emotional quality that facilitates the valuing of individuals and produces internalised feelings of self-worth that Hegtvedt envisages.[84]

5. *Voice*

Respect is easily detectable in a procedurally just interaction that prioritises voice.[85] According to procedural justice, police officers must offer citizens the opportunity to 'have their say'.[86] However, for citizens, the ability to control the outcome of that interaction

[81] Stephen L Darwall, 'Two Kinds of Respect' (1977) 88(1) Ethics 36.

[82] Karen A Hegtvedt, 'Justice Frameworks' in Peter J Burke (ed), *Contemporary Social Psychological Theories* (2nd edn, Stanford University Press 2006) 50 (hereafter Hegtvedt, 'Justice Frameworks').

[83] Jackson et al, 'Why Do People Comply with the Law?' (n 31) 1053.

[84] Hegtvedt, 'Justice Frameworks' (n 82).

[85] On respect and voice as among the most important 'building blocks' of procedural justice, see Bradford, 'Voice, Neutrality and Respect' (n 5).

[86] See, eg, Tom R Tyler, 'Trust and Legitimacy: Policing in the USA and Europe' (2011) 8(4) European Journal of Criminology 254 and Loader, 'In Search of Civic Policing' (n 69).

is not central. More important is the sense that they have participated and articulated their position on a given matter. On this view, citizens prefer that their input has been solicited and considered by the police, who are then sensitive to their concerns in arriving at an appropriate resolution.

When a police officer prioritises voice, he respects the citizen as a free and self-governing agent whose views are to be taken seriously.[87] In so doing, he implies that it is not enough to respect a citizen by virtue of his abstract rights and formal equality. Rather, his concrete identity, differentiating attributes, and individual views are worthy objects of respect. Respect is also detectable to the extent that citizens *feel* valued, in a subjective sense, as a result of having articulated their position.[88]

Recent work on the role and value of voice in procedural justice is instructive here. While earlier theorising on voice was strictly instrumental in nature—concerned with how the prioritisation of voice might enhance the likelihood of achieving a desired outcome—subsequent research has sought to develop an understanding of the non-instrumental mechanisms that inform reactions to voice. It has been suggested that while voice has an important instrumental meaning, this instrumentality does not explain why individuals value having a voice in the process.[89] One possibility is that respect—as an ethical notion implicit in the idea of procedural justice itself—can offer a convincing explanation for the non-instrumental value of voice.

(a) Instrumentalism and intrinsic values

As we have seen, procedural justice has the potential to incorporate a range of intrinsic values, yet recent efforts to theorise, let alone realise, them have been more than a little superficial. It is notable, for example, that while the word 'respect' is routinely invoked at the level of official discourse, in research and practice, it has been reduced to a weak side-constraint on the pursuit of instrumental outcomes. This is despite its status as an 'interaction-regulating value' and its capacity to mediate between a range of

[87] See further, Wood, 'Respect and Recognition' (n 79).

[88] Bird, 'Status, Identity, and Respect' (n 44).

[89] John Angus D Hildreth, Don A Moore, and Steven L Blader, 'Revisiting the Instrumentality of Voice: Having Voice in the Process Makes People Think They Will Get What They Want' (2014) 27(2) Social Justice Research 209.

other core intrinsic values at play, namely, neutrality, transparency, fairness, recognition, and voice.[90]

Without discrediting the crime control function that procedural justice purports to perform, there is a marked preoccupation with the instrumental over the non-instrumental, and a pervasive misunderstanding of the ways in which they might interact. We might even say that there is an implied consensus, at least among procedural justice scholars, as to the nature of this form of justice, how it operates, and what it is for. Such neglect is not simply a matter of disciplinary emphasis or style but a means of entrenching a particular status quo, consistent with that described by Zedner and Hough et al for whom criminological scholarship has long been comprised of both simple—even simplistic—models of crime control and models that have more texture and depth.[91] While there will always be competing ideologies as to how procedural justice should be realised, scholars and practitioners must be equally attentive to—and, ideally, recognise the reciprocal nature of the relationship between—instrumental and non-instrumental concerns. Only then might we invest procedural justice with new significance, and reflect coherently on its meaning, possibilities, and limits.

[90] We might extend to respect Fraser's analogy of recognition as an 'interaction-regulating value': Nancy Fraser, 'Rethinking Recognition' (2000) 3 New Left Review 107, 115.

[91] Zedner, 'Useful Knowledge?' (n 11) and Hough et al, 'Procedural Justice' (n 17).

3

Stop and Search as a Respectful Encounter

In this chapter, there is a shift in focus to the statutory power of the police to stop and search, the controversial status of which is not new.[1] Less well documented, however, is that stop and search is highly relevant to the study of respect, since the practice tends to undermine the value, if not render it conspicuously absent.

The chapter is organised as follows. The opening section explores how we might sharpen our critique of stop and search by framing it in terms of respect. Stop and search—a common form of adversarial contact between the police and the public—taps into deep and ingrained tensions between preventive policing, the exercise of coercive state authority, due process, and crime control. Among the most incisive criticisms of the power are its disproportionate and discriminatory exercise in relation to minority ethnic groups,[2] its role in eroding police legitimacy,[3] and

[1] The police power of stop and search in the UK has a long and contentious history, which is amply described elsewhere. See, eg, Ben Bowling and Coretta Phillips, *Racism, Crime and Justice* (Longman 2002); Ben Bowling and Coretta Phillips, 'Disproportionate and Discriminatory: Reviewing the Evidence on Police Stop and Search' (2007) 70(6) The Modern Law Review 936 (hereafter Bowling and Phillips, 'Disproportionate and Discriminatory'); Rebekah Delsol and Michael Shiner, 'Regulating Stop and Search: A Challenge for Police and Community Relations in England and Wales' (2006) 14(3) Critical Criminology 241 (hereafter Delsol and Shiner, 'Regulating Stop and Search'); and Rebekah Delsol and Michael Shiner (eds), *Stop and Search: The Anatomy of a Police Power* (Palgrave Macmillan 2015) (hereafter Delsol and Shiner (eds), *Anatomy of a Police Power*).

[2] See, eg, Bowling and Phillips, 'Disproportionate and Discriminatory' (n 1).

[3] See, eg, Ben Bradford, *Stop and Search and Police Legitimacy* (Routledge 2016) (hereafter Bradford, *Stop and Search and Police Legitimacy*).

Respect and Criminal Justice. Gabrielle Watson, Oxford University Press (2020). © Gabrielle Watson.
DOI: 10.1093/oso/9780198833345.001.0001

the invasion of privacy and violation of bodily integrity necessitated by the search itself.[4] In all three instances, police officers operate—whether by neglect or intent—with a narrow understanding of respectful relations, where respect operates as a weak side-constraint on a power that is exercised for narrowly instrumental reasons. Were the police to incorporate respect into the very purposes and rationale of stop and search, the 'wrongs' of the practice that attract regular criticism could be partly, if not wholly, counteracted.

The next section assesses three prominent proposals for the reform of stop and search—procedural justice training for police officers,[5] tighter legal regulation of the power,[6] and abolition[7]—in terms of respect. First, the language of respect offers a promising means by which to enhance procedural justice training. Second, respect provides a point of entry into the debate on the legal regulation of stop and search. Of note, however, is the capacity of respect to evaluate the third—and boldest—of the reform proposals. When the abolitionist position is assessed in terms of respect, there is scope to argue that if the power of stop and search cannot be exercised respectfully, it should not be exercised at all. Although there are important limits to such a view, we are left in no doubt as to the flexibility of respect as a concept of critical enquiry for policing and criminal justice.

[4] See, eg, Equality and Human Rights Commission, *Stop and Think: A Critical Review of Stop and Search Powers in England and Wales* (Equality and Human Rights Commission 2016) (hereafter Equality and Human Rights Commission, *Stop and Think*).

[5] Ben Bradford, Jonathan Jackson, and Mike Hough, 'Police Futures and Legitimacy: Redefining Good Policing' in Jennifer M Brown (ed), *The Future of Policing* (Routledge 2014) (hereafter Bradford et al, 'Police Futures and Legitimacy').

[6] Michael Shiner, 'Regulation and Reform' in Delsol and Shiner (eds), *Anatomy of a Police Power* (n 1) (hereafter Shiner, 'Regulation and Reform').

[7] Home Office, *Police Powers of Stop and Search: Summary of Consultation Responses and Conclusions* (Home Office 2014) s 3.10 Campaign groups and organisations. See also Femi Oyeniran, 'Stop and Search: It's Time for the Police to Abolish this Ineffective and Damaging Procedure' *The Independent* (21 July 2013) <www.independent.co.uk/voices/comment/stop-and-search-its-time-for-the-police-to-abolish-this-ineffective-and-damaging-procedure-8724542.html> accessed 1 August 2019 (hereafter Oyeniran, 'Stop and Search').

A. Critique

The key criticisms of stop and search—those which pertain to its disproportionate and discriminatory application, its role in eroding police legitimacy, and the invasion of privacy and violation of bodily integrity necessitated by the search itself—can each be reduced to a critique of the manner in which respect is understood. It is worth noting, however, that these criticisms are not entirely discrete—the issue of racial discrimination is especially pervasive—and there is inevitably a degree of overlap in the argument that follows.

As a widely proclaimed value and feature of official discourse, we might assume that respect is already a resource internal to policing and intrinsically valuable to the practice of stop and search.[8] Yet respect does not accrue to all. While the intrusive nature of stop and search has been justified, at least in part, on the grounds that it is conducted respectfully,[9] a recent review of the power confirmed that 47 per cent of respondents 'felt they were not treated with respect' when they were stopped and searched.[10]

[8] See, eg, Home Office, *Revised Code of Practice for the Exercise by Police Officers of Statutory Powers of Stop and Search and Police Officers and Police Staff of Requirements to Record Public Encounters: Police and Criminal Evidence Act 1984 Code A* (The Stationery Office 2014) (hereafter Home Office, *PACE Code A*) 3.1 'All stops and searches must be carried out with courtesy, consideration and respect for the person concerned.'

[9] College of Policing, *Definition of a Fair and Effective Stop and Search Encounter* (College of Policing 2016) 1, 'The person understands why they have been searched and feels that they have been treated with respect.' Home Office, *A Consultation on Police Powers of Stop and Search* (Home Office 2013) 11, 2.12 'The power of stop and search … must demonstrate respect for the people being searched.' Home Office, *Police Powers of Stop and Search: Summary of Consultation Responses and Conclusions* (Home Office 2014) 16, 'Concerning the proper use of the power, [there is] a requirement to explain the reasons for the search and to conduct it in a courteous and respectful way.'

[10] Her Majesty's Inspectorate of Constabulary, *Stop and Search Powers: Are the Police Using Them Effectively and Fairly?* (Her Majesty's Inspectorate of Constabulary 2013) (hereafter Her Majesty's Inspectorate of Constabulary, *Stop and Search Powers*). cf Her Majesty's Inspectorate of Constabulary, *2017 PEEL Assessment* (Her Majesty's Inspectorate of Constabulary 2017) 'We were pleased to find that police leaders continue to have a clear understanding of the value of treating the public with fairness and respect, and are succeeding in establishing this approach throughout their workforces' quoted in Sarah Pepin, *Effect of Police Stop and Search Powers on BAME Communities* (House of Commons Library 2018, no. CDP-2018-0125) 3–4.

Deeply implicated in the individual criticisms of stop and search is a reductive understanding of respect on the part of the police—and, for some commentators, a clear commitment to undermine the value—that warrants articulation and clarification.

1. The instrumental aims of stop and search

There appear to be two approaches—we might call them *dominant* and *emerging*—to understanding the instrumental aims of stop and search. It will be necessary to provide a brief sketch of both approaches because it is in pursuing either or both of them so eagerly that respectful relations are compromised. While the aim is not to discredit the instrumental functions of stop and search *per se*, the most prominent criticisms of the practice flow directly from the tendency of the police to overstate this function and understate intrinsic values such as respect.

The dominant approach, popular in policy documentation, posits stop and search as an instrumental mechanism of crime prevention and detection.[11] On this view, the purpose of stop and search is to enable police officers to detain suspects temporarily for the purposes of questioning and investigation. The power thus allows officers to allay or confirm what must be genuine and well-founded suspicions about them, without proceeding directly to arrest them.[12] The practice is deemed effective when suspicion is allayed and an unnecessary arrest is prevented or, conversely, when suspicion is confirmed and an object is found or a crime detected.[13]

While crime prevention and detection are sold as ends whose pursuit legitimates stop and search, recent scholarship has called into doubt whether the practice is instrumentally effective at all. Bradford and Loader have argued that crime prevention and detection are best understood as 'legitimating fictions' of stop

[11] Ben Bradford and Ian Loader, 'Police, Crime and Order: The Case of Stop and Search' in Ben Bradford, Beatrice Jauregui, Ian Loader, and Jonny Steinberg (eds), *The SAGE Handbook of Global Policing* (SAGE 2016) (hereafter Bradford and Loader, 'The Case of Stop and Search').

[12] Home Office, *PACE Code A* (n 8) 1.4.

[13] It is notable, then, that irrespective of the manner in which the police officer proceeds, the exercise is classed as effective. See, eg, Her Majesty's Inspectorate of Constabulary, *PEEL: Police Legitimacy 2017. A National Overview* (Her Majesty's Inspectorate of Constabulary 2017) 19.

and search, and that the practice has no more than a marginal purchase on the problem of controlling crime.[14] Their claim finds expression in research published by the Home Office, which verified that large increases in weapons-related stops and searches across ten London boroughs from 34,154 in 2007–08 to 123,335 in 2008–09 had no discernable effect on crime reduction.[15] Bowling and Phillips have echoed these sentiments, contending that there is no compelling 'business case' for such heavy reliance on stop and search. Its limited role in disrupting crime, deterring others, and maintaining community safety does little to legitimate the practice.[16] Meanwhile, Delsol has challenged claims to instrumental success on the grounds that, despite decades of research, it remains unclear what effectiveness—especially in preventive terms—means in this context or how it should be measured.[17]

The tenuous claims of the police to success in crime prevention and detection arguably conceal a more complex picture. Evidence on the social and spatial distribution of stop and search invites an alternative conception of stop and search as radically discretionary. An emerging school of thought posits the—rather less explicit—instrumental aims of stop and search to include the assertion of order,[18] the regulation of marginal populations, and the monitoring of those who are 'known' to the police, 'based on who they are, not how they behave'.[19] Although there is no basis in law for the police to use the power in this way, for

[14] Bradford and Loader, 'The Case of Stop and Search' (n 11).

[15] Rhydian McCandless, Andy Feist, James Allan, and Nick Morgan, *Do Initiatives Involving Substantial Increases in Stop and Search Reduce Crime? Assessing the Impact of Operation BLUNT 2* (Home Office 2016) 19, Table 5: Weapons-related stop and searches, by tier and search type, 2007–08 to 2008–09.

[16] Bowling and Phillips, 'Disproportionate and Discriminatory' (n 1) 959 and Matteo Tiratelli, Paul Quinton, and Ben Bradford, 'Does Stop and Search Deter Crime? Evidence from Ten Years of London-Wide Data' (2018) 58(5) The British Journal of Criminology 1212.

[17] Rebekah Delsol, 'Effectiveness' in Delsol and Shiner (eds), *Anatomy of a Police Power* (n 1).

[18] Satnam Choongh, *Policing as Social Discipline* (Clarendon Press 1997).

[19] Bradford and Loader, 'The Case of Stop and Search' (n 11) 257. See also PAJ Waddington, Kevin Stenson, and David Don, 'In Proportion: Race, and Police Stop and Search (2004) 44(6) The British Journal of Criminology 889 (hereafter Waddington et al, 'In Proportion').

some commentators, there is little motivation to remain within its parameters. Stop and search practices are characteristically 'low visibility'.[20] Despite—or perhaps because of—this reality, Bowling and Phillips consider these extra-legal practices to be widespread.[21]

There is a clear historical trajectory to such a belief. The earliest instances of stop and search sought to regulate and discipline those from marginalised communities and exploit the notion of the racially or culturally defined 'other'. Prominent examples include the North American 'Black Codes' which prohibited slaves from travelling without a ticket or the Pass Laws which were promulgated under the South African Apartheid regime.[22] In the UK, stop and search powers first appeared in laws aimed at controlling vagrancy: the 1824 Act furnished an officer with the power to stop and search an individual on the basis of his suspicion alone. It is against this background that modern stop and search powers evolved.[23]

(a) Disproportionate and discriminatory application

A defining feature of the critical debate on stop and search is the disproportionate and discriminatory manner in which it is exercised. Bowling and Phillips are unconvinced that respect can shed explanatory light on—or allow us to make significant advances in relation to—discriminatory practices in stop and search. Where discrimination is concerned, the authors attach little value to

[20] Ben Bradford and Jonathan Jackson, 'Enabling and Constraining Police Power: On the Moral Regulation of Policing' in Jonathan Jacobs and Jonathan Jackson (eds), *The Routledge Handbook of Criminal Justice Ethics* (Routledge 2016) (hereafter Bradford and Jackson, 'Moral Regulation of Policing').

[21] Bowling and Phillips, 'Disproportionate and Discriminatory' (n 1). See also Satnam Choongh, 'Policing the Dross: A Social Disciplinary Model of Policing' (1998) 38(4) The British Journal of Criminology 623.

[22] Markus Dubber, *The Police Power: Patriarchy and the Foundations of American Government* (Columbia University Press 2005). On the racially or culturally defined 'other,' see Stuart Hall, Charles Critcher, Tony Jefferson, John Clarke, and Brian Roberts, *Policing the Crisis: Mugging, the State and Law and Order* (2nd edn, Palgrave Macmillan 2013).

[23] Vagrancy Act 1824. See also Leanne Weber and Ben Bowling, 'Valiant Beggars and Global Vagabonds: Select, Eject, Immobilise' (2008) 12(3) Theoretical Criminology 355.

respect, whether understood as a weak side-constraint or a foundational value of policing:

> Despite the importance that we would attach to the need for courtesy and respect in the use of police powers, we feel that this point is *at a distance* from the main issues of discrimination in the use of the power and that no improvement in the manner in which the power is used will compensate for the more fundamental issues at stake.[24]

Yet there are good grounds for discounting such a view, and supposing that the polar opposite is the case. It is simply not possible, let alone desirable, to disassociate respectful treatment from the issue of racial discrimination in the manner that the authors suggest. Respect—far from being 'at a distance'—is deeply implicated in discriminatory policing practices and intensely felt by those targeted in this way. When respect is viewed as intrinsically valuable in making sense of stop and search and as a means by which to sharpen our critique of this discriminatory practice, its contribution becomes clear.

Home Office statistics reveal the striking empirical reality that, in the year ending March 2017, individuals from black and minority ethnic (BME) groups were just under four times as likely to be stopped than those who identified as white, while those who identified specifically as black (or black British) were over eight times more likely to be stopped than those who identified as white. In 71 per cent of cases, no further action was taken.[25] The Home Office explains away this racial disparity—and dismisses concerns about the over-policing of BME communities—by drawing attention to resident populations. The disparities are explained with reference to the disproportionately high levels of stop and search in the London Metropolitan Police District relative to the rest of the country, where a large proportion of residents identify as BME.[26]

The issue with interpreting the statistics through the lens of resident populations, however, is that it risks transforming a suspected problem of racial discrimination into one of urban policing.

[24] Emphasis added. Bowling and Phillips, 'Disproportionate and Discriminatory' (n 1) 960.

[25] Jodie Hargreaves, Hannah Husband, and Chris Linehan, *Police Powers and Procedures in England and Wales*, year ending 31 March 2017 (2nd edn, Home Office 2017) (hereafter Hargreaves et al, *Police Powers and Procedures*).

[26] ibid.

A focus on urban conditions can serve to legitimise high rates of stop and search, by deferring to the simple—even reductive—narrative that more policing is required in difficult and disadvantaged areas of the city.[27] Yet stop and search has long exposed and exacerbated racial tensions in England and Wales and the wealth of research on this issue reveals a complex, highly racialised picture.[28] Implicated in this concerning trend is a tendency of the police to undermine respect for BME suspects. When those from BME groups are disproportionately and repeatedly targeted for reasons of crime prevention and detection, the maintenance of order, or social management, we might infer that respect has operated as peripheral to—rather than as a foundational value of—the police-public interaction itself.

The utilitarian ethos of stop and search was reaffirmed in the 2015 Supreme Court judgment on section 60 of the Criminal Justice and Public Order Act 1994, which dismissed the argument that stop and search was intrinsically discriminatory. The court held that there are 'great benefits to the public in such a power' and particularly to 'black and minority ethnic groups'.[29] Strikingly, the court assumed this stance despite evidence of direct and indirect stereotyping, the disproportionate targeting of ethnic

[27] On the counterproductive effects of regulating behaviour closely in urban areas, see Jon Bannister and Ade Kearns, 'Tolerance, Respect and Civility amid Changing Cities' in Andrew Millie (ed), *Securing Respect: Behavioural Expectations and Anti-social Behaviour in the UK* (Policy Press 2009). This approach to explaining away racial disparities in the use of stop and search has the potential to reinforce what Anderson calls the 'iconic ghetto'. Anderson explains that the ghetto has come to be defined as the area where '"black people live," symbolising an impoverished, crime-prone … and violent area of the city'. When the ghetto assumes the 'iconic' status that Anderson describes, it defines black citizens even when they reside far from these areas: Elijah Anderson, 'The Iconic Ghetto' (2002) 642(1) The ANNALS of the American Academy of Political and Social Science 8.

[28] The extensive discourse on race and ethnicity in stop and search stands in stark contrast to the literature on procedural justice, which is remarkably silent on the issue. See, eg, Bowling and Phillips, 'Disproportionate and Discriminatory' (n 1) and Paul Quinton, 'Race Disproportionality and Officer Decision-Making' in Delsol and Shiner (eds), *Anatomy of a Police Power* (n 1).

[29] *R (Roberts) v Comr of Police of the Metropolis* [2015] UKSC 79, para 41. In the first appeal of its kind, the Supreme Court ruled unanimously that s 60, which allows suspicionless searches, is in accordance with the law and compatible with the European Convention on Human Rights.

minorities for suspicionless searches,[30] and the requirement that the power must be used 'fairly, responsibly, *with respect* for people being searched and without unlawful discrimination'.[31] This explicit call for respect loses much of its potential force, however, and even begins to sound thin and trite, when made indiscriminately, and without more detailed context. In Dworkin's terms, respect remains abstract in that it contains no specification of how it is to be 'weighed or compromised in particular circumstances'.[32] Whether respect was intended to be understood as a foundational value of stop and search in the statutory Code of Practice would be a question for those who drafted it, however, it is clear that it has not been interpreted by the judiciary as such.

The pragmatic response of the court makes clear that the word 'respect' functions as a weak side-constraint on a debate about preventive rationales. This is underwhelming, not least because respect is inherently reciprocal and, if taken seriously, might mediate fraught interactions between the police and the BME community. In particular, respect can mitigate the conditions of structured status inequality that characterise everyday police work, allowing us to dispense with any concerns about the relative positioning of parties to that interaction.[33] The concerning implication of the court judgment, however, is that status matters, and that the inconvenience experienced by a minority—and the attendant risk that they are not intrinsically valued—is necessary in order to 'prevent violent crime' and appeal to the greater public good.

The challenging conceptual territory into which the court ventures is deserving of further consideration. The restrictive understanding of respect to which the court subscribes—if only implicitly—might be summarised as follows. Those policing measures that contribute to the good of an individual—irrespective of his views on the matter—are in his best interests.[34] If the court's

[30] Ben Bowling and Estelle Marks, 'The Rise and Fall of Suspicionless Searches' (2017) 28(1) King's Law Journal 62.

[31] Emphasis added. Home Office, *PACE Code A* (n 8) 1.1.

[32] Ronald Dworkin, *Taking Rights Seriously* (Duckworth 1977) 93.

[33] Richard Sennett, *Respect: The Formation of Character in an Age of Inequality* (Penguin 2004) (hereafter Sennett, *Respect*).

[34] Adam Barnett, 'Britain's Supreme Court says targeting young black men for stop-and-search "benefits them"' *The Independent* (17 December 2015) <www.independent.co.uk/news/uk/crime/britain-s-supreme-court-says-targeting-young-black-men-for-stop-and-search-benefits-them-a6777651.html> accessed 1 August 2019.

interpretation of respectful policing is correct, the concerning implication is that we must flatly reject the BME suspect's view that it is not in his best interests to be searched intrusively and repeatedly in the name of crime prevention or detection. Yet such an approach to respect is incompatible with the idea that to respect a suspect as a human being is to defer to his own understanding—provided it is 'informed and coherent'—of what it means to respect and be respected.[35] Any plausible conception of respect for policing must move beyond a standard that is, strictly speaking, formal or procedural, as detailed in the statute. Rather, it must also make space for an individual's subjective experience of respect.

There are strong ethical reasons for developing stop and search policies that are sensitive to the views of BME suspects, whose experiences of respect—or lack thereof—have long been dismissed. But there is also a tension that must be managed, between the desire to reassure the public—for example, through visible, assertive policing—and to offer respect to those BME suspects who are most often or most heavily policed.[36]

In this way, race matters profoundly in any enquiry into respect in stop and search. Scholarship by Bourgois and Ahmed is relevant here, which shows how respect is highly valued among BME groups and those whose sense of belonging and social possibility in society are precarious. It also highlights the frequency with which expressions of respect are misinterpreted by particular subgroups, whose members may view the police as representatives of a group to which they do not belong.[37]

[35] On giving priority to a person's choices or preferences in a respectful interaction, provided they are 'informed and coherent', see Kalle Grill, 'Respect for What? Choices, Actual Preferences, and True Preferences' (2015) 41(4) Social Theory and Practice 692, 693..

[36] Respect should be paramount in stop and search irrespective of the 'availability' argument, namely, that certain structural factors render young black men more accessible to the police: Waddington et al, 'In Proportion' (n 19). See also Amy E Lerman and Vesla Weaver, 'Staying Out of Sight? Concentrated Policing and Local Political Action' (2014) 651(1) The ANNALS of the American Academy of Political and Social Science 202.

[37] Philippe Bourgois, *In Search of Respect: Selling Crack in El Barrio* (CUP 1995) and Sara Ahmed, *On Being Included: Racism and Diversity in Institutional Life* (Duke University Press 2012). See also Douglas' comments on those individuals who occupy a 'marginal state' and are 'somehow left out in the patterning of society, who are placeless': Mary Douglas, *Purity and Danger: An Analysis of the Concepts of Pollution and Taboo* (Routledge and Kegan Paul 1966) 95.

Respectful treatment has important implications for our own sense of cultural identity, effectively affirming, undermining, or even denying it. If we are to extend respect to individuals who are disproportionately subject to stop and search, there must be a serious effort to look afresh at the features of their cultures that they consider to be crucial to their identities.[38] The deficit of respect for BME groups in stop and search might be attributable, in part, to the tendency of police officers to assess the quality of an interaction exclusively from the perspective of their own culture. Yet to understand respect within certain cultural parameters is a risky strategy in complex, pluralist societies. Although it serves to limit understanding and skew the judgement of police officers, it *does not* alleviate their responsibility to confront and diminish their prejudices. The police must be willing to fulfil this particular responsibility if we are to respect them as legitimate actors too.

If there is a predisposition to cultural bias in stop and search, we might make progress by giving priority to the voices of those who suffer most frequently from it. This strategy would ensure that police relations with ethnic minorities and other disadvantaged populations are, as Loader suggests, treated as 'core' to police activity rather than marginal or secondary to it. In time, respectful relations might become institutionally embedded in policing agencies and working cultures.[39] It is essential, then, that the police aspire to meaningful expressions of respect. Without the openness stimulated by appreciation of varied cultural experiences of respect, they might proclaim commitment to the value but fail to see when and how it gives them reasons for acting—and for restraint—in instances of cultural conflict.

Although much of the scholarship on stop and search coalesces around the issue of race, it would prove unhelpful—even counterproductive—to evaluate stop and search exclusively in

[38] On respecting others in their difference, see, eg, Peter Balint, 'Respect Relationships in Diverse Societies' (2006) 12(1) Res Publica 35 (hereafter Balint, 'Respect Relationships'); John Tomasi, 'Kymlicka, Liberalism, and Respect for Cultural Minorities' (1995) 105(3) Ethics 580, and Bethan Loftus, *Police Culture in a Changing World* (OUP 2009) ch 5 (hereafter Loftus, *Police Culture*).

[39] Ian Loader, 'Policing, Recognition, and Belonging' (2006) 605(1) The ANNALS of the American Academy of Political and Social Science 201, 214 (hereafter Loader, 'Recognition and Belonging').

these terms.[40] Analyses of stop and search must be open to a range of interpretational possibilities and acknowledge the multiple forms of direct and indirect discrimination at play relating to, for example, age, gender, and socio-economic class, as well as the intersectionality between these different forms.[41] Analyses must speak to the statistical reality that those most likely to be stopped and searched frequently and aggressively—and, we might infer, those most likely to feel devalued as a result—display a variety of socio-demographic characteristics. Not only are these individuals most likely to be black but they are also most likely to be young, male, and socially marginalised. According to a 2017 report entitled *No Respect*, almost 1.5 million young BME people believe that their communities have been unfairly targeted. There is a real sense that stop and search has a corrosive impact on their interactions with the police, and that they feel 'hunted' irrespective of innocence or guilt.[42]

(b) Erosion of police legitimacy

Police legitimacy is the dominant concept in the contemporary discourse on stop and search.[43] Stop and search is regularly described as a litmus test of police-public relations,[44] yet critics routinely draw attention to the role of the police power in eroding them. While the argument that stop and search can present

[40] Delsol and Shiner, 'Regulating Stop and Search' (n 1); Delsol and Shiner (eds), *Anatomy of a Police Power* (n 1); and Genevieve Lennon and Kath Murray, 'Under-regulated and Unaccountable? Explaining Variation in Stop and Search Rates in Scotland, England and Wales' (2018) 28(2) Policing and Society 157.

[41] On the 'significant interaction' between gender and minority status in police stops (whereby white women were *more* likely to be stopped than their minority group counterparts), see Bradford, *Stop and Search and Police Legitimacy* (n 3) 108.

[42] Peter Keeling, *No Respect: Young BAME Men, The Police and Stop and Search* (Criminal Justice Alliance 2017).

[43] See, eg, Bradford, *Stop and Search and Police Legitimacy* (n 3) and Tom R Tyler, Jeffrey Fagan, and Amanda Geller, 'Street Stops and Police Legitimacy: Teachable Moments in Young Urban Men's Legal Socialization' (2014) 11(4) Journal of Empirical Legal Studies 751 (hereafter Tyler et al, 'Teachable Moments').

[44] See, eg, Delsol and Shiner, 'Regulating Stop and Search' (n 1) and House of Commons, *BAME Communities: Stop and Search* (HC Deb 23 May 2018, vol 641, col 357WH).

significant material costs for police legitimacy is well rehearsed,[45] the relevance of respect is not.

In the literature, respect is treated as a kind of moral axiom—likened, far too quickly, to politeness, courtesy, or dignity—with the result that it is introduced to debates on stop and search and police legitimacy in diverse and conflicting ways. In one much-cited contribution, Tyler et al observe that when police officers treat citizens *inter alia* with 'dignity and respect', they are *rewarded* with enhanced legitimacy.[46] By contrast, Bowling and Phillips claim that when stop and search is conducted improperly, it *undermines* the 'legitimacy of, and respect for, the police'.[47]

It would appear, then, that respect functions in a manner that is so subtle in stop and search it has yet to be fully appreciated. When we juxtapose the views of Tyler et al and Bowling and Phillips, we find two abbreviated—and sharply contrasting—accounts as to the role and value of respect. They reveal a tension between what I term *respect as process* and *respect as outcome*. For Tyler, respect is implicated in proper police treatment and thereby in the *process* of stop and search itself. On this view, respectful treatment can contribute directly to perceptions of police legitimacy.[48] By contrast, for Bowling and Phillips, improper police treatment *results* in declining respect for the police, and so respect is viewed as an outcome to which we might aspire.[49]

This chapter focuses, as do Tyler et al, on the role and value of respect in shaping the process of stop and search itself. We might even hypothesise that respect functions as the key construct in linking stop and search to a diminished sense of police legitimacy. While this conceptualisation of respect in stop and search has yet to be articulated elsewhere, let alone empirically verified,

[45] Ben Bradford, 'Unintended Consequences' in Delsol and Shiner (eds), *Anatomy of a Police Power* (n 1) and Bradford, *Stop and Search and Police Legitimacy* (n 3).

[46] Tyler et al, 'Teachable Moments' (n 43).

[47] Bowling and Phillips, 'Disproportionate and Discriminatory' (n 1) 939.

[48] Tyler et al, 'Teachable Moments' (n 43). A Police Foundation briefing on stop and search also subscribes to a view of respect as implicated in the interaction itself. 'Officers who treat an individual fairly and with respect inspire greater confidence and trust': The Police Foundation, *The Briefing* (Series 2, edn 3, The Police Foundation 2012) 7.

[49] Bowling and Phillips, 'Disproportionate and Discriminatory' (n 1).

the research by Tyler and colleagues is subtly indicative of this trend.[50]

(c) Invasion of privacy and violation of bodily integrity

When Bowling and Weber claim that 'the manner in which searches are conducted is a primary source of dissatisfaction and feelings of having been treated with disrespect', they imply that respect is a value to which the physical search might legitimately aspire, but gloss over the intricacies of what constitutes a respectful search.[51] Again, in this context, the meaning of respect has been diluted and needs to be reclaimed.

Were respect to be treated as a foundational value of policing, it would play a pivotal role in countering a key criticism of the conduct of the search itself: namely, that it does not protect the privacy and bodily integrity of the suspect.[52] While every suspect, by virtue of his humanity, has a claim to respect,[53] it is easy to imagine a case in which the—often speculative and inadequately grounded—physical touching of a suspect 'on the streets' is not respectful and instead constitutes a state-legitimised affront to his privacy and bodily integrity.[54] In this way, the physical search provides a particularly striking example of the tendency of the police to treat respect as a weak side-constraint on the pursuit of instrumental outcomes.

Guidance from the Metropolitan Police states that 'it is legitimate for an officer of any sex to stop and search a person of any sex, provided the search is in public and restricted to a superficial examination of outer garments'.[55] According to the guidance, a police officer can place his hand inside the pockets of outer

[50] See, eg, Tyler et al, 'Teachable Moments' (n 43) and Jason Sunshine and Tom R Tyler, 'The Role of Procedural Justice and Legitimacy in Shaping Public Support for Policing' (2003) 37(3) Law & Society Review 513.

[51] Ben Bowling and Leanne Weber, 'Stop and Search in Global Context: An Overview' (2011) 21(4) Policing and Society 480, 481.

[52] See, eg, Equality and Human Rights Commission, *Stop and Think* (n 4) 71.

[53] Robin S Dillon, 'Respect' in Edward N Zalta (ed), *The Stanford Encyclopedia of Philosophy* (Stanford University 2018) <http://plato.stanford.edu/entries/respect/> accessed 1 August 2019 (hereafter Dillon, 'Respect').

[54] See, eg, Anne Phillips, *Our Bodies, Whose Property?* (Princeton University Press 2013) (hereafter Phillips, *Our Bodies, Whose Property?*)

[55] Metropolitan Police, *Stop and Search of People of Different Gender to the Searching Officer* (Metropolitan Police 2016) 1.

clothing, inside collars, socks and shoes, and may also search the suspect's hair, if this is reasonably necessary in the circumstances of a particular search. Any search involving the removal of more than an outer coat, jacket, gloves, footwear, or any other item concealing identity, must only be made by an officer of the same sex. Otherwise, the commitment of the Metropolitan Police to respect is limited to an empty and otherwise unelaborated requirement that 'all stops and searches must be carried out with … respect for the person concerned'.[56] As ever, the value is too little examined and too quickly dismissed, and is further complicated by the author's dated—even provocative—tendency to conflate 'gender identity' and 'sex'.

The literature in political philosophy on self-ownership provides a novel means by which to elucidate the significance of respect in relation to the conduct of the search itself.[57] This is the concept of property in one's own person, which is often expressed as the moral right of a person to have bodily integrity and be in exclusive control of his own body. Clearly, self-ownership places moral constraints on what can permissibly be done to others. It also possesses many of the features that societies find so appealing when subscribing to the liberal ideal, such as liberty of individual action, a set of inalienable moral rights, and a government that exercises only limited power over its citizens.[58] One plausible application of the concept of self-ownership, then, is to show that

[56] ibid.

[57] On self-ownership, see Cécile Fabre, *Whose Body is it Anyway? Justice and the Integrity of the Person* (OUP 2006) ch 1 (hereafter Fabre, *Whose Body is it Anyway?*). Fabre offers an original account of the rights individuals have over their own bodies and others' bodies. The account relies on a conception of justice that emphasises sufficiency, autonomy, and respect for persons. For Fabre, the idea of 'respect for persons' implies that, in a just society, there should be opportunities for individuals to cultivate 'self-respect' in addition to the 'basic respect' which they are owed from others. See also Carole Pateman, 'Self-Ownership and Property in the Person: Democratisation and a Tale of Two Concepts' (2002) 10(1) The Journal of Political Philosophy 20 (hereafter Pateman, 'Self-Ownership and Property in the Person'). cf Kasper Lippert-Rasmussen, 'Against Self-Ownership: There Are No Fact-Insensitive Ownership Rights over One's Body' (2008) 36(1) Philosophy & Public Affairs 86 (hereafter Lippert-Rasmussen, 'Against Self-Ownership').

[58] Fabre, *Whose Body is it Anyway?* (n 57); Pateman, 'Self-Ownership and Property in the Person' (n 57); and Lippert-Rasmussen, 'Against Self-Ownership' (n 57). See also Phillips, *Our Bodies, Whose Property?* (n 54).

it accords with our intuitions about the injustice of various acts involving the invasion of privacy and the violation of bodily integrity by the state.

The suspect who is stopped and searched has a 'moral jurisdiction' over his person that is deserving of respect. In other words, he has a moral entitlement—if not a legal one—that an officer refrains from interfering with it without explicit permission.[59] In this way—rather than simply asserting that respect is owed to all suspects in stop and search—the literature on self-ownership allows us to ground the requirement for respect in relation to the body itself.

2. The respect deficit

It has been possible to expose a severe respect deficit in stop and search, which has been raised only tangentially elsewhere. Regrettably, the value is not as 'simple' or as 'easy to implement' as Tyler claims.[60] Nonetheless, the advantage of integrating a deeper understanding of respect into stop and search would be its role in partly, if not wholly, counteracting the considerable critique that it attracts.

The intrinsic case for respect is that it should be a foundational value of stop and search irrespective of whether it generates instrumental outcomes because it builds into the practice an ethical awareness that is valued in a liberal democracy.[61] Even if empirical evidence showed categorically that conducting stop and search respectfully guarantees its instrumental effectiveness, this alone would not be enough to justify holding it as a deep, necessary feature of a framework for deliberating about the practice. While it is a welcome fact that respect—however vaguely articulated in policy documentation and achieved in practice—seems to promote instrumental outcomes, the version of respect advanced in this book stands independently of this fact. A respectful stop and search should be concerned primarily with process rather

[59] The process is inevitably intrusive; even confrontational. If necessary, the police officer is empowered to use reasonable force to conduct the search: see Home Office, *PACE Code A* (n 8) 3.2.

[60] Tom R Tyler, 'Trust and Legitimacy: Policing in the USA and Europe' (2011) 8(4) European Journal of Criminology 254, 260.

[61] Loader, 'Recognition and Belonging' (n 39).

than outcome. It matters *how* we pursue various instrumental aims, not just that we do so.[62]

But this is not to dismiss outcomes entirely and, in particular, what overall patterns of distribution reveal about current approaches to respect. As we have seen, the proportion of BME citizens who are stopped and searched is substantially higher than the proportion of white citizens reporting such encounters.[63] The literature has produced two kinds of response—we might call them strong and weak—to this statistical reality. For some commentators, the appropriate response is to view the disparity in the use of stop and search as indicative of stereotyping, racial prejudice, and—more radically—ethnic profiling.[64] For others, stop and search is better viewed as a practice that succumbs to racial stereotypes but is not exclusively shaped by them. On this view, a more complex and subtle explanation is required.[65] Irrespective of whether we subscribe to the strong or weak response, the statistics imply that respect is not freely available in the context of stop and search, and that a selective approach to the value is at play.

The wildly disproportionate exercise of stop and search towards certain ethnic groups implies that it is not enough for the state to respect what citizens have in common—in other words, to respect them by virtue of their humanity. They should also, where appropriate, respect—or, at least, acknowledge—their differences. In this context, police officers would be required to take into account the minority status of certain citizens and filter that status into their decisions to refrain from—or, where appropriate, proceed with—stop and search. There is an inevitable risk, however, that this approach serves not to promote respect within an increasingly multicultural context but to simplify group identities drastically and increase the frequency and intensity of ethical

[62] ibid and Ian Loader, 'Why do the Police Matter? Beyond the Myth of Crime-Fighting' in Jennifer M Brown (ed), *The Future of Policing* (Routledge 2014). On the 'special moral obligations' of the police, see Jake Monaghan, 'The Special Moral Obligations of Law Enforcement' (2017) 25(2) The Journal of Political Philosophy 218.

[63] Hargreaves et al, *Police Powers and Procedures* (n 25).

[64] See, eg, Alistair Henry, 'Policing and Ethnic Minorities' in Alistair Henry and David J Smith (eds), *Transformations of Policing* (Ashgate 2007).

[65] Waddington et al, 'In Proportion' (n 19) 905.

disagreements.[66] Such are the constraints and freedoms of respect. Were police officers to work towards alleviating the disparities in the use of stop and search and were they to do so with a respectful attitude towards all those they are charged to police, their actions could function as much as a form of redress to ethnic minority groups as an expression of respect.

B. Beyond Critique

It has become a truism that stop and search, as it is currently constituted, is deeply problematic and in need of major revision at the levels of theory, policy, and application.[67] The concept of respect permits an expansive approach to the issue of how best to reform this discredited tactic. This section evaluates three prominent reform proposals—procedural justice training for police officers, tighter legal regulation, and abolition—in terms of respect. The first and second proposals accommodate the idea—if largely implicitly—that respect must become central to stop and search if it is to be adequately reformed. Implicit in the third proposal is an alternative argument that stop and search must be abolished on the grounds that it simply cannot be conducted respectfully.

From time to time, this task will involve reading respect into specific proposals from which the idea is *prima facie* absent. While it is true that the proposals are rarely couched in the language of respect, its traces are still so clearly evident there. The value is regularly presupposed in the content of the proposals themselves but, if made explicit, would offer a coherent ethical framework for guiding discussion on the reform proposals and mediating conflicts of opinion contained within them.

1. Proposals for reform

(a) Procedural justice training

In stop and search, procedural justice is indispensable, not least in helping to resolve tensions generated by a practice which is so often reduced to a dialogue of claims and counter-claims to status. Against this background, respect might be posited as an

[66] See further Balint, 'Respect Relationships' (n 38).
[67] Bradford et al, 'Police Futures and Legitimacy' (n 5).

innovation—and elevated to a consistent running theme—of all procedural justice training programmes.

One inspection report revealed that most police officers were untrained in the use of stop and search powers and only twenty-one forces provided any form of refresher training.[68] Those forces which had made significant investments in training had done so because of external pressure from oversight bodies including the Equalities and Human Rights Commission. Given the inconsistency in training provision, it was found that police officers had instead refined their practice through informal mentoring processes. While this can be a valuable approach if mentors are skilled and engaged, it can also lead to the proliferation of procedurally unjust, inadequately respectful, and even unlawful practices, including searches carried out without reasonable grounds for suspicion.[69]

The evidence suggests that there is a need for a structured procedural justice training programme for all police officers entrusted with the power of stop and search. For Bradford et al, the police must give citizens the impression that they would 'treat them with respect' and that they are '"out there" making decisions in a procedurally fair manner'.[70] Meanwhile, Sennett's scholarship provides some ideas as to the form that respect might take. As we have seen, he eschews the traditional Kantian view of respect based on simple egalitarianism (we should treat others with respect *because* we are considered to be of equal status) and suggests a form of respect that is readily adaptable to stop and search (we should treat others with respect *despite* the fact we are of unequal status).[71]

There is scope for Sennett's ideas on respect to find expression in procedural justice training programmes. According to Hough, there is a need for training that explicitly addresses the issue of authority: its use and legitimation as well as how best to respond to suspects inclined to challenge it.[72] It is well documented that, in

[68] Her Majesty's Inspectorate of Constabulary, *Stop and Search Powers* (n 10).

[69] ibid.

[70] Bradford et al, 'Police Futures and Legitimacy' (n 5) 84.

[71] Sennett, *Respect* (n 33). For an overview of the Kantian position, see Thomas E Hill Jr, *Respect, Pluralism, and Justice: Kantian Perspectives* (OUP 2000).

[72] Mike Hough, 'Procedural Justice and Professional Policing in Times of Austerity' (2013) 13(2) Criminology & Criminal Justice 181.

many urban communities, police-public relations are adversarial in nature. This is especially so in communities where stop and search is exercised improperly and without legal authority. Once an adversarial approach to stop and search becomes dominant, the police are likely to have only limited scope to revert to a style of policing grounded in principles of procedural justice.[73] Were procedural justice training programmes to be framed in terms of respect, police officers would be introduced to an idea that has intuitive appeal—almost everyone has an opinion on respect—but which also has praxis, offering a coherent ethical framework for the practice of stop and search.

Yet there are also anticipated barriers to implementing a 'soft' reform strategy of this kind. It is conceivable, for example, that this proposal may run against some of the most fundamental aspects of police organisational culture, especially given its sense of internal solidarity. The culture of the police organisation itself—'suspicious, isolationist, conservative, cynical'[74]—is often cited as a key barrier to improving the quality of police-public relations.[75] If the police environment is dismissive of the relevance of 'soft skills' such as enhancing knowledge of and sensitivity to respect, full implementation of this reform could be precluded. Bradford et al cite these and other barriers while also conceding that they are likely to inhibit officers' propensities to treat all citizens they encounter 'in a respectful and open manner'.[76]

(b) Tighter legal regulation

In England and Wales, stop and search is legally mandated and exceptionally broad in scope.[77] Some commentators have called

[73] ibid.

[74] Bradford et al, 'Police Futures and Legitimacy' (n 5) 87. See also Jerome H Skolnick, *Justice without Trial: Law Enforcement in a Democratic Society* (Wiley 1966) and Loftus, *Police Culture* (n 38) ch 1.

[75] For an alternative account of police culture as highly relevant to rule-formulation and as a potential resource in the development of new police powers and practices, see Andrew Goldsmith, 'Taking Police Culture Seriously: Police Discretion and the Limits of Law' (1990) 1(2) Policing and Society 91.

[76] Bradford et al, 'Police Futures and Legitimacy' (n 5) 88. See also Wesley G Skogan, 'Why Reforms Fail' (2008) 18(1) Policing and Society 23.

[77] The police are empowered to stop and search citizens under a broad range of legislative acts. For a comprehensive list, see College of Policing, *Stop and Search: Legal Basis* (College of Policing 2018) <www.app.college.police.uk/app-content/stop-and-search/legal/legal-basis> accessed 1 August 2019.

for tighter legal regulation of the power.[78] One reform option would be to revise and frame the relevant statutory provisions in terms of respect. These provisions could expressly codify respect by offering a clear definition as well as illustrations of good practice in the respectful conduct of stop and search. The flaw in this approach, however, is its formal adherence to legalism, whereby respect is effectively reduced to a matter of rule-following and respectful relationships to a series of duties and rights determined by rules. By implication, we are at risk of giving effect to that most obviously hierarchical aspect of law that Lacey describes: its creation of duties and standard-setting devices.[79]

There is also a deeply contested question as to whether stop and search can be subject to effective legal regulation at all. For Young, the statutory power does not preclude abuse of police discretion, especially given the regularity with which the norms and working practices of police officers are prioritised over external legal regulation.[80] For Bradford and Loader, the law has failed spectacularly in subjecting stop and search to effective control and it is therefore unhelpful to make sense of the power in terms of its detailed legal framework.[81] Lustgarten draws attention to research which shows that 'reasonable suspicion' is frequently absent in stop and search practices that expressly require it. In view of the relevant provisions in the Police and Criminal Evidence Act 1984, these searches are unlawful.[82] Quinton's empirical findings reveal that the law does not feature strongly in decision-making processes and functions instead as little more than a resource for asserting authority and 'disciplining' citizens, especially those in 'long-standing relationships' with the police.[83] This scholarship

[78] On creating the conditions for effective legal regulation, see David Dixon, *Law in Policing: Legal Regulation and Police Practices* (OUP 1997).

[79] Nicola Lacey, 'Criminalization as Regulation: The Role of Criminal Law' in Christine Parker, Colin Scott, Nicola Lacey, and John Braithwaite (eds), *Regulating Law* (OUP 2004). See also Judith N Shklar, *Legalism: Law, Morals, and Political Trials* (Harvard University Press 1964).

[80] Jock Young, *Policing the Streets: Stops and Searches in North London* (Middlesex University 1994).

[81] Bradford and Loader, 'The Case of Stop and Search' (n 11).

[82] Laurence Lustgarten, 'The Future of Stop and Search' [2002] Criminal Law Review 603 and Home Office, *PACE Code A* (n 8) 2.1–2.11.

[83] Paul Quinton, 'The Formation of Suspicions: Police Stop and Search Practices in England and Wales' (2011) 21(4) Policing and Society 357, 366.

makes clear that the social reality of stop and search is complex and messy and that the decentring of legal regulation might be a plausible move.[84] The idea that the law should not have a monopoly on the regulation of stop and search—and, in particular, that regulation could instead occur informally, within the police and between the police and other actors—is now gaining momentum. If the aim is meaningful reform, then there is some potential—though also real risks—to integrating respect into the legal framework of stop and search.

(c) Abolition

For Bowling and Phillips, the discourse on stop and search is sharply divided between 'apologists' and others—especially those protesting racial injustice—who have mooted the possibility of abolishing the power altogether.[85] It would appear that the arguments of abolitionists contain an unarticulated view that the practice of stop and search is profoundly antithetical to respect. And so, the argument goes, if the coercive power cannot be exercised respectfully, it should not be exercised at all.[86]

Yet it is doubtful that abolition is even feasible. We might focus instead on reimagining stop and search as a respectful encounter, whereby every citizen is deserving of respect: full recognition as a person, with the same basic moral worth as any other.[87] Even though scholars, practitioners, and activists might legitimately disagree about how best to achieve it, we must remain committed to the idea that respect is realistically attainable and need not function as a weak side-constraint on the pursuit of instrumental outcomes.

A power that so often prompts highly charged interactions between the police and the public is unlikely to disappear simply because we forbid its exercise. Bradford and Loader have observed,

[84] In this context, the term 'decentring' refers to the gradual removal of government and administration from policing: Julia Black, 'Decentring Regulation: Understanding the Role of Regulation and Self-regulation in a "Post-Regulatory" World' (2001) 54(1) Current Legal Problems 103.

[85] See, eg, Oyeniran, 'Stop and Search' (n 7).

[86] This argument would proceed on the basis that the modest demands of the Equalities and Human Rights Commission for 'good enough policing' simply cannot be met: Equality and Human Rights Commission, *Stop and Think* (n 4) 71, 'Our vision of "good enough" policing'.

[87] Dillon, 'Respect' (n 53).

for example, that abolition would do little to prevent 'informal' stops and 'formal' ones would doubtless be replaced by more intrusive practices and an increased number of arrests.[88] In other words, divesting the police of the power of stop and search could result in increasingly disrespectful police-public encounters. The preferred role for abolitionism—as a theoretical perspective and political movement—should be in reinforcing stop and search, prompting reform, and demanding a more robust justification for its continued use.

One advantage of retaining stop and search and reimagining it as a respectful encounter might be its role in giving effect to the 'moral rights of policing' that Miller envisages.[89] For Miller, the purpose of policing is to realise a collective good. The good in question involves two kinds of moral right: human rights and institutional (moral) rights. The former are held by individuals solely by virtue of their humanity. The latter are held by individuals in part by virtue of their humanity and in part by virtue of their membership of a community or morally legitimate institution. Miller argues that the protection of moral rights should not only be a feature of policing but an important guiding principle of the practice.[90] Although respect is not included in his original typology, it could easily be posited as an additional institutional moral right to which all individuals who are stopped and searched—as members of a liberal polity—have a claim.

2. Prospects for reform

Shiner explores the prospects for the reform of stop and search and addresses the seeming inability of successive administrations and bodies to regulate what is a highly discretionary, low-visibility tactic. For Shiner, barriers to reform relate principally to

[88] Bradford and Loader, 'The Case of Stop and Search' (n 11).

[89] Seumas Miller, 'Political Theory, Institutional Purpose and Policing' in Ben Bradford, Beatrice Jauregui, Ian Loader, and Jonny Steinberg (eds), *The SAGE Handbook of Global Policing* (SAGE 2016) (hereafter Miller, 'Political Theory, Institutional Purpose and Policing'). See also Seumas Miller, 'Moral Rights and the Institution of the Police' in Tom Campbell and Seumas Miller (eds), *Human Rights and the Moral Responsibilities of Corporate and Public Sector Organisations* (Kluwer Academic 2004) and Seumas Miller, *The Moral Foundations of Social Institutions* (CUP 2010) ch 9.

[90] Miller, 'Political Theory, Institutional Purpose and Policing' (n 89).

organisational resistance and structural inequalities that are conducive to stereotyping as well as a larger politics of denial within and beyond the police service.[91]

It is underwhelming—though, to some extent, anticipated—that the voluntary Code of Conduct on stop and search does not adopt the vocabulary of respect, nor does it appeal explicitly to the value. Instead, as is the recurring theme of this chapter, the Code is framed in terms of instrumental effectiveness, facilitating the 'strategic' use of the power by regulating it more strictly, and increasing paperwork to ensure accountability.[92] The Code is somewhat less concerned with the quality of the police-public interaction itself. This tentative attempt at reform is indicative of the highly politicised and outcome-driven context in which stop and search operates.

Nonetheless, given the renewed political interest in stop and search, there is ample opportunity for scholars and practitioners to advance a compromise between continued use of the power in its current form and outright abolition. But that will require a sense of what is possible in the political moment: of what rhetoric will work, what interests can be mobilised and defeated, and what bureaucracies can achieve.[93] In this context, policing scholarship is most helpful when it raises key issues—framed through particular conceptual resources—that need to be borne in mind in shaping policy.

Respect proves helpful in deciding which reform proposals we should endorse, how they are to be interpreted, and what exceptions we should make. While procedural justice training for police officers and tighter legal regulation offer two possible—though imperfect—means by which to cultivate and uphold respect, there are other possibilities. Drawing lessons from the unpopular and contested implementation of the Macpherson recommendations

[91] Michael Shiner, 'The Politics of the Powers' in Delsol and Shiner (eds), *Anatomy of a Police Power* (n 1).

[92] Home Office, *Best Use of Stop and Search Scheme* (Home Office 2014) 2..

[93] On political mobilisation, see Kwame Anthony Appiah, *The State and the Shaping of Identity*, The Tanner Lectures on Human Values delivered at Clare Hall, University of Cambridge (Tanner Humanities Center, University of Utah 2001). On securing public support for stop and search, see BBC News, 'Stop and Search: Police Code of Conduct Launched' (BBC News 26 August 2014). 'People would support [stop and search] if searches were well-targeted and carried out with respect.' <www.bbc.co.uk/news/uk-28923242> accessed 1 August 2019.

on stop and search,[94] Shiner explores the possibility of initiating a sustained dialogue with those unfairly targeted, as well as the triggering of punitive measures—from disciplinary action through to dismissal—in instances of police misconduct.[95] Bowling suggests that objective decision-making could be enhanced by means of a 'reasonable person' test, which would require police officers to articulate their reasons for targeting an individual. He also recommends that redress be made available for those disproportionately affected by stop and search, beyond the current option of civil action against the police.[96] Bradford and Jackson argue for the 'ethical curtailment' and 'redirection' of stop and search 'on the ground.' They set out the benefits of increased police visibility and recently-instituted forms of bureaucratic regulation that aim to encourage police officers to behave ethically (reward and disciplinary schemes, civilian oversight, and Police and Crime Commissioners).[97] Meanwhile, Bradford and Loader make a persuasive case for increased scrutiny as a condition of the continued use of stop and search. Given its social and moral complexity, the police power must be surrounded by 'as much monitoring, exposure, argument and contestation as possible'.[98] In other words, there must be a preference for 'heated' environments of active discussion and debate, as opposed to 'cool' neglect.[99]

Reform is essential and—irrespective of the regulatory model adopted—a significant reconfiguring of the relationship between stop and search and respect is required with some degree of urgency. A deeper awareness of the persisting significance of respect, in both conceptual and concrete terms, would prove valuable in any such reform process. The concept is sufficiently elastic as to

[94] Sir William Macpherson, *Report of the Stephen Lawrence Inquiry* (Cm 4262-I, Home Office 1999). See also House of Commons Home Affairs Committee, *The Macpherson Report—Ten Years On*. Twelfth Report of Session 2008–09 (HC 427, The Stationery Office 2009).

[95] Shiner, 'Regulation and Reform' (n 6).

[96] Ben Bowling, 'There is Still Much to Do on Stop and Search' *Centre for Crime and Justice Studies* (7 May 2014) <www.crimeandjustice.org.uk/resources/there-much-still-do-stop-and-search> accessed 1 August 2019.

[97] Bradford and Jackson, 'Moral Regulation of Policing' (n 20) 278.

[98] Bradford and Loader, 'The Case of Stop and Search' (n 11) 257.

[99] Ian Loader and Richard Sparks, *Public Criminology?* (Routledge 2010) chs 3 and 4.. See also Kath Murray and Diarmaid Harkin, 'Policing in Cool and Hot Climates: Legitimacy, Power and the Rise and Fall of Mass Stop and Search in Scotland' (2017) 57(4) The British Journal of Criminology 885.

facilitate wide-ranging dialogue on stop and search but not excessively so as to result in unproductive ambiguity or the dilution of meaning.

It is no novel insight that respect matters greatly. At present, however, there is symbolic investment in respect with no real guarantee of its expression in practice.[100] This being so, we must question the form and function of every public commitment of the police to uphold a moral value. Who are its advocates and beneficiaries and what are their intentions and ideologies? A reformed version of stop and search must engage meaningfully with the value and not simply appeal to the word 'respect' when it is expedient to do so.[101] That said, there is cause for cautious optimism. Even if we were to concede that a *fully* respectful version of stop and search is unlikely to be achieved in the current political climate, we might nonetheless go some way towards highlighting respect, and consigning instrumental concerns to their proper place.

[100] On the symbolic power of the police, see Ian Loader, 'Policing and the Social: Questions of Symbolic Power' (1997) 48(1) The British Journal of Sociology 1. On the police as a 'public affirmation of civility', see John Keane, *Violence and Democracy* (CUP 2004).

[101] Lacey's claim that 'no one in the [criminal justice] system should hide beyond jargon' is apt here: House of Commons Justice Committee, *Cutting Crime: The Case for Justice Reinvestment.* First Report of Session 2009–10, Volume 1 (HC 94-I, The Stationery Office 2010) 93.

PART II

On Respect and Prison Life

4

Penal Policies and Institutional Sociologies

The concept of respect can both inspire and unsettle, not least by modifying our approach to criminal justice and eroding established categories and presumptions. As before, the overarching concern is to demonstrate that this is the case, though the object of enquiry now shifts from the police-public encounter to the prison. Despite a shift in focus, the core claim of this book—that respect provides a means by which to advance an incisive critique of criminal justice—should now be familiar.

Given that respect is, almost without exception, one of the first values to emerge in conversations with inmates about 'what matters' in prison,[1] one could be forgiven for assuming that scholars had given the issue thorough attention. This is not the case.[2] This chapter—the first of two on prisons—situates a number of institutional sociologies of the prison in relation to the key trends in penal policy with which they coincided. In so doing, it offers a critique of the current approach to respect in prisons in England and Wales and identifies moments in recent history when respect—however reductively understood—was especially pronounced.

There are important reasons for a dual focus on penal policy and prison sociology. The first relates to the comprehensive and wide-ranging critique of respect that it facilitates. An analysis of policy would tell only an official story. A dual focus allows the

[1] Susie Hulley, Alison Liebling, and Ben Crewe, 'Respect in Prisons: Prisoners' Experiences of Respect in Public and Private Sector Prisons' (2012) 12(1) Criminology & Criminal Justice 3, 6 (hereafter Hulley et al, 'Respect in Prisons').

[2] For two notable exceptions, see Michelle Butler and Deborah H Drake, 'Reconsidering Respect: Its Role in Her Majesty's Prison Service' (2007) 46(2) The Howard Journal of Criminal Justice 115 and ibid.

Respect and Criminal Justice. Gabrielle Watson, Oxford University Press (2020). © Gabrielle Watson.
DOI: 10.1093/oso/9780198833345.001.0001

official story to be supplemented with a series of alternative—but no less serious or authoritative—accounts of imprisonment. The second reason relates to the flexibility of respect itself. While respect is *prima facie* universal and enduring, in practice, it is a historical and transitory product of the context in which it is expressed. On this view, what it means to act respectfully in prisons is neither exact nor fixed, and if the policy context changes, then respect and the particular institutional conditions of its existence are likely to change too.[3]

It is noteworthy that HM Prison and Probation Service has committed, at the level of official discourse, to treating offenders with 'decency and respect' and designated humanity as one of its core values.[4] Yet the evidence suggests that to varying degrees and in various guises, within and between prisons and across time, respect has not been treated as a declared value of the prison, to be pursued in and of itself. Rather, it has functioned as a weak side-constraint on the pursuit of the institution's instrumental outcomes.[5] The implication is that respect is far from being assiduously cultivated and imprisonment practices are deeply at odds with the Rawlsian notion that respect is an entitlement that social institutions are required by justice to support and maintain.[6] Liebling's claim that respect is 'gained

[3] For Laursen and Laws, respect covers a 'wide repertoire of interactions', from daily greetings and cordial acknowledgments to forms of positive appraisal: Julie Laursen and Ben Laws, 'Honour and Respect in Danish Prisons: Contesting "Cognitive Distortions" in Cognitive-Behavioural Programmes' (2017) 19(1) Punishment & Society 74.

[4] Her Majesty's Prison and Probation Service, *Annual Report and Accounts 2017–18* (HC 1175, The Stationery Office 2018) 5 (hereafter Her Majesty's Prison and Probation Service, *Annual Report and Accounts 2017–18*). Respect also features as one of four tests of a 'healthy establishment' in inspections conducted by Her Majesty's Chief Inspector of Prisons for England and Wales. See, eg, Her Majesty's Chief Inspector of Prisons for England and Wales, *Annual Report 2017–18* (The Stationery Office 2018) 1–2. See also Part 3, Men in Prison, *Poor living conditions and reduced staffing affect respect outcomes.*

[5] In a bolder version of the argument advanced here, Liebling, following Garland, suggests that a concern with 'technical efficacy' has come to replace the promotion of moral values in prison entirely: Alison Liebling, 'Perrie Lecture: The Cost to Prison Legitimacy of Cuts' (2011) 198 Prison Service Journal 3, 9. See also David Garland, *Punishment and Modern Society* (Clarendon Press 1990).

[6] John Rawls, *A Theory of Justice* (Belknap Press of Harvard University Press 1971).

slowly but may be lost in an instant' is suggestive of an unethical practice whereby respect is extended and then withdrawn from prisoners, as well as an institutional failure to regulate fraught relationships between prisoners in which respect is often the core value at stake.[7]

Rather than facilitating the pursuit of more progressive imprisonment policies and practices, it is possible that the language of respect has interfered with that task. Once the prison became enamoured with the idea that respect could function as a keyword or slogan, it lost track of its meaning. The notion that respect—described by some scholars as a 'fundamental moral right'—might have become implicated in a culture of moral indifference seems, at first, implausible.[8] Yet, within an institution that is concerned primarily with what it '*does*, rather than what … it *achieves*', it is almost inevitable.[9]

A. Institutional Sociologies of the Prison

Imprisonment occupies a prominent place in contemporary criminal justice scholarship, much of which takes the form of institutional sociology. The authors of these studies are often motivated by a liberal concern to contribute to more humane practices of punishment. In order to deepen our critical stance on respect in contemporary imprisonment, this chapter revisits six landmark contributions to the genre: Sparks, Bottoms, and Hay's *Prisons and the Problem of Order*;[10] Bosworth's *Engendering Resistance*;[11] Liebling's *Prisons and their Moral Performance*;[12] Crewe's *The*

[7] House of Commons Justice Committee, *Written Evidence: Role of the Prison Officer.* Memorandum submitted by the Institute of Criminology, University of Cambridge (Justice Committee Publications 2009) 9.

[8] See, eg, Robin S Dillon, 'Respect' in Edward N Zalta (ed), *The Stanford Encyclopedia of Philosophy* (Stanford University 2018) <http://plato.stanford.edu/entries/respect/> accessed 1 August 2019 (hereafter Dillon, *Respect*).

[9] David Garland, 'The Limits of the Sovereign State: Strategies of Crime Control in Contemporary Society' (1996) 36(4) The British Journal of Criminology 445, 458.

[10] Richard Sparks, Anthony E Bottoms, and Will Hay, *Prisons and the Problem of Order* (Clarendon Press 1996) (hereafter Sparks et al, *Problem of Order*).

[11] Mary Bosworth, *Engendering Resistance: Agency and Power in Women's Prisons* (Ashgate 1999) (hereafter Bosworth, *Engendering Resistance*).

[12] Alison Liebling, *Prisons and their Moral Performance: A Study of Values, Quality, and Prison Life* (OUP 2004) (hereafter Liebling, *Moral Performance*).

Prisoner Society;[13] Phillips' *The Multicultural Prison*;[14] and Bennett's *The Working Lives of Prison Managers*.[15]

There are three reasons—one jurisdictional, one temporal, the other conceptual—behind the selection of these studies for examination. First, those well acquainted with the field will note that these studies were conducted exclusively in England and Wales. This is a necessary precondition for their alignment with English and Welsh policy developments, but it is not to overlook the fact that prison sociology is primarily an American phenomenon whose origins are in Clemmer's study of the Menard Branch of the Illinois State Penitentiary.[16] Clemmer's *The Prison Community* was followed by two more American studies of note, namely, Sykes' *The Society of Captives*, a study of New Jersey State Prison,[17] and Goffman's *Asylums*, a study of a psychiatric facility in Washington DC.[18] Given the frequency with which these works frame and influence modern contributions to the genre, it would have been difficult—even impossible—for the studies discussed in this chapter to remain insulated from them. Sparks et al, for example, draw attention to the implications of their research on the 'problem of order' for the tradition of sociological interest in the 'prison community'. In this way, their study is best viewed as a deliberate attempt to recover and update the American tradition of institutional sociology for a criminological audience, drawing not only on American but also on Scandinavian resources.[19]

Second, these studies—published between 1996 and 2015—have been selected because they respond to a clear policy trajectory from the Woolf Report and its broadly enthusiastic reception in the early 1990s, to the various—largely unsuccessful—attempts to

[13] Ben Crewe, *The Prisoner Society: Power, Adaptation, and Social Life in an English Prison* (OUP 2009) (hereafter Crewe, *Prisoner Society*).

[14] Coretta Phillips, *The Multicultural Prison: Ethnicity, Masculinity, and Social Relations among Prisoners* (OUP 2012) (hereafter Phillips, *Multicultural Prison*).

[15] Jamie Bennett, *The Working Lives of Prison Managers: Global Change, Local Culture and Individual Agency in the Late Modern Prison* (Palgrave Macmillan 2015) (hereafter Bennett, *Prison Managers*).

[16] Donald Clemmer, *The Prison Community* (Christopher Publishing House 1940).

[17] Gresham M Sykes, *The Society of Captives: A Study of a Maximum Security Prison* (Princeton University Press 1958).

[18] Erving Goffman, *Asylums: Essays on the Social Situation of Mental Patients and Other Inmates* (Doubleday & Co 1961).

[19] Sparks et al, *Problem of Order* (n 10).

'humanise' prisons over the next two decades and the rise of managerialism over the same period, to present-day concerns, three decades on from *Woolf*.[20] Woolf's recommendations were hailed by commentators at the time as the introduction of 'decency and justice' into prisons when conditions had become intolerable. The period from *Woolf* onwards, then, provides a particularly rich context in which to launch a critique of respect in prisons, not least because of the increased use of liberal, moralistic language by HM Prison Service during this period.[21]

These studies might be said to be *in conversation* with penal policy, but only in a limited sense. Although not solely concerned with the narrow demands of policy relevance, the studies actively respond to a policy trajectory, even if they play a marginal role in influencing its direction. Insofar as they have exposed a deficit of respect or other moral values in prisons, the content and direction of penal policy has remained broadly—though not exclusively—indifferent to them.[22] Liebling's Measuring the Quality of Prison Life (MQPL) and Staff Quality of Life (SQL) surveys, and her study of moral performance from which they emerged, are important exceptions.[23]

Third, these studies have been selected because each has a discrete contribution to make, variously challenging or aligning with the central claims of this book and offering some insight into the

[20] Home Office, *Prison Disturbances April 1990: Report of an Inquiry by The Rt Hon Lord Justice Woolf (Parts I and II) and His Honour Judge Stephen Tumim (Part II)* (Cm 1456, The Stationery Office 1991) (hereafter Home Office, *The Woolf Report*); Prison Reform Trust, *The Woolf Report: A Summary of the Main Findings and Recommendations of the Inquiry into Prison Disturbances* (Prison Reform Trust 1991); and Mark Day, Alex Hewson, and Charles Spiropoulos, *Strangeways 25 Years' On: Achieving Fairness and Justice in our Prisons* (Prison Reform Trust 2015) (hereafter Day et al, *Strangeways 25 Years' On*).

[21] See, eg, Liebling, *Moral Performance* (n 12); Nicki Jameson and Eric Allison, *Strangeways 1990: A Serious Disturbance* (Larkin Publications 1995), and Emma Kaufman, *Punish and Expel: Border Control, Nationalism, and the New Purpose of the Prison* (OUP 2015) ch 1.

[22] On the significance of values in contemporary imprisonment, see, eg, Rob Allen, Andrew Ashworth, Roger Cotterrell, Andrew Coyle, RA Duff, Nicola Lacey, Alison Liebling, and Rod Morgan, *A Presumption Against Imprisonment: Social Order and Social Values* (British Academy 2014) and Alison Liebling, Ben Crewe, and Susie Hulley, 'Values and Practices in Public and Private Sector Prisons: A Summary of Key Findings from an Evaluation' (2011) 196 Prison Service Journal 55.

[23] Liebling, *Moral Performance* (n 12).

modes of thought with which respect has come to be associated or contrasted. This is true whether their engagement with respect is express or implied. *Prisons and the Problem of Order* provides important context for the commissioning, publication, and reception of the Woolf Report; *Engendering Resistance* suggests that the experience of respect in prison might rest, at least in part, on gender; *Prisons and their Moral Performance* engages explicitly with respect and raises challenging questions about its empirical measurement; *The Prisoner Society* exposes the definitional ambiguities of respect in an institution characterised by status hierarchies and penal power; *The Multicultural Prison* suggests that respect must be interpreted through a racialised prism; and *The Working Lives of Prison Managers* offers a new perspective on the contemporary prison's managerialist aims. The aim is not to review these studies in detail, not least because each was enthusiastically received and reviews are widely available elsewhere.[24] In any case, such extensive retelling would threaten to obscure the main line of argument. Rather, the aim is to use each study as a 'sounding board' for a critique of respect and, in so doing, challenge and extend existing knowledge and not simply rewrite it.

Moreover, these studies—notwithstanding their subtlety, scope, and authority—are not treated as definitive or as the only suitable studies for this task. Instead, they are treated as key exemplars of how individuals negotiate the complex moral terrain of the prison. Respect, however, does not figure to the same degree in early sociologies of the prison, such as the now canonical works by Clemmer in *The Prison Community*, Sykes in *The Society of Captives*, Goffman in *Asylums*, and Cohen and Taylor

[24] See, eg, John Pratt, 'Review of Richard Sparks, Anthony E Bottoms, and Will Hay, *Prisons and the Problem of Order* (1996)' (1998) 38(1) The British Journal of Criminology 179; Barbara Hudson, 'Review of Mary Bosworth, *Engendering Resistance: Agency and Power in Women's Prisons* (1999)' (2002) 11(1) Critical Criminology 83; Dirk van Zyl Smit, 'Review of A Liebling, *Prisons and their Moral Performance: A Study of Values, Quality, and Prison Life* (2004)' (2005) 45(5) The British Journal of Criminology 765; Marguerite Schinkel, 'Review of Ben Crewe, *The Prisoner Society: Power, Adaptation, and Social Life in an English Prison* (2009)' (2010) 57(3) Probation Journal 343; Jamie Bennett, 'Review of Coretta Phillips, *The Multicultural Prison: Ethnicity, Masculinity, and Social Relations among Prisoners* (2009)' (2013) 17(3) Theoretical Criminology 422; and Louise Brangan, 'Review of Jamie Bennett, *The Working Lives of Prison Managers: Global Change, Local Culture and Individual Agency in the Late Modern Prison* (2015)' (2017) 17(2) Criminology & Criminal Justice 226.

in *Psychological Survival*.[25] Nor does it figure to the same degree in contemporary abolitionist works, such as Scraton, Sim, and Skidmore's *Prisons under Protest*[26] and Sim's *Punishment and Prisons*.[27] An examination of respect based on Clemmer, Sykes, Goffman, Cohen and Taylor, Scraton et al, or Sim, though plausible, would necessarily centre less on a critique of respect and more on its absence in the studies themselves, prompting an alternative line of enquiry into the sociology of knowledge. One possibility would be to study the social, disciplinary, and institutional contexts within which dominant discourses on the prison are produced and reproduced. It is well established that discourse extends beyond the written word, encompassing a set of formal and informal rules about what can be said, how it can be said, and who can say what to whom.[28] The content of the dominant discourse is often less interesting than the range of rules and practices that have supported it and excluded other emerging discourses—such as those on respect—from positions of prominence.

B. The *Woolf* Report

The publication of *Prisons and the Problem of Order* intersected with the commissioning and largely appreciative reception of the Woolf Report in prisons in the early 1990s. Both publications offer a point of preliminary enquiry in tracing the lineage—and current limitations—of respect in contemporary imprisonment.[29]

The Woolf Report represented the culmination of an unprecedentedly wide-ranging formal inquiry into the Strangeways prison riot and the associated disturbances of 1990.[30] Woolf concluded that the prolonged period of unrest had been prompted by a widespread sense of prisoner dissatisfaction and shared sense of injustice over chronic overcrowding, unsanitary conditions,

[25] Stanley Cohen and Laurie Taylor, *Psychological Survival: The Experience of Long-Term Imprisonment* (Penguin 1972).

[26] Phil Scraton, Joe Sim, and Paula Skidmore, *Prisons under Protest* (Open University Press 1991).

[27] Joe Sim, *Punishment and Prisons: Power and the Carceral State* (SAGE 2009).

[28] See, eg, Sara Mills, *Discourse: The New Critical Idiom* (Routledge 2004).

[29] Sparks et al, *Problem of Order* (n 10) and Home Office, *The Woolf Report* (n 20).

[30] Elaine Player and Michael Jenkins (eds), *Prisons after Woolf: Reform through Riot* (Routledge 1994) (hereafter Player and Jenkins, *Reform through Riot*).

and indecent treatment by staff. The report fell squarely within the tradition of official reports insofar as it accepted the parameters of a continuing prison estate and excluded fundamental questions about its purpose or legitimacy. However, Woolf's recommendations—which were framed for implementation without a new Act of Parliament—had clear moral ambitions. They ranged from specific measures such as revised procedural protections and mechanisms for complaint, improved sanitation in cells, more constructive regimes, and increased contact with families, to an ambitious reform agenda, which would see a fully integrated criminal process and accredited standards throughout HM Prison Service.[31] In this way, the report provided the most significant point of departure for the formation of penal values and policy in the period that followed. It is the single most significant document for an examination of respect in prisons, in that it fully embraced the idea—if only, on occasion, the vocabulary—of respect.

Prisons and the Problem of Order is based on extensive empirical research in two contrasting English dispersal prisons, conducted in the year prior to the major prison disturbances of 1990. It was a year that, incidentally, had seen the beginnings of institutional reform and reflection on the nature of imprisonment. The extent of reform, however, had been modest and its value base unclear.[32] The timing of the publication itself is also significant. Published in 1996, it helpfully maps the intellectual terrain and nature of the political debate on prisons pre and post-*Woolf*.

Sparks et al systematically compare the institutional order of both prisons—including the differing control strategies employed in each—from the point of view of both staff and prisoners. The study is typically discussed in relation to its landmark finding that only legitimate social conditions within prison—perceived as such by prisoners—generate normative commitments towards

[31] See, eg, Liebling, *Moral Performance* (n 12) and Rod Morgan, 'Imprisonment: Current Concerns and a Brief History Since 1945' in Mike Maguire, Rod Morgan, and Robert Reiner (eds), *The Oxford Handbook of Criminology* (2nd edn, OUP 1997).

[32] Kathleen McDermott and Roy D King, 'A Fresh Start: The Enhancement of Prison Regimes' (1989) 28(3) The Howard Journal of Criminal Justice 161. For reflections on these developments, see Liebling, *Moral Performance* (n 12) and Crewe, *Prisoner Society* (n 13).

compliant behaviour. In short, the idea is that order flows from legitimacy.[33] While political analysts take for granted that power relations can only achieve stability if naked power is transformed into authority by processes of legitimation, Sparks et al confirm that this widely held view obtains in the complex moral context of the prison.

A sceptical reader may consider it a curious move to align *Woolf* with *Prisons and the Problem of Order*, given that they are concerned with essentially opposite phenomena. While *Woolf* was concerned with a series of riots—a 'special problem' and relatively rare form of disruption—Sparks et al were concerned with the 'perennial problem' of securing and maintaining order.[34] The advantage of aligning them is that they provide a broad sense of the tenor and direction of the imprisonment debate in the early 1990s. Throughout this period, respect was invoked in the context of entitlements to due treatment from others, especially those which promoted a sense of justice. A prominent theme to run throughout the Woolf Report, for example, was that of 'justice in prisons secured through the exercise of responsibility and respect'.[35] For Woolf, respect was deeply implicated in the act of securing justice in prisons which, once achieved, would enhance 'security and control': two issues with which Sparks et al were principally concerned. In this way, the publications

[33] The study drew on Weber's political theory and his understanding of collective participation and belief: Max Weber, *The Theory of Social and Economic Organization* (William Hodge & Co 1947) and Max Weber, *Economy and Society: An Outline of Interpretive Sociology* (Bedminster Press 1968). See also Richard Sparks, 'Can Prisons Be Legitimate? Penal Politics, Privatization, and the Timeliness of an Old Idea' (1994) 34(S1) The British Journal of Criminology 14; Richard Sparks and Anthony E Bottoms, 'Legitimacy and Order in Prisons' (1995) 46(1) The British Journal of Sociology 45 (hereafter Sparks and Bottoms, 'Legitimacy and Order'); Anthony E Bottoms, 'Interpersonal Violence and Social Order in Prisons' (1999) 26 Crime and Justice 205; and Richard Sparks and Anthony E Bottoms, 'Legitimacy and Imprisonment Revisited: Some Notes on the Problem of Order Ten Years After' in James M Byrne, Donald Hummer, and Faye S Taxman (eds), *The Culture of Prison Violence* (Pearson 2008) (hereafter Byrne et al, *Prison Violence*).

[34] Sparks et al, *Problem of Order* (n 10) 2 and Home Office, *The Woolf Report* (n 20). On the tendency of prison sociologists to focus on the 'stable' rather than the 'non-stable' aspects of the social structure, see Thomas Mathiesen, 'The Sociology of Prisons: Problems for Future Research' (1966) 17(4) The British Journal of Sociology 360.

[35] Home Office, *The Woolf Report* (n 20) paras 14.437–14.438.

actually complement each other—prompting deeper reflection on the role and value of respect—in a manner that has not yet been appreciated.

Of note is the manner in which *Prisons and the Problem of Order* documents the importance of 'human qualities' in daily routines.[36] It is an observation that accords with a claim later made by Woolf that 'superficial' or 'cosmetic' changes to the practice of imprisonment would not suffice, and that more attention must be paid to the social and institutional dynamics within and between prisons.[37] From the perspective of one prison officer at HMP Long Lartin, fair and equal treatment, if afforded consistently, can be instrumental in cultivating respect between prisoners and the authorities:

> If you are fair, you give them what they are entitled to, and make sure every inmate gets the same. Don't give it to one and take it from another. Make sure you're seen to be fair to every inmate whom you mix with. They'll accept you, and they'll say, well—they may call you names occasionally whether you've given them everything or not—but they'll still respect you … for being fair.[38]

The prison officer's comments are encouraging since they suggest that respect is realistically attainable, despite the common conception that all social relations in prisons are characterised by practices of subordination.[39] He appeals to the well-established idea—already encountered in chapter one—of respect as a mode of recognition, which involves respecting a prisoner by virtue of his humanity. This can be distinguished from another common usage of respect, namely, that which involves a positive appraisal or evaluation of some kind. This form of respect—from which the officer is keen to distance himself—would require him to single out particular prisoners for differential treatment, for example,

[36] Sparks and Bottoms, 'Legitimacy and Order' (n 33) 45, discussing research developed later in Sparks et al, *Problem of Order* (n 10).

[37] Home Office, *The Woolf Report* (n 20) para 1.12 and Elaine Player and Michael Jenkins, 'Introduction' in Player and Jenkins, *Reform through Riot* (n 30) 10.

[38] Sparks et al, *Problem of Order* (n 10) 146–47.

[39] See, eg, Richard Sennett, *Respect: The Formation of Character in an Age of Inequality* (Penguin 2004) (hereafter Sennett, *Respect*) and Michael Ignatieff, 'State, Civil Society, and Total Institutions: A Critique of Recent Social Histories of Punishment' (1981) 3 Crime and Justice 153.

following good behaviour. In the former case, a citizen is respected solely by virtue of the fact that he is a human being capable of autonomous agency while, in the latter case, the moral merits of an individual or the virtues of his character or conduct are valued.[40] Treating prisoners with respect does not necessarily require simple egalitarianism—that they are treated equally in a literal sense—though this appears to have been underappreciated at HMP Long Lartin.

Meanwhile, at HMP Albany, staff members encountered respect in a diluted form. From the perspective of one prisoner, an attitude of respect towards prison officers was coupled with an inability or unwillingness to cultivate an excessively close relationship with them:'I really try to avoid speaking to officers unless I have to. I respect them for what they do, but I think they're still opposition.'[41]

The prisoner's comments imply a disconnect between the attitude of respect and the act of respect. While he adopts an attitude of respect towards staff, he is either unwilling or unable to act 'out of' respect. Certainly, respect is partly about adopting a certain attitude towards another. But the expressive act of respect also matters greatly, not least because it allows outsiders to assess whether respect is present at all.[42] We can only speculate as to whether the prisoner's preference for attitude over action is indicative of a reductive approach to respectful relations within the institution more generally.

A reading of Sparks et al prompts consideration of whether respect is a matter not only of interaction but also inaction. They observe, for example, that for many prisoners, the 'defining

[40] Allen W Wood, 'Respect and Recognition' in John Skorupski (ed), *The Routledge Companion to Ethics* (Routledge 2010) (hereafter Wood, 'Respect and Recognition') and Stephen L Darwall, 'Two Kinds of Respect' (1977) 88(1) Ethics 36 (hereafter Darwall, 'Two Kinds of Respect').

[41] Sparks et al, *Problem of Order* (n 10) 194.

[42] Stephen L Darwall, *The Second-Person Standpoint: Morality, Respect, and Accountability* (Harvard University Press 2006). cf Lægaard's suggestion that institutions should focus on 'public features' or expressions of respect without attending to attitudinal questions or internal motivations. In so doing, institutions might nonetheless be described as respectful: Sune Lægaard, 'Attitudinal Analyses of Toleration and Respect and the Problem of Institutional Applicability' (2015) 23(4) European Journal of Philosophy 1064.

feature' of a good prison officer is one who 'leaves (them) alone as much as possible'. When contact is necessary, it is 'civil, good-humoured and fair'.[43] The idea of respect as non-interference hints at a complex relationship in which the prison officer must act in accordance with negative constraints and not only positive requirements. He must defer to the prisoner's understanding of what it means to respect and be respected and accept that non-interference is a desirable means by which to recognise his intrinsic worth.[44]

It was essential for Woolf to temper traditional concerns about security and control with a concern for justice and respect, and he did so by suggesting that the former were predicated on the existence of the latter. The discussion in Sparks et al is invaluable, first, in drawing out the subtle relationship between these concepts and, second, in confirming that they were prominent concerns prior to the disturbances and certainly before they were articulated in *Woolf*. This is not to discredit the importance of *Woolf*—a publication that is both explicitly and implicitly supportive of respect in prisons—but simply to point to the fact that the ideas contained therein were not new.

C. The Shaping of Modern Imprisonment

The chapter now moves on to examine—again, by means of a dual focus on prison policy and institutional sociology—the role and value of respect in the period following *Woolf*. The period between 1990 and 2003 was one of protracted indeterminacy for HM Prison Service, in view of a series of largely unsuccessful attempts to 'humanise' prisons. Although there was a sustained effort to transform penal practices, values, and sensibilities and initiate a liberal penal project, aspirations for a more respectful form of imprisonment were soon compromised.[45] Respect was not treated as a precondition for justice and, by extension, security and

[43] Sparks et al, *Problem of Order* (n 10) 193.

[44] See further Joseph Raz, *Value, Respect, and Attachment* (CUP 2001) ch 4. On the importance of respecting a person's choices and preferences, see Kalle Grill, 'Respect for What? Choices, Actual Preferences, and True Preferences' (2015) 41(4) Social Theory and Practice 692.

[45] Liebling, *Moral Performance* (n 12).

control—as Woolf had envisaged—but as a weak side-constraint on the pursuit of managerialist aims.

1. The rise of managerialism

Managerialism had developed incrementally in the years pre-*Woolf*, but there was a marked intensification of such practices in prisons in the early 1990s. By 1995, it had fully shaped the prison's commitment to instrumental effectiveness and replaced long-term, normatively oriented policy debates. As an organising ideology, managerialism is characterised by greater accountability and the search for the best use of resources in pursuit of stated objectives. It ensured that the prison was transformed into a hierarchical, market based, performance oriented institution, and its core activities were enabled through budgets, strategic plans, data collection and analysis, audits, and ratings. Every institutional challenge became a technical problem to be solved.[46]

The first performance measures were introduced to HM Prison Service in 1992 and played a key role in reconfiguring the prison's approach to moral values. The measures were based on a conception of accountability that reflected high trust in the market and private business methods and low trust in professionals and public servants, ensuring that the economy of prison management became a central concern. But their introduction was also viewed as an attempt to 'moralise' prison management by appealing to value plurality. This was achieved by including measures of decency and dignity alongside measures of public security, operational effectiveness, and cost. As managerialism gained traction, however, the

[46] On managerialism and instrumental outcomes, see, eg, Malcolm M Feeley and Jonathan Simon, 'The New Penology: Notes on the Emerging Strategy of Corrections and its Implications' (1992) 30(4) Criminology 449; Liebling, *Moral Performance* (n 12); Alison Liebling, 'Prisons in Transition' (2006) 29(5) International Journal of Law and Psychiatry 422 (hereafter Liebling, 'Prisons in Transition'); Bennett, *Prison Managers* (n 15); Dominique Robert, 'Managerialism' in Mary Bosworth (ed), *Encyclopedia of Prisons and Correctional Facilities* (SAGE 2005) (hereafter Robert, 'Managerialism'); Thomas Klikauer, 'What is Managerialism?' (2015) 41(7–8) Critical Sociology 1103 and Pat O'Malley, *Risk, Uncertainty and Government* (GlassHouse 2004). On ideology and its relationship to theory and practice, see Michael Freeden, *Liberal Languages: Ideological Imaginations and Twentieth-Century Progressive Thought* (Princeton University Press 2005) ch 12.

conflict between managerialist imperatives and organisational values—including respect—became increasingly pronounced.[47]

When management was transformed into an 'ism', it joined a family of 'isms' that have apparently clear philosophies, but which also accommodate a range of informal and often unspecified practices.[48] In prison scholarship, the term is often used pejoratively to imply an inappropriate or even dictatorial use of hierarchical power. When more power flows, more effectively, especially at the top of the organisation, managerialism can become a tool not only for target-setting but also for the assertion of control and, as Bennett observes, the othering of prisoners.[49] There are implications for staff too. Managerialism is often associated with a particular conception of staff as a homogenous resource like any other. They are rarely consulted and have limited professional discretion. Their work is also increasingly shaped by human resource management techniques such as recruitment, reward, appraisal, development, communication, and consultation.[50]

The flaws of the managerialist approach were brought into sharp focus in the context of women's imprisonment. These institutions subscribed to policies and procedures which were presented as gender-neutral but were considered by many to be designed for the guidance, regulation, and performance of men. There were even attempts to manufacture the consent of female prisoners and enlist their support for such policies.[51] The result was that respect was far from an animating principle in women's prisons. Despite the consensus among scholars that female prisoners are deserving of a 'particularist ethic of care', institutions frequently subsumed

[47] On performance measures, see Liebling, *Moral Performance* (n 12) and Andrea Mennicken, '"Too Big to Fail and Too Big to Succeed:" Accounting and Privatisation in the Prison Service of England and Wales' (2013) 29(2) Financial Accountability & Management 206 (hereafter Mennicken, 'Accounting and Privatisation').

[48] On 'isms', see Raymond Williams, *Keywords: A Vocabulary of Culture and Society* (Fontana 1976).

[49] Liebling, 'Prisons in Transition' (n 46) and Bennett, *Prison Managers* (n 15).

[50] Bennett, *Prison Managers* (n 15) and David Garland, *The Culture of Control: Crime and Social Order in Contemporary Society* (OUP 2001) (hereafter Garland, *Culture of Control*).

[51] Robert, 'Managerialism' (n 46). On the gendered nature of prison management structures, see Eamonn Carrabine and Brian Longhurst, 'Gender and Prison Organisation: Some Comments on Masculinities and Prison Management' (1998) 37(2) The Howard Journal of Criminal Justice 161.

their needs under those of men, and conveniently glossed over the ways in which their confinement may be less amenable to a managerialist framework.[52]

In the two decades following *Woolf*, managerialism eroded a range of moral values, including respect, and inhibited numerous opportunities for liberal-humanitarian prison reform. This was attributed, in part, to a notable lack of open, democratic, reflective discourse between senior management and ground-level staff around each prison's unique purposes, and how best to realise them.[53]

2. *'Decent, but austere'*

During the mid to late 1990s, there was a shift—concurrent with the rise of managerialism—towards a new penal policy emphasis. There was a strident return to notions of security and control and a renewed interest in the prison as a means of incapacitation, even though this led to a significant rise in the population. Deeply implicated in this new phase was a significant limiting of the moral ambitions of the prison. In stark contrast to the preceding period and the ambitions set out in *Woolf*, perceptions of fairness and justice fell drastically among prisoners and, in some prisons, staff violence returned.[54] It was a reimagined penal sensibility best encapsulated by the sentiments of the then Home Secretary, Michael Howard, and his opinion that prisons should be—in the service of deterrence—'decent, but austere'.[55] Yet the superficiality of Howard's claim was soon exposed when, in practice, the latter

[52] See, eg, Bosworth, *Engendering Resistance* (n 11) 38; Mary Bosworth and Emma Kaufman, 'Gender and Punishment' in Jonathan Simon and Richard Sparks (eds), *The SAGE Handbook of Punishment and Society* (SAGE 2013) and Barbara Owen, James Wells, and Joycelyn Pollock, *In Search of Safety: Confronting Inequality in Women's Imprisonment* (University of California Press 2017).

[53] Player and Jenkins, *Reform through Riot* (n 30). See also Martin Parker, *Against Management: Organization in the Age of Managerialism* (Polity 2002) and Thomas Klikauer, *Managerialism: A Critique of an Ideology* (Palgrave Macmillan 2013).

[54] Liebling, *Moral Performance* (n 12) and Crewe, *Prisoner Society* (n 13).

[55] Michael Howard, *Speech to the Conservative Party Conference* (Bodleian Library: Conservative Party Archive 6 October 1993) 12. See also Anthony E Bottoms, 'Theoretical Reflections on the Evaluation of a Penal Policy Initiative' in Lucia Zedner and Andrew Ashworth (eds), *The Criminological Foundations of Penal Policy: Essays in Honour of Roger Hood* (OUP 2003).

invariably outweighed the former. His sentiments converged with the disarray of HM Prison Service and a political moment in which punitive public opinion was open to being readily exploited.[56]

Bosworth's *Engendering Resistance,* a study conducted in three women's prisons in England, intersected with this change in policy direction. The basic premise of the study is that processes of power and resistance in prison are invariably gendered. For Bosworth, works of institutional sociology had been, up to that point, shaped detrimentally by a masculinist rationality which served to exclude, distort, or discredit the experiences of women.[57]

Bosworth proposes the concept of identity as a challenging corrective to this work, and this proves valuable for several reasons. First, the concept is well equipped to connect the experiences of women to the structuring principles of gender, class, sexuality, and ethnicity. Second, it allows Bosworth to introduce with relative ease the cognate concepts of agency, power, and resistance by showing how—within certain boundaries, and even when tightly controlled—the women found ways to resist control and create atmospheres more to their liking. Third, it facilitates a critique of earlier accounts of legitimacy in men's prisons, arguing that legitimacy, as it was then configured, excluded issues of identity.

It is possible to glean much more about respect in prisons from *Engendering Resistance* than would be possible from a policy review alone. While the dominant narrative is that imprisonment came to be defined once more by punitive sentiments, Bosworth hints at the ways in which respect maintained a limited presence during this period. We learn that the women variously negotiated, resisted, modified, and affirmed their feminine identities, and it is likely that the search for respect would have been deeply implicated in their actions.[58]

There is little new in the idea that individual and collective identities—especially those of stigmatised groups—are negotiated on a continual basis. Our identity tells us who we think we are and announce to others. It also provides others with a sense of what they can expect and how they might respond to us, and we to them. The value of Bosworth's study is in showing that identity in prison is much more than a self-reference point. Identity

[56] Crewe, *Prisoner Society* (n 13).

[57] Bosworth, *Engendering Resistance* (n 11).

[58] ibid.

can become a resource and focal point for rewards, competition, and conflict. And although acknowledged only tangentially by Bosworth, a prisoner's identity also offers a means by which to gain respect.[59]

It is conceivable that those who have their choices and liberties curtailed by means of imprisonment might find it difficult to appeal to a generalised notion of respect, preferring instead to draw attention to their concrete needs. Of note, however, is one woman's appeal to an idealised notion of femininity—her identity as a mother—in order to resist a stigmatised criminal identity and present herself as more than 'just' a prisoner. Motherhood indicated to peers that she had responsibility and legitimacy, qualities for which, according to Bosworth, she 'deserved a little respect'.[60]

Such a claim is suggestive of Young, for whom respect involves 'granting and fostering' in individuals the 'liberties and capacities to be autonomous'. It also involves protecting them 'from the tyranny of those who might try to determine (their) choices ... because they control resources on which (they) depend for their living'.[61] Certainly, Bosworth details some minor victories whereby women were concerned not only to 'undo' but actively subscribe to an idealised notion of femininity for their own social or material benefit.[62] Whether they were protected from the 'tyranny' that Young describes is questionable, since Bosworth does not provide concrete evidence of meaningful institutional acknowledgment—let alone respect—of the women's choices to present themselves in this way. But we might reasonably assume that the women's attempts to cultivate new, non-criminal identities were disrupted by

[59] Bosworth, *Engendering Resistance* (n 11). See also Lora Bex Lempert, *Women Doing Life: Gender, Punishment and the Struggle for Identity* (New York University Press 2016) and Colin Bird, 'Status, Identity, and Respect' (2004) 32(2) Political Theory 207 (hereafter Bird, 'Status, Identity, and Respect').

[60] Mary Bosworth, 'Gender, Race, and Sexuality in Prison' in Barbara H Zaitzow and Jim Thomas (eds), *Women in Prison: Gender and Social Control* (Lynne Rienner Publishers 2003) 144. This chapter is based on research conducted for Bosworth, *Engendering Resistance* (n 11).

[61] Iris Marion Young, *Intersecting Voices: Dilemmas of Gender, Political Philosophy, and Policy* (Princeton University Press 1997) 126. For another important account of autonomy along these lines, see Jennifer Nedelsky, 'Reconceiving Autonomy: Sources, Thoughts and Possibilities' (1989) 1(1) Yale Journal of Law and Feminism 7.

[62] See further Judith Butler, *Undoing Gender* (Routledge 2004).

the institution's pursuit of managerialist outcomes and its reliance on techniques of security and control.

3. The Decency Agenda and a new moral vocabulary

When Martin Narey was appointed Director General of HM Prison Service in 1999, he sought to reinsert a moral vocabulary—based on the notion of decency—into the domain.[63] His aims *inter alia* were to enhance social relations by challenging staff racism and brutality, strive for humane treatment through improved hygiene standards and healthcare provision and redefine the prison as a site of reformation. Respect is implicated in the idea of decent imprisonment and it is noteworthy that the value came to the fore once again as an explicit concern and a focal policy issue.[64] By 2000–01, the Decency Agenda emerged as a key theme in the development of HM Prison Service's measures of prison quality.[65]

How might we evaluate the Decency Agenda? The narrative in official discourse is that the agenda had a 'substantial and enduring' effect on prisons. Decency became one of seven strategic priorities identified in HM Prison Service's Five-Year Strategy. The agenda itself supported the introduction of the Safer Custody Programme, the achievement of overcrowding targets and drug testing, and the confirmation through audit of prisoner access to 'reasonable conditions'.[66]

Yet those in the academic community have queried whether penal practices, values, and sensibilities were genuinely transformed: in short, whether the project was successful at all. Of note was the prison's misguided tendency to treat decency and respect as synonymous throughout this period, when there are clear distinctions that can and should usefully be made between them. The prison's weak approximation of decency and respect might be interpreted as a reflection of the indeterminacy that flowed from the use of liberal, moralistic language in the penal context during

[63] Liebling, *Moral Performance* (n 12) and Crewe, *Prisoner Society* (n 13).

[64] See, eg, House of Commons Justice Committee, *Written Evidence: Role of the Prison Officer.* Memorandum submitted by Helen Arnold, Institute of Criminology, University of Cambridge (Justice Committee Publications 2009).

[65] Liebling, *Moral Performance* (n 12).

[66] House of Commons Justice Committee, *Written Evidence: Role of the Prison Officer.* Memorandum submitted by the Ministry of Justice (Justice Committee Publications 2009) s 3.2.41.

this period. For many, the Decency Agenda was characterised by a lack of clarity, on the part of those working in and managing prisons, about the nature of important terms such as 'justice', 'liberal', and 'care' and how they might be realised in practice. The terms were frequently used, partially operationalised, but seldom fully understood.[67]

The publication of Liebling's *Prisons and their Moral Performance*—a case study of the contemporary search for public sector reform—not only intersected with these policy developments; the body of qualitative and quantitative information it generated enabled the launch of the Decency Agenda itself.[68] Moral performance pertains to the emotional texture of the prison and the quality of moral treatment—by which Liebling means the quality of interpersonal and material treatment—of prisoners. Her research hypothesises a direct link between the moral performance of prison regimes and the experiences of prisoners in such a way that successfully operationalises the concept of legitimacy advanced by Sparks et al.[69]

The monograph itself is presented in two parts. In the first part, Liebling introduces a major empirical study conducted in five prisons in England and Wales which aimed, first, to establish which values mattered to staff and prisoners and, second, to employ the values derived from this part of the study to assess how five different prisons were performing in terms of imbuing their everyday practices with those values. In the second part, Liebling considers how best to develop a meaningful way of evaluating the intangible—and thus difficult-to-measure—moral dimensions of the prison experience such as humanity, justice, and respect. She explores these dimensions in meticulous empirical detail by implementing complex investigative methods in the style of appreciative inquiry. This methodology—drawn from the field of organisational development—allows Liebling to identify and explore the positive aspects of working practices

[67] Liebling, *Moral Performance* (n 12).

[68] ibid. For further reflections on Liebling's study of moral performance, see Ben Crewe, Alison Liebling, and Susie Hulley, 'Staff Culture, Use of Authority and Prisoner Quality of Life in Public and Private Sector Prisons' (2011) 44(1) Australian & New Zealand Journal of Criminology 94.

[69] Liebling, *Moral Performance* (n 12) and Sparks et al, *Problem of Order* (n 10).

in prisons in order to facilitate institutional change (for Liebling, prisons are settings with the potential, at least, to become 'moral communities').[70]

Liebling's efforts to refine the situational meanings given to moral values including respect and explore the difficulties of 'moral measurement'[71]—of operationalising them in investigative research—are perhaps the most compelling aspects of the study. But even the term 'moral *performance*' implies a certain orientation towards functions and outcomes, and there is compelling evidence that respect continued to be treated as a weak side-constraint on the pursuit of managerialist outcomes throughout this period.

(a) The situational meanings of respect

When Liebling published *Prisons and their Moral Performance*, there had been little theoretical or empirical exploration of prisoners' experiences of respect. With few exceptions, this remains the case. Of the few contributions to the literature, interpretations of respect tend to be narrow, focusing on the quality of interpersonal relationships between staff and prisoners and whether they exemplify a degree of courtesy and consideration.[72]

In a manner reminiscent of Sennett,[73] Liebling considers respect to be relational and dialogical, and a means by which to establish and mediate interactions between individuals. For two prisoners in Liebling's study, respect involves mutual recognition:

> They talk to me like a human being, not "do this! Do that!" They have a chat; it is nice just to talk.[74]

[70] Liebling, *Moral Performance* (n 12) 475. See also Carla Bagnoli, 'Respect and Membership in the Moral Community' (2007) 10(2) Ethical Theory and Moral Practice 113. On appreciative inquiry, see, eg, Charles Elliot, *Locating the Energy for Change: An Introduction to Appreciative Inquiry* (International Institute for Sustainable Development 1999); Anne T Coghlan, Hallie Preskill, and Tessie Tzavaras Catsambas, 'An Overview of Appreciative Inquiry in Evaluation' (2003) 100 New Directions for Evaluation 5; and Gervase Bushe, 'Appreciative Inquiry: Theory and Critique' in David M Boje, Bernard Burnes, and John Hassard (eds), *The Routledge Companion to Organizational Change* (Routledge 2011).

[71] Liebling, *Moral Performance* (n 12) 325.

[72] Hulley et al, 'Respect in Prisons' (n 1).

[73] Sennett, *Respect* (n 39).

[74] Prisoner, HMP Wandsworth, cited in Liebling, *Moral Performance* (n 12) 209. See also Wood, 'Respect and Recognition' (n 40).

Some staff show respect, respect for you as an individual, then it is natural to show it back. One officer says 'hello' or 'good morning', asks if you are OK and never just walks past you; it's the way he asks, you know he means it and he's interested.[75]

The prisoners imply that respect is important because of the implicit acceptance that it signals for their status and intrinsic worth. Yet, in Liebling's study, comments of this kind were something of a rarity, since the prisoners were at greater ease describing disrespect than respect. This is revealing in light of Crewe's claim that the vocabulary used by prisoners to describe the prison experience is a good guide to its qualities.[76] That a sense of disrespect—a denial of the recognition to which a person is entitled—was so widespread among prisoners provides an important hint that respect was a peripheral concern in an institution preoccupied with instrumental outcomes.

It is tempting to focus narrowly on simple interpersonal exchanges when examining a moral value as subtle and complex as respect. Yet it is worth reflecting on whether there may be exceptional circumstances in which a form of disrespect could be deemed—if not ideal—at least satisfactory. An action that is *prima facie* disrespectful—confiscating surplus food obtained by a prisoner and disposing of it instead—might be the only option to prevent a broader sense of injustice among onlookers. Assuming that he is being provided with a nutritionally adequate diet, the key question is whether the confiscation of surplus food—especially if he is hungry—constitutes 'surface disrespect' or a deeper form of disrespect that philosophers insist we must always denounce.[77] Given the 'problem of order' that Sparks et al describe,[78] surface disrespect might be justifiable on some occasions in order to prevent conflict and ensure a legitimate regime, and provided that prison officers have a strong moral commitment to respect for prisoners on most occasions.

[75] Prisoner, HMP Belmarsh, cited in Liebling, *Moral Performance* (n 12) ibid.

[76] Ben Crewe, 'Depth, Weight, Tightness: Revisiting the Pains of Imprisonment' (2011) 13(5) Punishment & Society 509.

[77] On surface and deeper forms of disrespect, see Thomas E Hill Jr, *Respect, Pluralism, and Justice: Kantian Perspectives* (OUP 2000) 143.

[78] Sparks et al, *Problem of Order* (n 10).

(b) Quantifying values

Liebling's MQPL survey arose from her study of moral performance and was adopted by HM Prison Service Standards Audit Unit in 2004, having been resisted initially due to its complexity. The MQPL survey is now used in routine performance and audit measurement of all prisons in England and Wales. Its purpose is to measure the presence of non-instrumental values in prison—including respect—as well as regime dimensions such as fairness, order, safety, personal development, and family contact. It draws directly on the views and experiences of prisoners, who are invited to respond to over 100 questions scored on a five-point Likert scale.[79] Although the MQPL survey marked some progress where respect and other moral values were concerned, it was not implemented as a stand-alone survey. Rather, it was situated alongside a range of other performance measures in a move which suggests that managerialism, not individual welfare, remained the institution's recurring motif and primary goal.

Since 2007, Liebling's SQL survey has also been used by HM Prison Service to assess the performance of its institutions and improve prison culture. Since 2011, it has been instrumental in developing the 'Every Contact Matters' initiative, which emphasises the potential rehabilitative value of every interaction and shapes the public sector's bids to operate prisons as efficiently as possible in a competitive environment.[80]

Both surveys prompt consideration of the extent to which quantification can be called upon as a mediating instrument where disparate values and rationalities such as respect and safety are at stake.[81] Liebling would likely be receptive to the

[79] See Liebling, *Moral Performance* (n 12). For a detailed commentary on the methodological tools for the MQPL survey, see Alison Liebling, Susie Hulley, and Ben Crewe, 'Conceptualising and Measuring the Quality of Prison Life' in David Gadd, Susanne Karstedt, and Steven F Messner (eds), *The SAGE Handbook of Criminological Research Methods* (SAGE 2011).

[80] On 'Every Contact Matters', see, eg, Alison Liebling, *Prisons Research: Measuring the Quality of Prison Life*. Impact Case Study prepared for the Research Excellence Framework (Research Excellence Framework 2014).

[81] On quantification as a moralising instrument, see, eg, Andrea Mennicken, 'The Quantification of Decency', transcript of presentation at *Moral Economies, Economic Moralities*, University of California, Berkeley (Society for the Advancement of Socio-Economics 2016); Mennicken, 'Accounting and

view held by Espeland and Stevens, for whom one virtue of quantification is its capacity to offer 'standardized ways of constructing proxies for uncertain and elusive qualities'.[82] Similarly, Miller considers quantification to be a powerful means by which to represent such values because performance numbers possess a 'neutrality and social authority' and are 'endowed with a legitimacy that seems difficult to contest or dispute'.[83] Much of the literature, then, suggests that we should be enthusiastic about performance metrics and not too swift to dismiss their potential for animating debate and initiating reform. Yet the literature routinely overlooks the prior question of whether moral values are amenable to empirical measurement at all. While it is now commonplace for prisons to measure a range of moral values—including respect—by means of the MQPL survey, it is far from clear that they should. To do so is to view respect, for example, as objective, fixed, and stable—and thus measurable—when it is best understood as subjective, malleable, and variable.[84]

We are left with the overwhelming sense that prisons direct too much attention towards measuring the existence of moral values and only limited attention towards forging better social relations that are generative of such values in the first place. At present, the institution's strategic and operational priorities are *constrained* but not *characterised* by respect in such a way that implies once more that instrumental outcomes and external accountability are its primary concerns.

Privatisation' (n 47); and Andrea Mennicken, 'Accounting for Values in Prison Privatization' in Susanna Alexius and Kristina Tamm Hallström (eds), *Configuring Value Conflicts in Markets* (Edward Elgar 2014).

[82] Wendy Nelson Espeland and Mitchell L Stevens, 'Commensuration as a Social Process' (1998) 24 Annual Review of Sociology 313, 316. See also Andrew Coyle, *Humanity in Prison: Questions of Definition and Audit* (International Centre for Prison Studies 2014) 9–12 and Wendy Nelson Espeland and Michael Sauder, 'Rankings and Reactivity: How Public Measures Recreate Social Worlds' (2007) 113(1) American Journal of Sociology 1.

[83] Peter Miller, 'Accounting and Objectivity: The Invention of Calculating Selves and Calculable Spaces' (1992) 9(1/2) Annals of Scholarship 61, 68–69. See also Peter Miller, 'Governing by Numbers: Why Calculative Practices Matter' (2001) 68(2) Social Research 379.

[84] See, eg, Dillon, 'Respect' (n 8).

4. Managerialism continues

Crewe conducted his empirical research between 2002 and 2003, at the height of the Decency Agenda. By the time the study was published in 2009, the agenda itself had waned, though decency remained a strategic priority of HM Prison Service and there was evidence too of a continued commitment to managerialism.[85]

The Prisoner Society, an ethnographic study of a medium-security men's prison in England, offers a perceptive insight into the ways in which the vocabulary of respect maintained a presence in prisons—albeit as a weak side-constraint on the pursuit of instrumental outcomes—throughout this period. Crewe provides a localised 'snapshot' of one prison's 'social anatomy' and the experiences that occur within it. He explores how the institution exercises its power, typically through individualising the prisoner community and demanding certain forms of compliance and engagement. Inevitably, the prisoners experience this exercise of power differentially. He then relates this process to the broader aims, means, and conditions of the institution. He describes how the 'prisoner society'—its norms, hierarchy, and social relationships—is shaped both by the conditions of confinement and the different backgrounds, values, and identities that inmates import into the prison environment.[86]

The Prisoner Society is of note for its discussion of the definitional ambiguities of respect in a prison framed and challenged by status hierarchies and penal power. Crewe observes, for example, that little attempt had been made to distinguish between cognate concepts such as power (influence or the capacity to achieve), status (social standing or prestige), and different forms of respect. He insists that definitional clarity is crucial, not least because the term 'respect' is employed by both staff and prisoners in diverse ways.[87]

[85] Crewe, *Prisoner Society* (n 13).

[86] ibid, ch 1, especially pp 3 and 8.

[87] ibid. In their research on inmate culture, Winfree et al invited participants to reflect on the differences between 'offender types' according to 'how much respect [they] would give them', without clarifying what it might mean to respect an individual, either in general or in the prison context: L Thomas Winfree Jr, Greg Newbold, and S Houston Tubb III, 'Prisoner Perspectives on Inmate Culture in New Mexico and New Zealand: A Descriptive Case Study' (2002) 82(2) The Prison Journal 213.

Crewe introduces Darwall's landmark scholarship—explored in detail in chapter one—which identifies two kinds of respect: recognition respect and appraisal respect.[88] He adapts Darwall's typology by proposing a third way in which respect is at work at HMP Wellingborough: not only as a mode of recognition and a form of appraisal but also as an instrumental requirement.[89]

As we have seen, recognition respect is an attitude of regard for others grounded in the Kantian notion that all persons are worthy of respect by virtue of their humanity. When prisoners request that prison officers treat them with respect, they appeal to this basic right to be taken into consideration. Appraisal respect is analogous to esteem. For Crewe, appraisal respect is easily translatable to the prison environment in view of Darwall's observation that it is possible to have appraisal respect for someone's ability without having moral regard for them. According to Crewe, respectful relations in prison might also be instrumental in nature. On this view, a prisoner may feel obligated to modify his behaviour in such a way that is based not on moral considerations but instead on fear or awe of another prisoner's social influence or physical potential. When a prisoner—usually in the interests of self-protection—acts in this way, he demonstrates that it is possible to show 'respect' towards another for strictly prudential reasons.[90]

Yet the question arises as to whether Crewe's instrumental respect should be labelled as respect at all. At best, it denotes a surface approach to respect or a performative action that lacks the proper intent. Moreover, when a key empirical finding—that there was admiration among some prisoners for behaviour that induces fear—effectively conflates appraisal and instrumental respect, we receive mixed messages from Crewe regarding the latter's explanatory scope.[91] His typology may require some fine-tuning—including an adequate differentiation between both forms of respect—if it is to be fully workable in a context as socially and morally complex as the prison. Alternatively, we might take the view that such rigid categorisations of respect are best avoided.

[88] Darwall, 'Two Kinds of Respect' (n 40).
[89] ibid and Crewe, *Prisoner Society* (n 13).
[90] Crewe, *Prisoner Society* (n 13).
[91] ibid.

Aside from the challenge of categorising forms of respect, we might infer from Crewe's analysis that the institution—preoccupied with managerialist outcomes as a new form of penal power—failed to regulate everyday social relations between prisoners in which respect was often the core value at stake. In examining the minutiae of social relations in prison, he shows how respect so often regulates horizontal relationships between prisoners and not simply vertical relationships between state and subject. Moreover, we learn that respect was routinely implicated in a struggle for status, power, and masculine veneration. Overtly masculine performances of physicality and violence were strategic resources for those prisoners concerned to gain respect, manipulate power relations, and alter the relative standing of their peers.[92]

5. The Rehabilitation Revolution

The coalition government's ambitions for the 'Rehabilitation Revolution' were outlined in 2010 in the form of a Green Paper, *Breaking the Cycle*, and an accompanying Evidence Report.[93] Its basic proposition can be simply articulated. Prior to the launch of the Rehabilitation Revolution, the argument goes, prisons were dominated by a 'command and control' agenda. A relentless focus on targets and micro-management removed scope for innovation and professional discretion. The Green Paper promised a 'fundamental shift' in the way rehabilitation was financed and delivered.[94] Prisons would become places of 'hard work and industry' and integrated offender management would improve outcomes for those suffering from drug and alcohol abuse or dependence.[95] The vision was not limited to prisons. Rather, it was situated within a broader context in which all criminal justice

[92] ibid.

[93] Ministry of Justice, *Breaking the Cycle: Effective Punishment, Rehabilitation and Sentencing of Offenders* (Cm 7972, The Stationery Office 2010) (hereafter Ministry of Justice, *Breaking the Cycle*) and Ministry of Justice, *Green Paper Evidence Report. Breaking the Cycle: Effective Punishment, Rehabilitation and Sentencing of Offenders* (Ministry of Justice 2010).

[94] Ministry of Justice, *Breaking the Cycle* (n 93) 38.

[95] ibid 1–2.

agencies were expected to play a pivotal role in realising these ambitions.[96]

In reality, however, these ambitions were not new. Many of the policies posited as innovative are better understood as a development and intensification of certain policy preoccupations of the previous government. And despite the emphasis on rehabilitation and moral progress, the implementation of 'Payment by Results' schemes in prisons as part of this 'revolutionary shift' is perhaps the most striking example of a system that continued to be driven by instrumental outcomes.[97]

The publication of Phillips' *The Multicultural Prison* intersected with these developments.[98] Against the background of research which exposed how ethnic minority prisoners experience greater 'weight' and 'pain',[99] Phillips sets out in ethnographic detail the relevance of diversity and multiculturalism to day-to-day social relations between male prisoners at HMYOI Rochester and HMP Maidstone. Phillips' is a sensitive and finely textured account, which raises valuable questions about what it means to respect diversity in conditions of confinement. We have become accustomed to these questions being too quickly dismissed, especially when matters of ethnic diversity are couched in 'us/them' language or when respect is invoked in vague terms.[100]

[96] ibid 38 and Richard Garside and Helen Mills, *UK Justice Policy Review: Volume 1, 6 May 2010 to 5 May 2011* (2011) 12–13 'The Rehabilitation Revolution'.

[97] Simon Bastow, 'Payment by Results in the Prison System: Challenges of Calibrating Success and Failure' (London School of Economics and Political Science, British Politics and Policy Blog 2013) <http://blogs.lse.ac.uk/politicsandpolicy/payment-by-results-in-the-prison-system-challenges-of-calibrating-success-and-failure/> accessed 1 August 2019.

[98] Phillips, *Multicultural Prison* (n 14).

[99] ibid, ch 6. See also Her Majesty's Inspectorate of Prisons for England and Wales, *Parallel Worlds: A Thematic Review of Race Relations in Prisons* (Her Majesty's Inspectorate of Prisons for England and Wales 2005); National Offender Management Service, *Race Review 2008. Implementing Race Equality in Prisons: Five Years On* (National Offender Management Service 2008); and David Lammy, *The Lammy Review: An Independent Review into the Treatment of, and Outcomes for, Black, Asian and Minority Ethnic Individuals in the Criminal Justice System* (Ministry of Justice 2017) (hereafter Lammy, *The Lammy Review*) 50: 'A lower proportion of BAME respondents believed staff treated them with respect, recalled staff members checking on their well-being or having a member of staff they felt they could turn to for help'.

[100] See further Lammy, *The Lammy Review* (n 99).

Arguments about deeply embedded racial tensions between inmates are so well rehearsed in the literature, that we might reasonably form the belief that diversity itself poses a challenge to the practice of imprisonment.[101] Phillips' study is refreshing in that it highlights moments when respect between prisoners of diverse ethnicities genuinely flourished, in a manner that suggests a degree of immediate synchronicity with the coalition government's rehabilitative ambitions. Gilroy's notion of 'multicultural conviviality' provides Phillips with an overarching framework within which to make sense of these relations. Gilroy offers a neat way of referring to the normality of moving across ethnic boundaries in our daily interactions.[102] For many prisoners, the diverse population was unremarkable and by no means at the forefront of their relations with others. The most striking example of multicultural conviviality was in the self-cook area at HMP Maidstone as a site that 'condensed and revealed the ethnic diversity of the prison' like no other.[103] This confined social space allowed prisoners to form alliances and bonds across religious and ethnic lines in the spirit of tolerance and mutual respect.

Somewhat predictably, however, Phillips also documents a sense of separatism and loose ethnic solidarity among a subset of prisoners. Diversity and multiculturalism were at the root of their conflictual relationships, exemplifying the very antithesis of the government's rehabilitative ambitions. In a manner reminiscent of Crewe's research, we learn that a violent form of masculinity was a prominent feature of both regimes and offered prisoners a means by which to resist institutional control and gain respect through intimidation, fear, and physical conflict.[104] In this way,

[101] See, eg, Crewe, *Prisoner Society* (n 13). In the US, race is cited as a 'risk factor' for inmate violence: Mark T Berg and Matt DeLisi, 'The Correctional Melting Pot: Race, Ethnicity, Citizenship, and Prison Violence' (2006) 34(6) Journal of Criminal Justice 631.

[102] Paul Gilroy, *After Empire: Melancholia or Convivial Culture?* (Routledge 2004).

[103] Phillips, *Multicultural Prison* (n 14) 89. See further Rod Earle and Coretta Phillips, 'Digesting Men? Ethnicity, Gender and Food: Perspectives from a "Prison Ethnography"' (2012) 16(2) Theoretical Criminology 141 (hereafter Earle and Phillips, 'Digesting Men? Ethnicity, Gender and Food').

[104] Phillips, *Multicultural Prison* (n 14); Earle and Phillips, 'Digesting Men? Ethnicity, Gender and Food' (n 103); and Crewe, *Prisoner Society* (n 13).

we should be careful too not to overstate the role of race and ethnicity and understate the role of masculinity in these fraught interactions.

Phillips' findings—in focusing exclusively on horizontal social relations between prisoners—throws into sharp relief the nature and limits of HM Prison Service's commitment to respect. When Phillips' study was published, the National Offender Management Service (since February 2017, HM Prison and Probation Service) had made a public commitment to treat its prisoners with respect but made no comparable commitment to regulate relationships between prisoners in which respect is often the core value at stake.[105] Several years on, this remains the case.[106] This limiting of institutional responsibility to securing respect in vertical relationships only will be revisited in chapter 6. For now, it is worth noting that HM Prison Service is invested in respect to the extent that it supports a set of strategic and operational priorities and is much less concerned—publicly, at least—with its role in structuring and legitimating social relations between its subjects.

6. A 'protean notion'

It has been possible, then, to trace a clear assertion of a value base or moral vocabulary in prisons—prompted by the recommendations of the Woolf Report—followed by various failed attempts to make sense of and sustain that vocabulary. We can discern a further attempt to reassert that vocabulary at the beginning of the next decade by means of the Decency Agenda and later by means of the Rehabilitation Revolution.[107] The organisational management of prisoners ensured that respect, together with decency and

[105] National Offender Management Service, *Annual Report and Accounts 2012–2013* (National Offender Management Service 2013) 6: 'In delivering offender management services, we will ... treat offenders with decency and respect.'

[106] Her Majesty's Prison and Probation Service, *Annual Report and Accounts 2017–18* (n 4).

[107] Liebling, *Moral Performance* (n 12) and Crewe, *Prisoner Society* (n 13). See also Alison Liebling and Ben Crewe, 'Prisons Beyond the New Penology: The Shifting Moral Foundations of Prison Management' in Jonathan Simon and Richard Sparks (eds), *The SAGE Handbook of Punishment and Society* (SAGE 2013) (hereafter Liebling and Crewe, 'Prisons Beyond the New Penology').

fairness, remained relevant throughout this period, if only in official discourse.

In effect, HM Prison Service has had a fluctuating relationship with respect, and there is ample evidence to suggest that the value has merely *constrained* and not *characterised* the institution's managerialist concerns since *Woolf*. That respect has been able to withstand this fluctuating relationship without disappearing entirely from sight is testament to its reputation as a 'protean notion' that may be 'used in multiple ways' as part of 'various discursive positionings'.[108] The prison has maximised—intentionally or otherwise—on the flexibility of respect and its capacity to drift between several potential meanings. As ever, it has appealed to the word 'respect' while neglecting to cultivate the value in practice.

D. Prisons after *Woolf*

Accounts of contemporary imprisonment tend to suggest that there was a clean historical break after *Woolf*. There is a familiar narrative that Woolf's recommendations were initially accepted by the government as a reform agenda for the next quarter of a century. This inspired a flurry of activity, including various attempts to 'humanise' prisons. But these attempts were ultimately unsuccessful and Woolf's moral ambitions for the prison were left unrealised. According to this narrative, *Woolf* assumed limited relevance soon after its publication and was consigned to history.[109]

Yet it is possible that such accounts have over-schematised a more complex story. There is scope to advance an alternative line of argument, namely, that there was no such historical break and that almost thirty years after the publication of the Woolf Report, its themes and recommendations are as—if not more—prescient.[110] The report continues to offer a powerful indictment

[108] On respect as a 'protean notion', see Richard Buttny and Princess L Williams, 'Demanding Respect: The Uses of Reported Speech in Discursive Constructions of Interracial Contact' (2000) 11(1) Discourse & Society 109, 110.

[109] See, eg, Crewe, *Prisoner Society* (n 13) and Phillips, *Multicultural Prison* (n 14).

[110] The Rt Hon Lord Woolf, 'Strangeways 25 Years' On: Achieving Fairness & Justice in Prison' transcript of speech delivered at The Honourable Society of the Inner Temple (Inner Temple 1 April 2015) and Day et al, *Strangeways 25 Years' On* (n 20).

of political complacency in the face of rapidly deteriorating moral and material conditions in prisons, and its continuing relevance for a critique of respect is more significant than has yet been appreciated.

This book's framing of *Woolf* then and now is a deliberate attempt to recover and explore the continuing relevance of Woolf's moral ambitions for the prison. Woolf, in recommending the introduction of a range of humane practices into prisons, fully embraced the idea—if only, on occasion, the language—of respect.[111] And far from being resisted in prisons as the dominant narratives on *Woolf* imply, respect continues to be embraced—albeit reductively—as a weak side-constraint on the pursuit of managerialist outcomes. It is an approach to respect that has so far been unable to mitigate against the polarising social dynamics of contemporary imprisonment.

One way of exploring the continuing relevance of *Woolf* is by examining Bennett's recent contribution to the genre of institutional sociology.[112] Such works have become rarer, with academic expertise increasingly receding from the public gaze. While studies have tended to focus either on prisoner characteristics or on the structural determinants of the prison experience, Bennett's is the first to focus exclusively on the experiences of prison managers.

The Working Lives of Prison Managers presents an ethnographic study of two medium-security prisons in England, where globalised changes in management practices had intersected with localised practices and occupational cultures. The study was published at a time when the prison had made 'heroic strides' in some areas—in management and the monitoring of prison performance—and regressed significantly in others. We learn that chronic overcrowding and a near doubling of the prison population since *Woolf* continue to impede efforts to rehabilitate offenders and cultivate a genuinely moral climate.[113]

Bennett's study is important for a critique of respect in prisons for two reasons. First, it provides a renewed perspective on managerialism in contemporary imprisonment, including how the philosophy has reconfigured the role of prison managers. Second, it hints at the ways in which prison managers—working under

[111] Home Office, *The Woolf Report* (n 20).
[112] Bennett, *Prison Managers* (n 15).
[113] ibid and Day et al, *Strangeways 25 Years' On* (n 20) 33.

managerialist constraints—are in a position to promote only a diluted form of respect based on civility and good manners.

1. The shifting nature of managerialism

Having been incorporated into the very fabric of the prison, managerialism has an established reputation for undermining moral values. Bennett documents the ways in which the prison's commitment to the managerialist project has shifted subtly in recent years, and there appear to be rather less subtle implications for respect.

As Bennett concluded his empirical work, Liebling's MQPL survey was implemented in prisons throughout the UK. He observes that while managerial control is not genuinely reconciled with progressive concerns about the humane treatment of prisoners, nor are these concerns entirely displaced, as Liebling and Crewe have suggested in recent years.[114] Rather, the prison's instrumental aims remain firmly in place but in altered form. Bennett proposes the term '*prison* managerialism' to refer to a more nuanced practice in which prison managers participate in an ongoing dialectical process between the competing demands of global managerialism and the local prison culture.[115] On this view, it makes sense that the prison would be in a position to deliver only a weak approximation of intrinsic values such as respect.

If we subscribe to Bennett's account, it follows that Garland's 'culture of control' thesis no longer prescribes as restrictive a phenomenon.[116] While Garland associates the culture of control with reduced professional discretion and increased monitoring

[114] ibid. Bennett distinguishes his position from that of Liebling and Crewe, who claim that prisons in England and Wales have shifted from 'managerialism-plus'—an approach that reconciles the structures of managerial control with progressive concerns about the humane treatment of prisoners—towards 'managerialism-minus' in which 'economy and efficiency are prioritised above any moral mission'. On this view, the prison has moved from delivering a weak approximation of intrinsic values such as respect, to a position whereby those values are entirely displaced: Liebling and Crewe, 'Prisons Beyond the New Penology' (n 107) 294.

[115] The implementation of the 'performance hub' in 2010 signalled a commitment to managerialism in altered form, encompassing *inter alia* externally driven measures, performance ratings for individual institutions, and a league table of prisons: Bennett, *Prison Managers* (n 15) ch 9 and Afterword.

[116] Garland, *Culture of Control* (n 50).

of practice, Bennett's prison managerialism implies that these practices have evolved in recent years. Managerialism is now concerned not only with regulation but also with developing self-regulation and not only with the actions of employees but also with their emotions, values, and identities.[117]

2. Enabling and constraining respect

Of note are Bennett's tangential references to the ways in which managerialism enabled and constrained opportunities for prison managers to cultivate respect. The managers were highly attuned to the value, citing their most deeply held concerns as 'reform, rehabilitation and humane treatment'. But these humanitarian concerns routinely came into conflict with the pursuit of 'professionalism' and 'punishment and security', and Bennett describes 'myriad' situations in which they prioritised managerialist imperatives, especially when manipulating performance data.[118]

One prison manager promoted civility and good manners as a means by which to cultivate respect:

> There are certain values that you can bring, like good manners. I think good manners are important. You can *instil* that and *insist* and get that from prisoners, providing you reciprocate that and speak to prisoners appropriately, address them appropriately—please, thank you … [There are] basic standards and values you can instil … and you can get the proper respect back from staff and prisoners. If you *insist* on that, they will respond.[119]

Two observations are in order here. First, while it is encouraging that the language of respect had found its way into this regime, the prison manager's concern to 'instil' and 'insist' on good manners in order that the prisoners showed 'proper respect' implies that he placed a premium on institutional compliance and control over the

[117] Bennett, *Prison Managers* (n 15).

[118] ibid 127–28. For the practical implications of this conflict, see, eg, Prison Reform Trust, *Bromley Briefings: Prison Factfile* (Prison Reform Trust 2017) 17: 'Inspectors find declines in nearly all areas—particularly safety and respect.'

[119] Emphasis added. Bennett, *Prison Managers* (n 15). For Liebling, the most respected officers were those who held typically masculine qualities and accentuated them during their social relations with prisoners. These officers mixed confidence and courage with a form of 'combative humour': Alison Liebling, 'Why Prison Culture Matters' in Byrne et al, *Prison Violence* (n 33).

pursuit of progressive practices and moral values. His comments evoke Garland's notion of 'responsibilization', whereby individuals are encouraged to behave in ways that align with state-directed standards of behaviour in order to enable the smooth running of an institution.[120] Respect need not be instilled or insisted upon, and is best cultivated in conditions of mutual understanding.[121] According to Bennett, those prison managers persuaded by the benefits of managerialism understood the incorporation of moral values into its philosophy as an 'enabling force'.[122] But there is also a sense in which this approach—whereby respect is treated as a weak side-constraint on the pursuit of instrumental outcomes—serves only to taint the quality of social relations.

Second, it is notable that the prison manager insists on civil relations and good manners as the primary means by which to cultivate respect. It is true that civility and good manners have some bearing on what it means to respect others. Good manners require that we consider others' feelings, express gratitude towards them, and, where appropriate, engage in tolerant restraint. But the term 'respect' admits of fine gradations which are too often overlooked, and it would be to the detriment of any prison regime to reduce respect to a matter of civility.[123] There are actions and dispositions—such as saying 'please' and 'thank you'—where respect seems to consist wholly in the fulfilment of a certain social ritual. A respectful attitude seems almost built into the social meaning of the action—as if it were 'frozen into the performance itself'—quite independently of an individual's thoughts or motives.[124] To demonstrate good manners is simply to rehearse a particular set of actions which by no means require critical

[120] Garland, *Culture of Control* (n 50) 124–27.

[121] Dillon, 'Respect' (n 8).

[122] Bennett, *Prison Managers* (n 15) 129.

[123] On civility, see Cheshire Calhoun, 'The Virtue of Civility' (2000) 29(3) Philosophy & Public Affairs 251; Richard Boyd, 'The Value of Civility?' (2006) 43(5–6) Urban Studies 863; Teresa M Bejan, *Mere Civility: Disagreement and the Limits of Toleration* (Harvard University Press 2017); Keith J Bybee, *How Civility Works* (Stanford University Press 2016); and Michael Walzer, 'Civility and Civic Virtue in Contemporary America' (1974) 41(4) Social Research 593. On respect as 'more than civility', see Liebling, *Moral Performance* (n 12) 210 and Ben Crewe and Alison Liebling, 'Are Liberal-Humanitarian Penal Values and Practices Exceptional?' in Thomas Ugelvik and Jane Dullum (eds), *Penal Exceptionalism? Nordic Prison Policy and Practice* (Routledge 2011).

[124] Bird, 'Status, Identity, and Respect' (n 59) 209–10.

reflection, still less a genuine attitude of respect. And given that civility is not subject to the same sincerity requirement as respect, it is best understood as a minimal, outward—and even, at times, hypocritical—virtue. Are we genuinely respectful if we engage in such performative modes of respect while lacking the proper intent? It is possible that the act of 'respecting' someone against one's own convictions is no real respect but, rather, manifests itself as an additional insult.

Given that—unlike other moral values—civility is primarily associated with the following of socially established rules, it is as much about formal compliance as it is about social relations.[125] This approach promotes a certain amount of superficial posturing and gesturing towards respect in its most basic form: enough for the prison to convince those external to the institution that its practices are minimally consistent with the value. Although wholly unsatisfactory where respect is concerned, it leaves the institution considerable scope to pursue its managerialist aims, which have remained in place to a greater or lesser degree since *Woolf*. Clearly, there is much left to do to disrupt the hierarchical opposition between instrumental and non-instrumental approaches to penal practice and understanding.

[125] See the report on the then privately run HMP Birmingham, where inspectors 'observed relaxed and courteous interactions, but they were usually superficial'. The prison was accordingly described as 'poor' in terms of respect. Her Majesty's Chief Inspector of Prisons for England and Wales, *Report on an Unannounced Inspection of HMP Birmingham* (Her Majesty's Inspectorate of Prisons for England and Wales 2017) s 2.. In August 2018, Her Majesty's Chief Inspector of Prisons for England and Wales, Peter Clarke, demanded urgent government action and an independent enquiry into the 'appalling' institution, where staff-prisoner relationships had 'deteriorated markedly': Her Majesty's Inspectorate of Prisons for England and Wales, *Urgent Notification: HMP Birmingham* (Her Majesty's Inspectorate of Prisons for England and Wales 16 August 2018) 2 and 13. On 20 August 2018, the prison was brought back under state control: Jim Pickard, 'G4S Stripped of Control over "Failed" Birmingham Jail' *Financial Times* (20 August 2018). Following the initial six-month intervention, and a subsequent extension of that period, the Prisons Minister confirmed on 1 April 2019 that the government's contract with G4S will end early, and HMP Birmingham will remain under state control: Ministry of Justice, Her Majesty's Prison and Probation Service, and Her Majesty's Prison Service, 'Birmingham Prison Contract Ended' (Ministry of Justice, Her Majesty's Prison and Probation Service, and Her Majesty's Prison Service 1 April 2018) <https://www.gov.uk/government/news/birmingham-prison-contract-ended> accessed 1 August 2019.

5

Respect at Prison Mealtime

This chapter continues to subject a series of unexamined beliefs on respect and criminal justice to critical scrutiny and challenge. There is a shift in focus to the quotidian experience of prison mealtime, whose pivotal role in shaping the experiences of prisoners has been considerably understated. The ritualised preparation and provision of prison food is imbued with considerable symbolic power.[1] While mealtime imparts the appearance of structure—and respectability—to the prison regime, it conceals a more complex reality in which respect is little more than an empty slogan in an institution preoccupied with managerialist imperatives and instrumental outcomes.

This chapter is prefaced with a short commentary on prison mealtime in historical context. It is then structured around three key stages of contemporary prison mealtime—*preparation, consumption*, and *resistance*—which I propose as organising categories for critiquing the practice. When the authorities treat respect as a weak side-constraint on the pursuit of instrumental outcomes rather than a foundational value of the regime itself, it

[1] On food as the 'symbolic medium par excellence', see Rod Earle and Coretta Phillips, 'Digesting Men? Ethnicity, Gender and Food: Perspectives from a "Prison Ethnography"' (2012) 16(2) Theoretical Criminology 141, 144 (hereafter Earle and Phillips, 'Ethnicity, Gender and Food'); Rebecca Godderis, 'Dining in: The Symbolic Power of Food in Prison' (2006) 45(3) The Howard Journal of Criminal Justice 255 (hereafter Godderis, 'Dining in'); and Amy B Smoyer and Giza Lopes, 'Hungry on the Inside: Prison Food as Concrete and Symbolic Punishment in a Women's Prison' (2016) 19(2) Punishment & Society 240 (hereafter Smoyer and Lopes, 'Prison Food'). On the centrality of food to the prison experience, see further Amy B Smoyer and Linda Kjær Minke, *Food Systems in Correctional Settings: A Literature Review and Case Study* (World Health Organization 2015). On food as a means by which to express the abstract significance of social systems, see Anne Murcott, 'The Cultural Significance of Food and Eating' (1982) 41(2) Proceedings of the Nutrition Society 203.

Respect and Criminal Justice. Gabrielle Watson, Oxford University Press (2020). © Gabrielle Watson.
DOI: 10.1093/oso/9780198833345.001.0001

undermines those responsible for preparing food, degrades prisoners who have no choice but to consume it, and exacerbates the experiences of those who—for reasons of religious belief, physical or mental ill-health, or in protest—resist or refuse it.[2]

Only a weak approximation of respect is detectable at prison mealtime. This is despite HM Prison and Probation Service having committed, at the level of official discourse, to treating offenders with 'decency and respect' and designating humanity as one of its core values.[3] And this is despite the findings of the Woolf Report—published three decades ago—in which 'monotonous, inedible, cold' food was the foremost complaint among volatile prisoners.[4] When the modern prison's flawed understanding and approach to respect is exposed, its support for the new corporate notion of 'Every Contact Matters' becomes less convincing.[5] This is especially so when its core idea—that meaningful day-to-day social contact between staff and prisoners, however fleeting, is significant for the social fabric of the institution—not only proceeds on the basis of a reductive understanding of respect but is promoted as part of a managerialist framework. Respect, then, is reduced to a kind of institutional *performance*.

Contributions to the literature on prison food have been occasional and diverse, and the categories of preparation, consumption, and resistance have the potential to expose new parallels and distinctions between them. The leading research includes Ugelvik on surreptitious food preparation, autonomy, and emotionality;[6] Smith on the pleasures, consolations, and quasi-domestic

[2] See, eg, Stefan Enggist, Lars Møller, Gauden Galea, and Caroline Udesen (eds), *Prisons and Health* (World Health Organization 2014) ch 3, 13–15, *Prison-Specific Ethical and Clinical Problems*: Prisoners who stop eating or go on hunger strikes (hereafter Enggist et al, *Prisons and Health*).

[3] Her Majesty's Prison and Probation Service, *Annual Report and Accounts 2017–18* (HC 1175, The Stationery Office 2018) 5 (hereafter Her Majesty's Prison and Probation Service, *Annual Report and Accounts 2017–18*).

[4] Home Office, *Prison Disturbances April 1990: Report of an Inquiry by The Rt Hon Lord Justice Woolf (Parts I and II) and His Honour Judge Stephen Tumim (Part II)* (Cm 1456, The Stationery Office 1991) 32.

[5] On 'Every Contact Matters', see Alison Liebling, *Prisons Research: Measuring the Quality of Prison Life*. Impact Case Study prepared for the Research Excellence Framework (Research Excellence Framework 2014).

[6] Thomas Ugelvik, 'The Hidden Food: Mealtime Resistance and Identity Work in a Norwegian Prison' (2011) 13(1) Punishment & Society 47 (hereafter Ugelvik, 'Hidden Food').

experiences that food—prepared and consumed in a women's prison—can cultivate,[7] and Phillips on cooking as a 'performance' of identity and mode of cultural exchange in two ethnically diverse English prisons.[8]

A sense of the general is as important as the particular. Having critiqued the constitutive elements of prison mealtime, the chapter concludes by situating prison mealtime within the practice of criminal justice more generally. The sustained period of fiscal austerity under which the prison is currently operating provides a point of entry into that broader debate. It is routinely assumed that diminishing resources equate to a diminution of prisoners' rights and liberties.[9] Yet, in requiring prisons to reorient their priorities, budget cuts might also create opportunities for respect at prison mealtime. One such opportunity is the authorisation of inmates to work in the prison kitchen over their civilian or prison officer counterparts, whereby significant savings are incurred.[10]

As ever, the aim is to demonstrate the flexibility of respect as a concept of critical enquiry for criminal justice by nominating for discussion just one of a number of prison practices it is capable of illuminating.[11] As in previous chapters, prison mealtime

[7] Catrin Smith, 'Punishment and Pleasure: Women, Food and the Imprisoned Body' (2002) 50(2) The Sociological Review 197.

[8] Coretta Phillips, *The Multicultural Prison: Ethnicity, Masculinity, and Social Relations among Prisoners* (OUP 2012) 89 (hereafter Phillips, *Multicultural Prison*). On eating and the formation of identities beyond the prison, see Sidney W Mintz and Christine M du Bois, 'The Anthropology of Food and Eating' (2002) 31 Annual Review of Anthropology 99 (hereafter Mintz and du Bois, 'Anthropology of Food and Eating').

[9] David Faulkner, *Criminal Justice and Government at a Time of Austerity* (Criminal Justice Alliance 2010).

[10] National Audit Office, *Serving Time: Prisoner Diet and Exercise* (HC 939, The Stationery Office 2006) 18, para 2.28 (hereafter National Audit Office, *Serving Time*). In the year ending 2018, on average, around 12,300 prisoners and detainees were working in custody at any one time across public sector prisons, privately managed prisons, and Immigration Removal Centres. They delivered around 17 million hours of work during the course of a year: Ministry of Justice, *Her Majesty's Prison and Probation Service Annual Digest 2017–18* (Ministry of Justice 2018) 1.

[11] There is a significant opening in the literature for an enquiry into respect at prison mealtime. However, given the flexibility of respect, the analysis might equally have been developed in relation to the prison visit, prison issue clothing and uniform, or the Incentives and Earned Privileges Scheme on the prohibition of reading and writing materials, popularly known as the 'prison book ban': see, eg, National Offender Management Service, *Incentives and Earned Privileges* (PSI

exposes the challenges involved—as well as the advances that could be made—in inscribing respectful relations between state and subject.

A. Historical Context

It is possible to draw some important connections between prison mealtime in historical context and the modern prison's managerialist objectives. It appears that centuries prior to the emergence of managerialism as an organising ideology, prison mealtime was implicated in the pursuit of various instrumental aims.

The dominant narrative in historical accounts of prison mealtime is that, pre-twentieth century, food was intended to 'punish, debilitate and degrade'.[12] The eighteenth century may have epitomised the most indecent of prison conditions, where a restricted diet was an explicit feature of punishment, and those restrictions could be removed only when the prisoner or his family offered payment.[13] Part of the reformative work of John Howard was to offer an incisive critique of the practice of charging prisoners for meals, proposing instead that they be provided with a daily allowance of food.[14] That respect should be a foundational value of prison mealtime—as opposed to being extended only once fees were met—was implicit in Howard's call for reform. Nonetheless, his vision for respect was strictly minimalist: 'I am not an advocate for an extravagant and profuse allowance to prisoners. I plead only for necessaries, in such a moderate quantity, as may support health and strength for labour.'[15]

By the beginning of the nineteenth century, the experience of imprisonment remained unimpeachably severe. Prison meals had seen no real improvement, and consisted chiefly of bread and thin

30/2013, National Offender Management Service 2013) and Alison Pratt and Gabrielle Garton Grimwood, *Prisoners: Incentives and Earned Privileges Scheme* (SN/HA/6942, House of Commons Library 2014).

[12] Maria Cross, 'Prisons' in Maria Cross and Barbara MacDonald (eds), *Nutrition in Institutions* (Wiley-Blackwell 2009) 277 (hereafter Cross, 'Prisons').

[13] ibid.

[14] RSE Hinde, *The British Penal System 1773–1950* (Duckworth 1951).

[15] John Howard, *The State of the Prisons in England and Wales, with Preliminary Observations, and an Account of Some Foreign Prisons* (Thoemmes Press 1777) 33. See also Robert Alan Cooper, 'Ideas and their Execution: English Prison Reform' (1976) 10(1) Eighteenth-Century Studies 73.

gruel or broths.[16] The Poor Law Amendment Act 1834 codified the principle of less eligibility, which stipulated that if imprisonment was to fulfil a deterrent function, the treatment of a prisoner must not be superior to that provided to a member of the lowest significant social class in free society.[17] There was cause for cautious optimism, however, following the introduction of prison inspections in 1835. Prison diet became a national scandal and inspectors made an explicit call for food to no longer act as an instrument of punishment.[18] Advances were made in the quantity—if not the quality—of prison food but an instrumentalist line of thought endured, in part, due to widespread public support for a retributive approach and the prevailing conservative ideology of the period. By 1840, the Regulations for Prisons in England and Wales continued to provide for a 'punishment diet' as a form of behavioural conditioning:

> 302. [*Punishment diet*]. Prisoners under punishment for offences within the prison shall have each an allowance of 1lb. of bread daily during such punishment, unless additional diet be ordered by the surgeon as necessary for health.[19]

Debates over the appropriate character of prison labour and diet continued.[20] By the mid-nineteenth century, prison food had once again been called into question, with leading physicians of the time recommending a substantial reduction in portion sizes on the grounds that the food provided was excessive and insufficiently

[16] Cross, 'Prisons' (n 12).

[17] Poor Law Amendment Act 1834. See also John Burnett, *Plenty and Want: A Social History of Food in England from 1815 to the Present Day* (Routledge 1989) and Edward W Sieh, 'Less Eligibility: The Upper Limits of Penal Policy' (1989) 3(2) Criminal Justice Policy Review 159.

[18] Edmund F Du Cane, *The Punishment and Prevention of Crime* (Macmillan 1885) 163 (hereafter Du Cane, *Punishment and Prevention of Crime*). See also Cross, 'Prisons' (n 12) 287–88; M Heather Tomlinson, 'Not an Instrument of Punishment: Prison Diet in the Mid-Nineteenth Century' (1978) 2(1) Journal of Consumer Studies and Home Economics 15 (hereafter Tomlinson, 'Not an Instrument of Punishment'); and Peter Higginbotham, *The Prison Cookbook* (The History Press 2010) ch 9, 'Changes in Prison Food 1800s–1860s' (hereafter Higginbotham, *Prison Cookbook*).

[19] Home Office, *Regulations for Prisons in England and Wales issued by the Secretary of State for the Home Department* (Shaw and Sons 1840).

[20] Leon Radzinowicz and Roger Hood, *The Emergence of Penal Policy in Victorian and Edwardian England* (Clarendon Press 1990).

penal. Women were to receive the same meals as men, but in more modest portions.[21] The food was to be of subsistence standard only for, as Zedner observes, to provide women with 'food sufficient to ensure good health would be to provide conditions of relative comfort, and the extremely poor with a positive incentive to crime'.[22] Later that century, reforms meant that good work and conduct were rewarded with gratuities and privileges but not with additional food, as such a prospect was thought to appeal to a prisoner's 'baser' instincts.[23]

In the twentieth and twenty-first centuries, a number of reforms—apparently eschewing the instrumental aims of imprisonment—were implemented. A move towards respect at prison mealtime, however, was punctuated by instances of prolonged force-feeding of political prisoners in the early twentieth century.[24] Integral to more progressive developments was the commissioning of a Departmental Committee on Diets in 1925.[25] Following the committee's investigation into prison food, the motivation to provide a nutritious diet to inmates was firmly established.[26] The following year, the commissioners made further calls for a 'more balanced and varied diet' which included 'the provision of regular vegetables', the replacement of prison 'cans' with aluminium trays and utensils, and opportunities for prisoners to dine in association in the hope that it might cultivate in them a sense of self-respect.[27] These reforms were indicative of a newly

[21] Philip Priestley, *Victorian Prison Lives* (Methuen 1985) and Valerie J Johnson, *Diet in Workhouses and Prisons 1835–1895* (Garland 1985).

[22] Lucia Zedner, *Women, Crime, and Custody in Victorian England* (OUP 1991) 115.

[23] Du Cane, *Punishment and Prevention of Crime* (n 18) 163.

[24] This practice was governed by the Prisoners (Temporary Discharge for Ill-Health) Act 1913. On political prisoners, see Alyson Brown, *English Society and the Prison: Time, Culture and Politics in the Development of the Modern Prison 1850–1920* (Boydell 2003).

[25] Prison Commission, *Report of Departmental Committee on Diets* (The Stationery Office 1925). See also Higginbotham, *Prison Cookbook* (n 18) ch 14, 'Prisons Enter the Twentieth Century' and ch 15, 'Prison Food After 1900'.

[26] Cross, 'Prisons' (n 12) and Tomlinson, 'Not an Instrument of Punishment' (n 18).

[27] Prison Commission, *Report of the Commissioners of Prisons and the Directors of Convict Prisons for the Year 1924–25* (Cmd 2597, The Stationery Office 1926) 20. See also John Pratt, *Punishment and Civilization: Penal Tolerance and Intolerance in Modern Society* (SAGE 2002) 71.

configured relationship between the state and its subjects, and a sustained attempt to afford prison mealtime 'a visibility and form' that brought it into line with a society that considered itself to be civilised.[28]

In the decades that followed, prison mealtime was transformed. Prisoners were given increased involvement in menu design, and meals were gradually made available for those with religious, ethnic, cultural, and medical requirements.[29] However, there is compelling evidence to suggest that, in prisons in England and Wales, food—if only implicitly—continues to form part of a penal strategy.[30] While the modern prison—in official discourse, at least—seeks to cultivate a certain humanitarian sensitivity, in reality, it continues to be defined by quite contradictory sentiments. Subtle institutional attempts at degradation through food persist and, for one commentator, daily meals serve as painful and periodic bodily expressions of the power that the institution exerts over the individual.[31] Even though respect appears to infuse the very purposes and rationale of prison mealtime—for example, in the *prima facie* civilised manner in which it is prepared and served—it is, in fact, accorded only instrumental value, operating as a weak side-constraint on the pursuit of managerialist outcomes.

While claims and counter-claims to respect at prison mealtime initially appear to have only contemporary relevance, they bear

[28] John Pratt, 'Norbert Elias and the Civilised Prison' (1999) 50(2) The British Journal of Sociology 271, 271.

[29] Cross, 'Prisons' (n 12).

[30] For an analogous argument in the American context, see Smoyer and Lopes, 'Prison Food' (n 1).

[31] Ugelvik, 'Hidden Food' (n 6). For a striking comparative example, see the punitive denial of conventional meals in selected American correctional facilities and their replacement with the highly controversial, much-litigated—yet currently constitutional—disciplinary loaf or Nutraloaf. Tasteless yet highly nutritious and eliminating the need for utensils, this meal is provided to inmates who refuse to adhere to prison-imposed rules of food distribution. The case of *Prude v Clarke* 675 F3d 732 (7th Cir 2012) is the most high-profile Supreme Court challenge to Nutraloaf, in which it was claimed that a punishment diet violates the Eighth Amendment in constituting 'cruel and unusual punishment'. See also *Borden v Hofmann* 974 A2d 1249 (Vt 2009) in which the court was required to determine whether placing an inmate on a Nutraloaf-and-water diet in response to misconduct constituted 'punishment' within the meaning of the Vermont Statutes (28 V.S.A. § 851).

comparison with a series of much earlier ideas and events that implicated food in the pursuit of the prison's instrumental objectives. In this way, the line of argument advanced here has a clear historical trajectory.

***

The core claim of this chapter—that respect provides a means by which to advance a critique of prison mealtime—will require some careful exposition. The categories of *preparation, consumption*, and *resistance* give shape to the limited and fairly disparate research and policy documentation on prison food and facilitate a critique of it. The discussion that follows is necessarily complicated by the fact that—beyond food safety laws, the Prison Rules, and catering regulations (developed originally by the National Offender Management Service (NOMS)) to which all public and private sector prisons must subscribe—it is not possible to make generalised claims about food in *all* prisons in England Wales, since responsibility for its preparation and management is devolved to individual prison governors.[32] And as explored in the previous chapter, the value orientations or penal styles of individual institutions also vary to a considerable degree and are shaped *inter alia* by its history, culture, and leadership.[33] That said, it is possible to identify some strong, recurring themes in relation to the preparation, consumption, and resistance of food in *most* prisons. Where necessary, exceptional practices—respectful or otherwise—are identified.

B. Preparation

1. *In the kitchen: Respect as a matter of rule-following*

Moving sequentially, this chapter begins with an exploration of the prison meal at the point of preparation. The Prison Rules provide a starting point and strategic context for the discussion. Rule 24(2) requires that the 'food provided shall be wholesome, nutritious, well prepared and served, reasonably varied and sufficient

[32] National Offender Management Service, *Freedom of Information Request, Reference 77329* (National Offender Management Service August 2012).

[33] Alison Liebling, 'Prisons in Transition' (2006) 29(5) International Journal of Law and Psychiatry 422 (hereafter Liebling, 'Prisons in Transition').

in quantity'.[34] However, the open texture of the Prison Rules in application makes inevitable an element of at least implicit discretion, and so supplementary guidance is issued to prison authorities on the proper implementation of these rules.[35]

All public and private sector prisons in England and Wales are also required to meet a range of standards contained within specifications known as Prison Service Instructions (PSIs)[36] and Prison Service Orders (PSOs).[37] The PSI on *Catering: Meals for Prisoners* sets out the minimum standards for the preparation and provision of 'safe' and 'acceptable' meals.[38] Of note are sections two and three of the PSI, which provide guidelines on 'food safety, management and security' and 'menu planning and meal provision' respectively. Section two includes requirements that all those engaged in food handling activities are competent to do so and, where prisoners are employed, that they are supervised and searched in line with local and national standards; that all food supply, transport, and storage procedures, as well as food facilities, processes, and practices comply with relevant food safety legislation; and that a food safety policy is displayed prominently in the main kitchen.[39] Section three includes requirements that prisoners, at minimum, are provided with three meals per day; that they have access to a multi-choice, pre-select menu (with a minimum of five choices) including a minimum of one substantial hot meal choice per day; that those choices reflect their 'diverse needs'; that menus rotate on a four-weekly basis; and that prisoners are consulted regularly on the quality of meals provided.[40]

To be distinguished from PSIs, which have a fixed expiry date, PSOs are long-term and mandatory. The PSO on *Women*

[34] The Prison Rules 1999, Rule 24(2).

[35] Nancy Loucks, *Prison Rules: A Working Guide* (4th edn, Prison Reform Trust 2000).

[36] Her Majesty's Prison and Probation Service, *Prison Service Instructions (PSIs)* <https://www.justice.gov.uk/offenders/psis> accessed 1 August 2019.

[37] Her Majesty's Prison and Probation Service, *Prison Service Orders (PSOs)* <http://www.justice.gov.uk/offenders/psos> accessed 1 August 2019.

[38] National Offender Management Service, *Catering: Meals for Prisoners* (PSI 44/2010, National Offender Management Service 2010) 1 (hereafter National Offender Management Service, *Catering*).

[39] ibid s 2.

[40] ibid s 3. HMP Leicester endeavours to provide a default meal option to new arrivals or those prisoners who refuse to select a meal: Independent Monitoring

Prisoners provided gender-specific guidance on prison diet and was among the most relevant documents to a study of respect, but was abolished in December 2018 and replaced with the *Women's Policy Framework*.[41] The PSO acknowledged, for example, that women require a lower carbohydrate diet than men and that this must be reflected in prison menus; that catering staff take into account the drug misuse histories of many female prisoners who are often, by implication, underweight; and that women on a detoxification programme for this reason are likely to crave sweet foods and that these must be made readily available. It also required that healthcare and catering staff liaise regularly to meet the needs of pregnant women and mothers, and women suffering from eating disorders.[42] While those responsible for drafting the PSO had shown sensitivity towards women prisoners as a group with a complex set of vulnerabilities and nutritional needs, it is striking that these guidelines have been removed entirely from the *Women's Policy Framework*.[43] It is a concerning move at odds with the findings of Lupton and de Graaf and Kilty, for example, which emphasise the importance not only of physical but also of emotional nourishment, and posit women's relationship with food as a social outlet through which they acculturate, discipline, and comfort others.[44]

While Prison Rule 24(3) provides for food to be inspected before and after cooking from 'time to time' by 'any person deemed by the Governor to be competent',[45] the PSI on catering goes

Board, *Annual Report of the Independent Monitoring Board at HMP Leicester 2015–2016* (Independent Monitoring Board 2016).

41 National Offender Management Service, *Women Prisoners* (PSO No 4800, Issue No 297, National Offender Management Service 2008) (hereafter National Offender Management Service, *Women Prisoners*) now replaced by Ministry of Justice and Her Majesty's Prison & Probation Service, *Women's Policy Framework* (Ministry of Justice and Her Majesty's Prison & Probation Service 2018) (hereafter Ministry of Justice and Her Majesty's Prison & Probation Service, *Women's Policy Framework*).

42 National Offender Management Service, *Women Prisoners* (n 41).

43 Ministry of Justice and Her Majesty's Prison & Probation Service, *Women's Policy Framework* (n 41).

44 Deborah Lupton, *Food, the Body and the Self* (SAGE 1996). See also Kaitlyn de Graaf and Jennifer M Kilty, 'You Are What You Eat: Exploring the Relationship Between Women, Food, and Incarceration' (2016) 18(1) Punishment & Society 27.

45 The Prison Rules 1999, Rule 24(3).

further. Specifically, it requires that, during inspections, prison staff demonstrate their strict adherence to its requirements.[46]

A key question to arise is whether it is possible to detect respect as it inheres in the rules and guidelines that provide a basis for the enactment of key procedural principles, such as the Prison Rules, PSIs, and PSOs. Those responsible for drafting the PSI on catering, for example, appear to have made a concerted effort to promote a form of respect towards prisoners and their basic dietary needs that is deeply procedural, by requiring staff to *show*, through strict rule adherence, that standards of meal preparation—and, by extension, relationships of respect—are being actively sustained. In this way, respect is not envisaged as a passive state. Rather, it is envisaged—if only implicitly—as a reciprocal practice that requires a degree of active participation, in a manner that is consistent with Sennett's understanding of respect as 'enacted' or 'performed' and involving a degree of 'expressive work'.[47]

Despite their attempts to embed respect as a foundational value, these specifications are likely to generate only empty, formalised, and legalistic transactions at the point of meal preparation. As in previous chapters, respect is reduced to a matter of rule-following, and respectful relationships to a series of duties and rights determined by rules.[48] That said, prison managers might consider it necessary to 'proceduralise' respect—and require its systematic 'delivery'—in order to manage the possibility that kitchen staff may not necessarily *feel* respectful of the prisoners whose meals they are responsible for preparing. As one prison officer has observed: 'A fundamental problem for staff in prisons is that it is not possible for them, anymore than anyone else, to manufacture respect for an individual who has just forfeited that respect in such a formal way.'[49]

[46] National Offender Management Service, *Catering* (n 38).

[47] Richard Sennett, *Respect: The Formation of Character in an Age of Inequality* (Penguin 2004) 59 (hereafter Sennett, *Respect*).

[48] See, eg, Nicola Lacey, 'Criminalization as Regulation: The Role of Criminal Law' in Christine Parker, Colin Scott, Nicola Lacey, and John Braithwaite (eds), *Regulating Law* (OUP 2004).

[49] Robert Hardy (convenor), *Respect in Prison.* Transcript of a conference held at Bishop Grosseteste College, Lincoln (Bishop of Lincoln (Robert Hardy) 1991). See also Michelle Butler and Deborah H Drake, 'Reconsidering Respect: Its Role in Her Majesty's Prison Service' (2007) 46(2) The Howard Journal of Criminal

While the view that prisoners can surrender their right to respect is misguided,[50] the quotation is illustrative of how hierarchical relations can be produced and legitimated within and through the words we speak. It is important to 'trace the relations' between an observation of this kind and the wider context in which it was uttered.[51] It is a comment that appears much less misguided when the context—an institution that treats respect as a weak side-constraint on the pursuit of managerialist outcomes—is taken into account.

2. In the kitchen: ethnic and cultural meals

The preparation of ethnic and cultural meals in prisons is a practice towards which a minimal degree of critical attention has been developed. While the PSI on catering is framed primarily in terms of procedural respect, in providing guidelines on special meals for religious beliefs (for example, Halal and Kosher foods) and cultural preferences (vegetarianism and veganism), it alludes—if only implicitly—to a richer form of respect.[52] The guidelines prescribe certain forms of behaviour, but they also announce certain moral values.

It is a 'fundamental requirement', for example, that prisoners are provided with meals that meet their religious beliefs and cultural preferences (HM Prison Service recognises eleven religious and cultural diets), and that all food is stored and prepared in an appropriate way.[53] Without exception, the multi-choice,

Justice 115 and Flora Fitzalan Howard and Helen Wakeling, *Analytical Summary 2019: Prisoner and Staff Perceptions of Procedural Justice in English and Welsh Prisons* (Her Majesty's Prison & Probation Service 2019).

[50] See, eg, Robin S Dillon, 'Respect' in Edward N Zalta (ed), *The Stanford Encyclopedia of Philosophy* (Stanford University 2018) <http://plato.stanford.edu/entries/respect/> accessed 1 August 2019 (hereafter Dillon, 'Respect'). On offering respect to those who may not offer it in return, see Mark Morris, 'The UK Prison Service Close Supervision Centres' in David Jones (ed), *Humane Prisons* (Radcliffe 2006) 97–98 'Respect and Openness'.

[51] Quentin Skinner, *Visions of Politics. Volume 1: Regarding Method* (CUP 2002) 87.

[52] National Offender Management Service, *Catering* (n 38).

[53] National Offender Management Service, *Catering Operating Manual: Meals for Prisoners in Custody at Annex B of PSI 44/2010 on Catering: Meals for Prisoners* (National Offender Management Service 2010) s 3.13, Religious Diets (hereafter National Offender Management Service, *Catering Operating Manual*).

pre-select menu must reflect prisoners' individual requirements.[54] The NOMS Catering Operating Manual provides examples of good practice during ethnic and cultural meal preparation. Suggested practices include the appropriate labelling of kitchen equipment; inviting faith chaplains into kitchens; providing fully for all religious festivals, for example, by ensuring that Muslim prisoners can observe Ramadan; and the involvement of prisoners from different religions and ethnicities in cooking and other kitchen work.[55] Advisory guidance on ethnic and cultural meals is also made available to all prisons, to be used by Catering Managers as a point of reference when engaged in meal preparation.[56]

The scope and content of both the PSI and the Catering Manual might be used as a broad index of the form of respect to which the prison aspires at the point of meal preparation. It is encouraging that both documents attempt—if only implicitly—to codify respect as a foundational value. Rather than treating everyone alike in a literal sense, respect provides a justification for various forms of differential treatment, special protections, and exemptions from otherwise uniform rights, duties, rules, and regulations. Even so, the composition of the PSI—in the form of rules and guidelines—is inevitably limiting and, again, capable of delivering, at best, a reductive—and strictly procedural—form of respect.

There is evidence to suggest that catering managers have even treated procedural forms of respect reductively and there has been a concomitant decline in trust among prisoners.[57] A research report published by the National Audit Office, for example, describes an emerging trend whereby catering staff meet the required standards for the preparation of religious and culturally sensitive

See also National Offender Management Service, *Faith and Pastoral Care of Prisoners* (PSI 05/2016, National Offender Management Service 2016).

[54] National Offender Management Service, *Catering* (n 38) s 3.1.

[55] National Offender Management Service, *Catering Operating Manual* (n 53) s 3.14.

[56] ibid s 3.15.

[57] Conceptually, trust is comparable to respect in that it requires a degree of action but also has a cognitive component: 'To say we trust you means we believe you have the right intentions toward us and that you are competent to do what we trust you to do': Russell Hardin, *Trust* (Polity 2006) 17.

food but encounter difficulties in convincing prisoners that this is the case. In particular, there are concerns among prisoners that standards for the storage and preparation of ethnic and cultural food are not met consistently.[58]

It seems that prisoners' lack of trust in this regard is not unfounded. The report confirms several cases in which prisoners had signed up in good faith to receive ethnic meals, which were later found to have been unethically prepared. Four out of sixteen prisons were unable to store halal meat separately from other meat (even though measures had been taken to avoid cross-contamination) and, in eleven prisons, kitchen equipment intended for those with Muslim diets was not labelled separately.[59]

The prisons concerned appear to have been only weakly constrained by procedural standards, not least because they engaged in a deeply unethical process of offering and then withdrawing respect for prisoners. But respect is not merely a matter of acting or not acting in a certain way. It is also—and perhaps more centrally—about assuming a certain attitude to the object of respect, and it is clear that, among those responsible for the preparation of ethnic meals, such attitudes were regularly absent.[60]

These practices make clear that it is possible for ethnic and religious groups to be recognised in a formal set of guidelines but for institutional indifference and abuses of power to persist, causing those concerned to feel disempowered, disenfranchised, and silenced.[61] They also make clear that while respect is by definition relational, it is not always reciprocal, whereby prisoners do not—even cannot—respect those responsible for preparing their food. Attending carefully to prisoners' requirements for ethnic meals—and not only gesturing at inclusion—necessitates a degree of mutual understanding between staff and prisoners that is fundamental to respectful relations. When prisoners are denied ethically prepared ethnic meals, they are likely to become too distracted

[58] National Audit Office, *Serving Time* (n 10).

[59] ibid.

[60] See, eg, Sune Lægaard, 'What Does "Respect for Difference" Mean?' in Peter Balint and Sophie Guérard de Latour (eds), *Liberal Multiculturalism and the Fair Terms of Integration* (Palgrave Macmillan 2013) (hereafter Lægaard, 'Respect for Difference').

[61] Phillips, *Multicultural Prison* (n 8) and, more generally, Margaret Davies, 'Exclusion and the Identity of Law' (2005) 5 Macquarie Law Journal 5.

by the conditions of their confinement to respond respectfully to prison authorities that so unethically denied them respect.[62]

Part of the reason for the institution's weak approximation of respect at prison mealtime is that the vocabulary of respect remains implicit in the Prison Rules, PSIs, and PSOs.[63] The challenge for prison officials is to find a reasonable way to elaborate on and operationalise respect and beyond basic connotations, for example, about the proper and humane treatment of individuals and their worthiness of consideration, the vocabulary of respect is challenging, open-textured, and capable of taking on diverse meanings.

3. In the kitchen: self-catering

An important issue to consider is whether and, if so, to what extent prisoners themselves should contribute to the provision of their own basic welfare and nutrition. The only real possibility to embed respect as a foundational value at the point of meal preparation would be to transfer partial or full responsibility to the prisoners themselves. This approach would approximate prison regimes, as far as possible, to everyday practices in free society. Preparing and consuming food from their respective cultures—refamiliarising themselves with its texture, colour, taste, shape, touch, and smell—would also allow prisoners to perform their ethnic identities and construct and maintain boundaries within the dominant prison culture.[64]

This was the case in one English prison, where communal self-cooking facilities were made available to inmates who held the

[62] See further Richard L Lippke, *Rethinking Imprisonment* (OUP 2007) ch 5 (hereafter Lippke, *Rethinking Imprisonment*).

[63] See Her Majesty's Prison and Probation Service, *Equality Objectives*: 'We insist on respectful and polite behaviour from staff [and] those in our care.' The vocabulary of respect promotes an ethical standard, yet its meaning is left unarticulated: <https://www.gov.uk/government/organisations/her-majestys-prison-and-probation-service/about/equality-and-diversity> accessed 1 August 2019. See also National Offender Management Service, *Equality of Treatment for Employees* (PSI 33/2010, National Offender Management Service 2011) and National Offender Management Service, *Ensuring Equality* (PSI 32/2011, National Offender Management Service 2011).

[64] See further Linda Keller Brown and Kay Mussell (eds), *Ethnic and Regional Foodways in the United States: The Performance of Group Identity* (University of Tennessee Press 1984). See, in particular, Part I, 'Food in the Performance of Ethnic Identity: Theoretical Considerations' and Part II, 'Food in the Performance

appropriate privileges. In addition to its primary function of providing facilities to prisoners with an interest in supplementing or substituting prison-provided meals, Phillips describes how the self-catering area became a significant feature of social relations. It provided prisoners with an important setting for cultural exchange and an opportunity to share food, tools, resources, ideas, and culinary techniques.[65]

Lippke observes that if we insist on punishing offenders because they have failed to act morally, then we must respect them by preserving their capacity to act morally during the course of that punishment. On this view, prison governors would be required to reconcile safety and security concerns with the fostering of what Lippke describes as an offender's 'moral personality': in this case, his capacity for self-restraint in the handling of knives and other kitchen utensils.[66] In a study by Earle and Phillips, carving knives—items which would otherwise be considered illicit—were made freely available during association periods in communal cooking areas. Far from being viewed as a threat to prison order, the open use of these utensils for their intended purpose and their return to officer-managed storage vividly exemplifies a situation whereby respectful relationships were valued, and an informal social contract was firmly in place.[67]

The House of Commons Select Committee recently drew analogy with open and closed prisons in Denmark, where—in stark contrast to the large institutional catering operations that dominate prisons in England and Wales—self-catering is almost universal, and prisoners are given a weekly budget to shop and cook for themselves. The committee recommended that NOMS examine the scope for introducing self-catering facilities to a greater number of prisoners in England and Wales.[68]

of Ethnic Identity: Field Studies'. See also Her Majesty's Inspectorate of Prisons for England and Wales, *Life in Prison: Food* (Her Majesty's Inspectorate of Prisons for England and Wales 2016) para 1.5.

[65] Phillips, *Multicultural Prison* (n 8).

[66] Lippke's observations are consistent with the intrinsic case for respect advanced in this book: Lippke, *Rethinking Imprisonment* (n 62) 111–12

[67] Earle and Phillips, 'Ethnicity, Gender and Food' (n 1).

[68] House of Commons Justice Committee, *Prisons: Planning and Policies*. Ninth Report of Session 2014–15 (HC 309, The Stationery Office 2015) para 143, 56–57 (hereafter House of Commons Justice Committee, *Prisons: Planning and Policies*).

It is unclear what has motivated an interest in a more liberal strategy at prison mealtime. Provided the committee is solely concerned with the welfare of prisoners, there is scope for respect to flourish. Self-catering would allow prisoners to interact with prison officers and with each other in ways that accommodate cultural differences. This is important since multiculturalism is—at the levels of both theory and political parlance—often formulated in terms of respect. While, at the political level, respect tends to be used as a rhetorical device, in theoretical terms, the claim is that respect provides strong support for policies that enhance multiculturalism.[69] It is notable, however, that the committee also raised the issue of cost-effectiveness.[70] Respect is unlikely to be realised at prison mealtime insofar as prisons continue to treat it as a weak side-constraint on the pursuit of instrumental outcomes.

C. Consumption

1. Time

In conditions of confinement, mealtime is routinely associated with the ritualised manner in which it is served and consumed. The rich interdisciplinary literature on food is instructive here, in which a ritual is understood as an action frequently repeated, in a form decided upon in advance.[71] The emphasis in the literature on mealtime as an 'event' is highly relevant. Among the factors that qualify mealtime as an event are our understanding of it as a 'purposeful action' (one which follows a 'script' regulating the strict sequencing and timing of dishes in order to achieve an intended effect), and a social occasion which creates meaning for the participants (a condition only likely to be fulfilled when inmates are afforded the privilege of 'dining out' in a communal space).[72]

In both the literature and policy documentation on prison food, there are frequent references to the strict scheduling and scripted

[69] See, eg, Lægaard, 'Respect for Difference' (n 60).

[70] House of Commons Justice Committee, *Prisons: Planning and Policies* (n 68).

[71] David Marshall, 'Food as Ritual, Routine or Convention' (2005) 8(1) Consumption, Markets & Culture 69 (hereafter Marshall, 'Food as Ritual, Routine or Convention').

[72] ibid 72–75. See also Godderis, 'Dining in' (n 1) and David Marshall and Rick Bell, 'Meal Construction: Exploring the Relationship Between Eating Occasion

or ritualised nature of mealtime. Although prisons are given discretion as to when meals are consumed, the PSI on catering highlights the importance of institutional momentum by requiring that all prisons serve food within forty-five minutes of its preparation.[73] However, it has been found that this standard is often not met, which means that the food is likely to lose some of its palatability and nutritional content. There are practical difficulties in meeting this requirement, such as kitchens accommodating large populations; the long distances between kitchens and prison wings; and, where prisoners have the opportunity to dine in association, queuing times of up to forty-five minutes.[74]

It is well established that confinement can seriously disrupt and distort a prisoner's sense of time.[75] This is further exacerbated by the Inspectorate's observation that, in 2016, many prison meals continued to be served unconventionally early.[76] At HMP Elmley, for example, lunch was served at 11.30am and the evening meal around 4.40pm.[77]

Despite being generally unpopular with prisoners and some catering staff due to their frugal content and nutritional value, pre-prepared breakfast packs are now distributed in most prisons. These poor quality breakfast packs—generally consisting of cereal, a piece of fruit, a bread roll, butter, jam, tea bags, and milk—can further extend the period between substantial meals, especially since they tend to be distributed the evening prior to their intended consumption. By implication, there are long intervals between meals, and many prisons do not meet the fourteen-hour

and Location' (2003) 14(1) Food Quality and Preference 53 (hereafter Marshall and Bell, 'Meal Construction').

[73] National Offender Management Service, *Catering* (n 38).

[74] National Audit Office, *Serving Time* (n 10).

[75] See, eg, Dominique Moran, *Carceral Geography: Spaces and Practices of Incarceration* (Ashgate 2015) and Dominique Moran, '"Doing time" in Carceral Space: Timespace and Carceral Geography' (2012) 94(4) Geografiska Annaler: Series B, Human Geography 305.

[76] Her Majesty's Chief Inspector of Prisons for England and Wales, *Annual Report 2015–16* (The Stationery Office 2016) (hereafter Her Majesty's Chief Inspector of Prisons for England and Wales, *Annual Report 2015–16*).

[77] Her Majesty's Chief Inspector of Prisons for England and Wales, *Report on an Announced Inspection of HMP Elmley* (Her Majesty's Inspectorate of Prisons for England and Wales 2015) (hereafter Her Majesty's Chief Inspector of Prisons for England and Wales, *HMP Elmley*) 40, 2.89.

interval standard between meals overnight. Prisoners can exercise a degree of choice as to when to consume the contents of these packs. Indeed, the ritual of mealtime is often circumvented by prisoners who consume the contents of their breakfast packs overnight, opting to wait a considerable amount of time for their next meal.[78] The pre-prepared breakfast packs were introduced in order that staff could be released from preparing, serving, and supervising breakfast in order to carry out other duties.[79] The result is that respect at prison mealtime is treated as a peripheral concern.

When served, the prison meal becomes a prism through which various messages, intentions, concerns, emotions, and values are channelled, all of which contribute both to the rich contextuality of the dining situation and our understanding of that situation as distinctively ritualistic.[80] This understanding of mealtime is consistent with Douglas on food as a 'code', where the code is found 'in the pattern of social relations being expressed'.[81] While the ritual of mealtime gives the impression of respect and civility, it serves only to detract from the prison's commitment to respect as a matter of crass instrumentality. For several commentators, the ritualised event of prison mealtime functions as a continuation of the more general attacks on identity that imprisonment entails.[82] It also becomes representative of the prisoner's restricted autonomy and an integral part of his experience of Sykes' 'pains of imprisonment'.[83]

Prisons have proved to be inflexible in terms of the scheduling of mealtime, claiming that only a 'major shift' in daily activities would allow the staffing of more suitable intervals between meals.

[78] Her Majesty's Chief Inspector of Prisons for England and Wales, *Annual Report 2015–16* (n 76) 35.

[79] National Audit Office, *Serving Time* (n 10).

[80] Mary Douglas, 'Deciphering a Meal' (1972) 101(1) Dædalus 61 (hereafter Douglas, 'Deciphering a Meal'); Mintz and du Bois, 'Anthropology of Food and Eating' (n 8); and Christina Fjellström, 'Mealtime and Meal Patterns from a Cultural Perspective' (2004) 48(4) Scandinavian Journal of Nutrition 161.

[81] Douglas, 'Deciphering a Meal' (n 80) 61.

[82] Ugelvik, 'Hidden Food' (n 6) and Jonathan Simon, 'Punishment and the Political Technologies of the Body' in Jonathan Simon and Richard Sparks (eds), *The SAGE Handbook of Punishment and Society* (SAGE 2013).

[83] Gresham M Sykes, *The Society of Captives: A Study of a Maximum Security Prison* (Princeton University Press 1958) ch 4 (hereafter Sykes, *Society of Captives*).

Instead, institutions have reached a compromise, whereby they are expected to provide additional snacks to prisoners on occasions when the fourteen-hour interval has been exceeded.[84]

That said, there are important exceptions to established mealtime rituals. The PSI on catering promotes respect as a foundational value by allowing prisoners to observe religious festivals. In order to allow prisoners to observe Ramadan, for example, it encourages sustained communication and cooperation between several departments including the Chaplaincy, Race Relations Management Team, Catering, and Security.[85]

2. Place

Place is an evolving concept that has been defined as a space to which both meaning and experience are attached. A place can be defined as much by the reiteration of practices on a daily basis—including practices of hierarchical structuring, inclusion and exclusion, boundaries, and transactions across those boundaries—as it is by the physical setting. To this extent, the notions of ritual and place are intimately connected.[86]

What is left out defines a space as much as what is included, and the setting in which the prison meal is consumed has the potential to both enable or constrain opportunities for respect. When prisoners dine in association, for example, there is scope to cultivate conditions of mutual respect. However, most institutions continue to understand respect so restrictively that it serves only to—quite literally—force prisoners apart. One of the consequences of the disturbances at Strangeways and other prisons in England and Wales in 1990 has been that the practice of prisoners eating together in communal spaces has largely disappeared.[87] This is despite longstanding recognition of the significance of spatial dynamics within

[84] National Audit Office, *Serving Time* (n 10) 40.

[85] National Offender Management Service, *Catering* (n 38).

[86] Tim Cresswell, *Place: A Short Introduction* (Blackwell 2004); David Sibley and Bettina van Hoven, 'The Contamination of Personal Space: Boundary Construction in a Prison Environment' (2009) 41(2) Area 198; and Sally Haslanger, *Good Food: Ethics and Politics of Food* (24.03, Massachusetts Institute of Technology: OpenCourseWare 2017) <http://ocw.mit.edu> accessed 1 August 2019 (hereafter Haslanger, *Ethics and Politics of Food*).

[87] Andrew Coyle, *Understanding Prisons: Key Issues in Policy and Practice* (Open University Press 2005) 109, 'Food'.

prison, which can be traced back at least as far as Bentham's notion that prisoner reform and well-being are achieved in part by a 'simple idea in architecture'.[88] Meals are delivered directly to cells or collected by prisoners from wing serveries to be consumed alone in their cells, inevitably next to a poorly screened or unscreened toilet and with inadequate seating.[89] The prison sends a strong message to those prisoners who must consume their meals in such conditions that they are as much 'where' they eat as 'what' they eat.[90] Recent inspections have confirmed that prison serveries, such as those at HMP Northumberland, are often understaffed and prisoners receive either overly generous or inadequate portion sizes.[91] These practices are replicated elsewhere: at HMP Swaleside, wing serveries often run out of food before all prisoners are served and, at HMP Elmley, inconsistent supervision of prisoners working at the serveries, with no regular prison officer in charge, leads to some abuse of power.[92]

Only limited redress is available to those prisoners left unsatisfied with this reality. The manner in which comments and complaints on food quality and delivery are logged is decided locally, but may include wing comment logs, individual comment slips, food bulletins, consultative committees, consumer questionnaires, annual surveys, and catering meetings.[93] A recent inspection of HMP Birmingham confirmed, however, that food comment books

[88] Miran Božovič (ed), Jeremy Bentham, *The Panopticon Writings* (Verso 1995) 31. See also Dominique Moran and Yvonne Jewkes, 'Linking the Carceral and the Punitive State: A Review of Research on Prison Architecture, Design, Technology and the Lived Experience of Carceral Space' (2015/2) no. 702–703 Annals de géographie 163.

[89] Her Majesty's Chief Inspector of Prisons for England and Wales, *Annual Report 2015–16* (n 76).

[90] Wilbur Zelinsky, 'You Are Where You Eat' in Barbara G Shortridge and James R Shortridge (eds), *The Taste of American Place: A Reader on Regional and Ethnic Foods* (Rowman & Littlefield 1998).

[91] Her Majesty's Chief Inspector of Prisons for England and Wales, *Report on an Unannounced Inspection of HMP Northumberland* (Her Majesty's Inspectorate of Prisons for England and Wales 2014) (hereafter Her Majesty's Chief Inspector of Prisons for England and Wales, *HMP Northumberland*).

[92] Her Majesty's Chief Inspector of Prisons for England and Wales, *Report on an Unannounced Inspection of HMP Swaleside* (Her Majesty's Inspectorate of Prisons for England and Wales 2016) and Her Majesty's Chief Inspector of Prisons for England and Wales, *HMP Elmley* (n 77).

[93] National Offender Management Service, *Freedom of Information Request, Reference 96015* (National Offender Management Service February 2015).

were not made available to all prisoners. To those prisoners given the opportunity to register their comments and suggestions, the dates of each entry showed sporadic bursts of activity, suggesting that these books could not be accessed freely on a day-to-day basis.[94]

Although dining in association is now an atypical institutional practice in male public sector prisons, there are important instances of this practice in women's prisons and those prisons managed by the private sector. It has been suggested that women prisoners—in view of their complex vulnerabilities—must have the opportunity to dine in association should they desire.[95] At HMP Grendon, prisoners also eat together in wing dining rooms in a manner that is consistent with the institution's therapeutic ethos.[96]

Following a recent inspection, Grendon's communal dining spaces were found to provide at least a superficial impression of respectability in that they were 'clean and well decorated'.[97] Yet the inspection report misses the important point that respect is not only evidenced externally. Respect—or lack thereof—can also provoke internal responses in prisoners which can be either cognitive or emotional in nature, and thus more or less rational.[98] The report provides little substantive commentary on inmates' personal responses to their treatment at Grendon. In this way, the Inspectorate's understanding of respect is almost as instrumental as that evidenced in the prisons it is charged to inspect. While it is encouraging that the Inspectorate has designated respect as one of four key conditions for a 'healthy prison', its preference for the terminology of 'respect outcomes' provides an important hint that its work is merely *constrained* and not *characterised* by respect.

One curious finding to emerge from the 2018 Annual Report is that 66 per cent of prisons inspected in 2017–18 achieved a 'good' or 'reasonably good' score for respect, despite the fact that,

[94] Her Majesty's Chief Inspector of Prisons for England and Wales, *Report on an Unannounced Inspection of HMP Birmingham* (Her Majesty's Inspectorate of Prisons for England and Wales 2014).

[95] National Offender Management Service, *Women Prisoners* (n 41).

[96] Her Majesty's Chief Inspector of Prisons for England and Wales, *Report on an Unannounced Inspection of HMP Grendon* (Her Majesty's Inspectorate of Prisons for England and Wales 2013).

[97] ibid 29.

[98] Dillon, 'Respect' (n 50).

at prison mealtime, experiences remained less than respectful.[99] There was much negativity about the quality of food—described in the report as 'unappetising' and 'meagre'—and most prisoners had no choice but to engage in individualised eating rituals within the confines of their cells.[100] Notably, the Inspectorate conceded that it 'cannot be confident' that prisons were as respectful as previous years, though a reading of earlier reports exposes sharply contrasting reports on respect year-on-year.[101] The 2011–12 report, for example, described respectful treatment as 'most often poor' for all inmates,[102] while the report published one year later claims that 'respect outcomes *remained* good or reasonably good in 73% of the prisons fully inspected'.[103] Vast disparities in 'respect scores' from one year to the next raises questions as to whether the current approach to measuring respect is problematic. Inspectors must, first, make a subjective decision as to the presence (or lack thereof) of respect and, second, quantify respect, by allocating a numerical score of 1, 2, 3, or 4 to prisons whose commitment to respect is 'poor', 'not sufficiently good', 'reasonably good', and 'good' respectively.[104] It is an approach to measuring respect that has the potential to complicate rather than facilitate the search for respect as a foundational value at prison mealtime. As explored in detail in the previous chapter, important questions are raised once again as to whether a moral value as fundamental—and elusive—as respect can be quantified at all.

Privately managed establishments are subject to the same levels of scrutiny by the Inspectorate but appear to place a higher premium on respect as a foundational value—to be pursued in and of itself—at the point of meal consumption. There are greater opportunities to 'dine out' in a communal space, though some regimes are currently more successful than others. At HMP Lowdham

[99] Her Majesty's Chief Inspector of Prisons for England and Wales, *Annual Report 2017–18* (The Stationery Office 2018) 29.

[100] ibid 30.

[101] ibid 29.

[102] Her Majesty's Chief Inspector of Prisons for England and Wales, *Annual Report 2011–12* (The Stationery Office 2012) 22.

[103] Emphasis added. Her Majesty's Chief Inspector of Prisons for England and Wales, *Annual Report 2012–13* (The Stationery Office 2013) 32.

[104] Her Majesty's Prison and Probation Service, *Annual Report and Accounts 2017–18* (n 3).

Grange, all prisoners are entitled to dine in association.[105] At HMP and YOI Bronzefield, the same privilege is made available to women.[106] At HMP Oakwood and HMP Northumberland, for logistical reasons, most prisoners eat in their cells despite the availability of communal dining spaces, but these shortcomings are being actively addressed.[107]

While these opportunities at prison mealtime do not constitute an argument in favour of privatisation, they provide an opportunity to be less romantic about public sector values and practices and the extent to which prisons are, in fact, committed to them. Liebling notes, for example, that the prisoners she interviewed tend to prefer private regimes where they are treated 'better and with more respect'.[108] It is ironic that the current era of contestability has produced a situation whereby private sector prisons appear to provide more humane regimes—especially at the point of food consumption—than their counterparts in the public sector. This is partly attributable to the fact that these prisons have more control over their own workforce and have specifically set out to outperform the public sector in areas in which it is weak.[109]

The broad consensus is that dining in association is an important cultural practice that has the potential, at least, to generate a sense of cohesion and connectedness around a meal.[110] That said, recent literature has questioned whether communal dining spaces always cultivate respect, drawing attention instead to the role of food in delineating the subordinate status of those in confinement.[111]

[105] Her Majesty's Chief Inspector of Prisons for England and Wales, *Report on an Unannounced Inspection of HMP Lowdham Grange* (Her Majesty's Inspectorate of Prisons for England and Wales 2015).

[106] Her Majesty's Chief Inspector of Prisons for England and Wales, *Report on an Unannounced Inspection of HMP and YOI Bronzefield* (Her Majesty's Inspectorate of Prisons for England and Wales 2015).

[107] Her Majesty's Chief Inspector of Prisons for England and Wales, *Report on an Announced Inspection of HMP Oakwood* (Her Majesty's Inspectorate of Prisons for England and Wales 2014) and Her Majesty's Chief Inspector of Prisons for England and Wales, *HMP Northumberland* (n 91).

[108] Liebling, 'Prisons in Transition' (n 33) 429.

[109] ibid. There are exceptional cases: on 20 August 2018, the prison was brought back under state control: Jim Pickard, 'G4S Stripped of Control over "Failed" Birmingham Jail' *Financial Times* (20 August 2018).

[110] Douglas, 'Deciphering a Meal' (n 80) and Haslanger, *Ethics and Politics of Food Choices* (n 86).

[111] Marshall and Bell, 'Meal Construction' (n 72).

Thomas describes how food, served and consumed in a highly regulated prison environment, comes to embody micro-relations of power in which the subordinate group resists the power of the dominant group.[112] In Godderis' study, the act of selecting a seat routinely occupied by another prisoner—a seemingly parochial concern yet considered to be a bold move, more common among the uninitiated—was 'a sign of disrespect'.[113] In Rowe's study of HMP Askham Grange, 'authoritarian' staff had considerable discretion both formally and informally. Rules were enforced selectively and staff placed restrictions on the styles of shoe to be worn by the women in the dining room. For Rowe, this constituted a 'functionally unnecessary' display of authority by staff, deployed where it was least needed, in order to regulate a group of already compliant women.[114] Although respect has the potential to obscure and alleviate status asymmetries between staff and prisoners, in this study, the polar opposite appears to have been the case. And while the dining room typically contributes a sense of sociality to the prison, it served instead as a context for claims and counter-claims to power, authority, status, and respect. In this context, Sennett's claim that settings that rely on a ritual performance of some kind invariably build mutual respect between actors of differing social status may not hold true.[115] At prison mealtime, then, the place and conditions of consumption are as important as the food that is consumed and the form as valuable as any functional considerations.[116]

D. Resistance

The various forms of public and private resistance that are prompted by prison food are exacerbated in an institution that is preoccupied with instrumental outcomes and makes only empty appeals to respect. Again, respect offers a means by which to

[112] Jim Thomas, 'Passing Time: The Ironies of Food in Prison Culture' in Lawrence C Rubin (ed), *Food for Thought: Essays on Eating and Culture* (McFarland 2008).

[113] Godderis, 'Dining in' (n 1) 263–64.

[114] Abigail Rowe, '"Tactics", Agency and Power in Women's Prisons' (2016) 56(2) The British Journal of Criminology 332, 344.

[115] Sennett, *Respect* (n 47).

[116] Marshall, 'Food as Ritual, Routine or Convention' (n 71).

advance a critique of the ways in which the institution manages those prisoners who resist or refuse food.

The prison is to be critiqued not only for its external performances of respect: in the quality of food that is prepared, the ritualised manner in which it is served, and the setting in which it is consumed. Every external act of respect—however adequate or inadequate—is likely to produce both cognitive and affective responses in the prisoner. Respect can prompt beliefs, perceptions, and judgements but it can also engender emotions, feelings, and ways of experiencing.[117] For those prisoners who engage in strategies of public resistance, affective responses of this kind are routinely at play.[118] But a lack of respect at prison mealtime can also prompt measured, self-reflective evaluations in prisoners about where they stand, and where they should stand, based on the value that has been ascribed to them by the institution. A measured response of this kind is evident in those prisoners who opt instead for forms of private resistance, including hidden practices of food preparation or, as is more common in England and Wales, the illicit brewing of alcohol.

Of the occasional contributions to the prison food literature, several are concerned with the influence of mealtime on power dynamics in prison, including the various forms of resistance that food engenders. Godderis suggests that food-based resistance in prison provides an insight into how prisoners use consumptive spaces to negotiate and contest the power inequalities inherent in the prison environment.[119] Ugelvik goes further in drawing analogy from Foucault, conceptualising power as a fluctuating relationship of forces, rather than a property of powerful groups or individuals. From this perspective, he suggests that food functions as a mode of prisoner 'identity work' through practices of hidden resistance.[120] On the reasoning of these scholars, food, *prima facie* an instrument and symbol of domination used by prison authorities to oppress, also has the paradoxical potential to become a tool of public and private resistance.[121] Relevant too is a body of

[117] Dillon, 'Respect' (n 50).

[118] The idea that food is related to a range of affective states is well established. See, eg, Edmund T Rolls, *Emotion and Decision-making Explained* (OUP 2013) ch 5, 'Food Reward Value, Pleasure, Hunger, and Appetite'.

[119] Godderis, 'Dining in' (n 1).

[120] Ugelvik, 'Hidden Food' (n 6) 47.

[121] ibid and Godderis, 'Dining in' (n 1).

literature that understands and explains prisoners' strategies of resistance more generally, with leading contributions from Sykes, Sparks et al, Bosworth, and Crewe.[122]

1. Public resistance

When the possibilities of dissent through voice are perceived to be limited and staff-prisoner interactions are overly reliant on forms of adversarial dialogue, some prisoners become disenfranchised and either incapable or unwilling to engage with the regime. The conditions of their confinement come to represent an embodied social milieu, shaping feeling and action in subtle ways. Some prisoners resort to their body as one of the few means by which to assert control.

The hunger strike is a practice of considerable expressive force and is likely to be symptomatic of an institution that treats respect as a weak side-constraint on the pursuit of instrumental outcomes. It offers prisoners a means by which to 'weaponise' their bodies in order to, for example, challenge the conditions of their confinement, gain leverage against prison authorities, or secure the respect of others.[123] As a result, a concern with prisoners' bodily autonomy or integrity and the degree to which it should be respected in the context of a hunger strike has motivated much of the criminal justice, legal, and medico-legal scholarship in this area.[124]

Chapter ten of the PSI on the *Management of Prisoners at Risk of Harm to Self, to Others and from Others* acknowledges the difficulties of understanding *why* prisoners might refuse to eat and drink and recommends a multidisciplinary approach in dealing with these cases. Respect is implicit in the PSI's assertion that a

[122] Sykes, *Society of Captives* (n 83); Richard Sparks, Anthony E Bottoms, and Will Hay, *Prisons and the Problem of Order* (Clarendon Press 1996); Mary Bosworth, *Engendering Resistance: Agency and Power in Women's Prisons* (Ashgate 1999); and Ben Crewe, *The Prisoner Society: Power, Adaptation, and Social Life in an English Prison* (OUP 2009) (hereafter Crewe, *Prisoner Society*).

[123] See, eg, Helena Flam and Debra King (eds), *Emotions and Social Movements* (Routledge 2005).

[124] Enggist et al, *Prisons and Health* (n 2) ch 3, 13–15, *Prison-Specific Ethical and Clinical Problems*, Prisoners who stop eating or go on hunger strikes. See also Steven C Bennett, 'The Privacy and Procedural Due Process Rights of Hunger Striking Prisoners' (1983) 58(5) New York University Law Review 1157.

prisoner's decision to refuse food, while in law constituting a form of self-harm, must be deemed valid, provided that the prisoner has the mental capacity to form such a decision.[125]

As before, it is possible to detect subtle shifts between different kinds of respect in the form and content of these guidelines. While the form—the information on food refusal, presented as a set of mandatory guidelines—appears to 'proceduralise' respect between professional and prisoner, the content of these rules—in showing consideration for the prisoner's identity, his individual attributes, and the distinctive nature of his case—appeals to respect as a foundational value.

As part of a multidisciplinary approach, the PSI encourages compliance with guidelines for the clinical management of individuals refusing food in prisons, all of which are, at least, procedurally respectful. The guidance provides health professionals with information on the aetiology and physical effects of food refusal, the most effective practical and clinical management of individuals who refuse to eat and drink, and legal considerations with reference to the Mental Capacity Act 2005.[126] Meanwhile, a PSI on the safeguarding of adults in prison explicitly prohibits exploitative practices including the withholding of food or drink and the force-feeding of prisoners. Such practices are defined in the PSI as acts of physical abuse that are explicitly at odds with a prisoner's human rights, bodily integrity, and well-being, and constitute the very antithesis of respect.[127]

2. Private resistance

Several studies explore the understated forms of food-related resistance that are also at work in the prison environment. Though these studies are not confined to England and Wales, they explore the various subtle practices of informally adapting to and resisting the institution. Prisoners aim to establish areas beyond the

[125] National Offender Management Service, *Management of Prisoners at Risk of Harm to Self, to Others or from Others (Safer Custody)* (PSI 64/2011 (revised 2013), National Offender Management Service 2013).

[126] Department of Health in collaboration with Mike Stroud, *Guidelines for the Clinical Management of People Refusing Food in Immigration Removal Centres and Prisons* (Department of Health 2009).

[127] National Offender Management Service, *Adult Safeguarding in Prison* (PSI 16/2015, National Offender Management Service 2015).

official system of control where they can—albeit temporarily—counter the threats to self and reinstate themselves as autonomous agents.[128] These practices disrupt the traditional dichotomy of the compliant and non-compliant prisoner that tends to occupy both the criminal justice literature and public imagination. Rather, they exemplify a third alternative, of the kind envisaged by Crewe, occupying a point on the spectrum between passive compliance and open rebellion.[129]

Ugelvik's work, for example, describes a subtle form of meal-time resistance that routinely takes place in one Norwegian prison, where respectful relationships are sustained with relative ease. Reporting the inmates' 'blatant aversion' to official prison food, Ugelvik examines their tendency to circumvent official rules through their involvement in an alternative 'hidden' food culture: covert practices of illegal or semi-legal meal preparation within prison cells.[130]

There is, potentially, a very subtle explanation for prisoners' involvement in these practices that moves beyond questions of individual taste or preference. For Ugelvik, these practices of hidden resistance provide a context in which prisoners can engage in 'identity work'.[131] By employing these strategies, prisoners can assert their autonomy by maintaining emotional connections with their families and experiencing a sense of continuity with the communities from which they originate.

Ugelvik describes three novel strategies of alternative meal preparation in which Norwegian prisoners routinely engage. Making use of the limited resources available to them, the prisoners demonstrate considerable ingenuity while engaging in these 'performances' of identity.[132] Their strategies vary in levels of conformity with official prison rules. The first strategy is relatively modest. It is concerned with modifying official prison food into a readily edible meal by enhancing its taste or altering it in such a way that is reminiscent of cuisine with which prisoners are more familiar. The second strategy involves the use of heat: this constitutes a

[128] See, eg, Erving Goffman, *Asylums: Essays on the Social Situation of Mental Patients and Other Inmates* (Doubleday & Co 1961).

[129] See, eg, Crewe, *Prisoner Society* (n 122).

[130] Ugelvik, 'Hidden Food' (n 6).

[131] ibid 55–56.

[132] Phillips, *Multicultural Prison* (n 8).

practice that is officially prohibited but routinely tolerated by staff. One novel approach, for example, is the preparation of pre-grilled chicken with the heat generated from a light bulb. The third strategy of covert food preparation is high-risk and explicitly forbidden. It involves the use of small, illegally made heaters or steamers in order to make simple dishes such as boiled rice, pasta, and omelettes. This advanced level of 'hidden' cooking can accomplish meals for which prisoners would otherwise require a kitchen.[133]

These practices might be situated in relation to Bosworth and Carrabine's conception of resistance in the prison regime, which they extend to everyday or routine actions and small-scale negotiations of power.[134] These inmates engage in an intelligent form of 'everyday' resistance, while remaining well placed to maintain a relationship of mutual respect with the prison authorities. This might be partly attributable to the fact that, unlike the hunger strike, these forms of resistance—covert by their very nature, and not publicly defiant—rarely generate negative and exacting responses from the prison authorities and thus rarely force them into taking immediate official action, implying that respectful relations are intrinsically valued.[135] It also indicates the presence of a form of cooperative interaction or mutuality of the kind Sennett describes.[136]

In England and Wales, food is less fully implicated in illicit trading and coercive transactions—perhaps due to the widespread availability of convenience food in the prison shop—but a recent inspection of HMP Northumberland confirmed that the practice of illicitly brewing alcohol or 'hooch' in cells continues.[137]

[133] Ugelvik, 'Hidden Food' (n 6).

[134] Mary Bosworth and Eamonn Carrabine, 'Reassessing Resistance: Race, Gender and Sexuality in Prison' (2001) 3(4) Punishment & Society 501.

[135] Ugelvik, 'Hidden Food' (n 6).

[136] Sennett, *Respect* (n 47).

[137] Her Majesty's Chief Inspector of Prisons for England and Wales, *HMP Northumberland* (n 91). By contrast, new research suggests that ramen noodles are replacing cigarettes as the most valuable currency in one American prison, a trend that is attributed to the rise of 'punitive frugality' at prison mealtime: Michael Gibson-Light, 'Ramen Politics: Informal Money and Logics of Resistance in the Contemporary American Prison' (2018) 41(2) Qualitative Sociology 199. On punitive frugality, see further Mona Lynch, *Sunbelt Justice: Arizona and the Transformation of American Punishment* (Stanford University Press 2009).

In England and Wales, these practices are much more likely to attract official action.[138]

In stark contrast to Norwegian practices, where prisoners and staff are 'seen, heard and respected as human beings',[139] there is only limited evidence of the prison's capacity to sustain respectful interactions at the point of meal resistance in England and Wales. When respect is in evidence, it is strictly procedural in nature. This appears to be due, in part, to the fact that the authorities in England and Wales allude intentionally—but not seriously—to the role and value of respect. Rather, the institution employs it as a slogan, appealing to the intuitive idea and, occasionally, the language of respect when it is expedient to do so. This reductive approach to respect is reproduced and shifted within and through the constitutive practices of food preparation, consumption, and resistance.

3. *Fiscal austerity at prison mealtime*

While there is clear analytic value in exploring the constitutive elements of prison mealtime in terms of respect, some distance from—and holistic assessment of—the practice is equally important. The sustained period of fiscal austerity under which the prison is currently operating provides a point of entry into a broader evaluation of the practice. HM Prison and Probation Service, on behalf of the Ministry of Justice, has overall responsibility for the allocation of food budgets to all adult public sector prisons in England and Wales. Prisons are exercising considerable fiscal restraint, having been allocated approximately £2.00 for a prisoner's daily meals in 2017–18.[140]

[138] See, eg, Her Majesty's Inspectorate of Prisons for England and Wales, *Changing Patterns of Substance Misuse in Adult Prisons and Service Responses* (Her Majesty's Inspectorate of Prisons for England and Wales 2015).

[139] Berit Johnsen, Per Kristian Granheim, and Janne Helgesen, 'Exceptional Prison Conditions and the Quality of Prison Life: Prison Size and Prison Culture in Norwegian Closed Prisons' (2011) 8(6) European Journal of Criminology 515, 516, commenting on Norwegian Ministry of Justice and the Police, *Punishment That Works – Less Crime – A Safer Society*. Report to the Storting on the Norwegian Correctional Services (Norwegian Ministry of Justice and the Police 2008). cf Liebling on 'punitive prisons which treat prisoners, and possibly prison staff, unfairly and with little or no respect': Liebling, 'Prisons in Transition' (n 33) 429.

[140] Prisons contracted to the private sector manage their own food budgets. On prison food expenditure, see National Offender Management Service, *Freedom of*

Liebling has described an intensification of 'economic rationality' as a governing value of the prison.[141] It is a governing value whose prominence is due, in part, to fiscal austerity, which has been the structuring context of imprisonment since the financial crisis of 2008. In this climate, there is a forceful insistence on the frugality and financial accountability of the prison. Imprisonment must be cost-effective, justifiable to a parsimonious public and, where appropriate, emulate commercial practices.[142]

It is routinely assumed that, when the logic of the market acts as the ideological basis for designing prison policy and practice, there is an erosion of prisoners' rights and liberties. The former Chief Executive of NOMS, in his Perrie Lecture on *Reducing Costs and Maintaining Values in Prison*, reaffirmed that dominant line of reasoning. Budget cuts prompted concerns about the reduced capacity of HM Prison Service to tackle internal deficiencies which, he anticipated, would adversely affect 'the experience of imprisonment for individuals, undermining our values and reversing the progress we have made'.[143]

Certainly, conditions of austerity might preclude penal reform and undermine foundational values. But in requiring prisons to reorient their priorities, austerity might also create opportunities to cultivate respect at prison mealtime. One such opportunity, now widely implemented—and endorsed by the National Audit Office for full implementation in open prisons and other low-risk settings—is the authorisation of inmates to work under supervision in prison kitchens over their civilian or prison officer counterparts, whereby significant savings are incurred.[144] Another proposal is to build dining areas adjacent to prison kitchens. Depending on the architecture of the prison, this strategy might involve major capital outlay but would generate a number of offset savings. Aside from the potential benefits of prisoners dining in association, delivery times would also

Information Request, Reference 92064 (National Offender Management Service July 2014).

[141] Alison Liebling, 'Perrie Lecture: The Cost to Prison Legitimacy of Cuts' (2011) 198 Prison Service Journal 3, 3.

[142] Crewe, *Prisoner Society* (n 122).

[143] Michael Spurr, 'Perrie Lecture: Reducing Costs and Maintaining Values' (2011) 198 Prison Service Journal 12, 14.

[144] National Audit Office, *Serving Time* (n 10) 18, para 2.28.

be reduced, thus retaining the nutritional quality of food that is consumed there.[145]

Both proposals bring into sharp focus a sense of why conceptual clarity matters in the evaluation of penal practice. The issue is not that instrumental and non-instrumental concerns are simultaneously at play. The institution's instrumental concerns must simply be held in their proper place. The optimistic view is that respect offers a straightforward means by which to ameliorate the negative effects of austerity policies which would otherwise serve to 'hollow out' everyday social relations. But there is the attendant risk that instances of respect are simply unintended upshots of those proposals. In the case of prisoners' kitchen work, we could reasonably imagine that, from the point of view of the institution, the most important aspect of their presence would not be *who* they are—as individuals who, by virtue of their humanity, are entitled to respect—but, rather, *what* they represent in the form of financial savings.[146] In this way, fiscal pressures might at once facilitate and undermine opportunities for respect at prison mealtime.

[145] John SA Edwards, Heather J Hartwell, and Joachim Schafheitle, 'Prison Foodservice in England' (2009) 20(4) Journal of Foodservice 157.

[146] See Arendt on the 'what' and the 'who': Hannah Arendt, *The Human Condition* (University of Chicago Press 1958).

6

Realising Respect

On 9 September 2010, Ann Juliette Roberts, a Youth Support Worker of African-Caribbean heritage with no previous convictions, travelled on the no. 149 bus in Tottenham, London with insufficient funds on her Oyster card to pay her fare. Police Constable Jacqui Reid attended. Mrs Roberts denied having any form of identification with her and, according to PC Reid, appeared nervous. PC Reid considered that Mrs Roberts was holding her bag in a suspicious manner and might have an offensive weapon inside it. She explained to Mrs Roberts that she would search her bag under section 60 of the Criminal Justice and Public Order Act 1994. Mrs Roberts asked to be searched in a police station. She did not want to be searched on the street because she was concerned that it might affect her reputation, since some of the young people with whom she worked might see it. PC Reid said that this was unnecessary and 'she would *do it there and then*.' No weapons were found.[1]

On 11 July 2018, HM Inspectorate of Prisons for England and Wales published its Annual Report, in which it documented two unannounced inspections that caused 'deep concern.'[2] HMP Wormwood Scrubs suffered from 'appalling' living

[1] Emphasis added. *R (Roberts) v Comr of Police of the Metropolis* [2015] UKSC 79, para 11. See also Home Office, *Code of Practice for the Exercise by Police Officers of Statutory Powers of Stop and Search and Police Officers and Police Staff of Requirements to Record Public Encounters: Police and Criminal Evidence Act 1984 Code A* (The Stationery Office 2009) 3.1 'Every reasonable effort must be made to minimise the embarrassment that a person being searched may experience.' (The 2009 Code was in force at the time of the encounter, and the most recent (2014) version retains the same provision.)

[2] Her Majesty's Chief Inspector of Prisons for England and Wales, *Annual Report 2017–18* (The Stationery Office 2018) 13 (hereafter Her Majesty's Chief Inspector of Prisons for England and Wales, *Annual Report 2017–18*).

Respect and Criminal Justice. Gabrielle Watson, Oxford University Press (2020). © Gabrielle Watson.
DOI: 10.1093/oso/9780198833345.001.0001

> conditions, violence, an almost complete lack of rehabilitative or resettlement activity, and seemingly intractable problems over repeated inspections. At 'squalid' and 'fundamentally unsafe' HMP Liverpool, inspectors found '*some of the worst conditions [they] had ever seen*.'[3] An impoverished regime, many cells lacked even the basic requirements for health and hygiene and the leadership and management focus on respect was '*inadequate at every level*.'[4] HM Chief Inspector of Prisons, Peter Clarke, insisted that such conditions had no place in the prison system of an advanced nation in the 21st century. He acknowledged the 'disappointing failure' of these prisons to act on previous recommendations, which were intended to ensure that prisoners were 'treated respectfully.'[5]

In criminal justice theory, policy, and practice, the issues of *respect in policing* and *respect in imprisonment* are rarely aligned—let alone discussed in relation to each other—despite their structural similarity and overlap.[6] On the basis of a joint construal of policing and imprisonment, it has been possible to critique the ways in

[3] ibid 13. Emphasis added.

[4] Emphasis added. Her Majesty's Chief Inspector of Prisons for England and Wales, *Report on an Unannounced Inspection of HMP Liverpool* (Her Majesty's Inspectorate of Prisons for England and Wales 2017) 15.

[5] Her Majesty's Chief Inspector of Prisons for England and Wales, *Annual Report 2017–18* (n 2) 7.

[6] There is a correspondingly isolationist approach to respect in criminal justice research. This is notable since many professional actors will have been exposed to—and potentially informed by—this research. With the exception of a general reflection on the role and value of respect in criminal justice published by Millie in 2016, studies of respect have focused on one aspect of the criminal process: policing, prisons, or anti-social behaviour. In the UK, see Susie Hulley, Alison Liebling, and Ben Crewe, 'Respect in Prisons: Prisoners' Experiences of Respect in Public and Private Sector Prisons' (2012) 12(1) Criminology & Criminal Justice 3; Michelle Butler and Deborah H Drake, 'Reconsidering Respect: Its Role in Her Majesty's Prison Service' (2007) 46(2) The Howard Journal of Criminal Justice 115 (hereafter Butler and Drake, 'Reconsidering Respect'); Michelle Butler, 'What are you Looking at? Prisoner Confrontations and the Search for Respect' (2008) 48(6) The British Journal of Criminology 856; and Andrew Millie (ed), *Securing Respect: Behavioural Expectations and Anti-Social Behaviour in the UK* (Policy Press 2009) (hereafter Millie (ed), *Securing Respect*). In the US, see Robert C Davis, Pedro Mateu-Gelabert, and Joel Miller, 'Can Effective Policing Also Be Respectful? Two Examples in the South Bronx' (2005) 8(2) Police Quarterly 229. For Millie's general reflection

which respect has been treated reductively in both contexts and, at best, as a weak side-constraint on the pursuit of instrumental outcomes. As ever, the challenge has been to remain committed to a bold, wide-ranging narrative on respect in criminal justice, while maintaining a degree of fidelity to the intellectual and institutional contexts within which the value is interpreted and realised.

A distinction is routinely drawn between, on the one hand, an approach to criminal justice that distances itself from practice and—in being pitched at a high level of abstraction—represents a mode of 'utopian critique' and, on the other hand, an approach to criminal justice that is fully immersed in the applied domain and constitutes itself as a tool of reconstruction and reform.[7] This pattern of working is well entrenched in criminal justice, and we would do well to challenge it. Accordingly, this chapter seeks to reconcile both forms of enquiry, and is organised as follows.

The first section draws together various strands of the critique presented in preceding chapters, identifies some recurring themes, and considers the implications of a reductive approach to respect for the liberal credentials of criminal justice.[8] While respect is a value whose importance in criminal justice many would endorse in principle, it would be overly optimistic to expect a stable consensus

on respect and criminal justice, see Andrew Millie, *Philosophical Criminology* (Policy Press 2016) ch 7, 'Respect'.

[7] On utopian critique, see David Garland and Richard Sparks, 'Criminology, Social Theory and the Challenge of our Times' in David Garland and Richard Sparks (eds), *Criminology and Social Theory* (Clarendon Press 2000) 13–14.

[8] On liberalism and criminal justice, see, eg, Ian Loader, 'Fall of the "Platonic Guardians": Liberalism, Criminology and Political Responses to Crime in England and Wales' (2006) 46(4) The British Journal of Criminology 561; Stanley Cohen, *Against Criminology* (Transaction Publishers 1988) 14; Jonathan Jacobs, 'Criminal Justice and the Liberal Polity' (2011) 30(2) Criminal Justice Ethics 173 (hereafter Jacobs, 'Criminal Justice and the Liberal Polity'); Ben Crewe and Alison Liebling, 'Are Liberal-Humanitarian Penal Values and Practices Exceptional?' in Thomas Ugelvik and Jane Dullum (eds), *Penal Exceptionalism? Nordic Prison Policy and Practice* (Routledge 2011); and AP Simester, Antje du Bois-Pedain, and Ulfrid Neumann (eds), *Liberal Criminal Theory: Essays for Andreas von Hirsch* (Hart 2014). See, in particular, Part 4: Criminal Justice in a Liberal State. On criminal 'justice', see Nicola Lacey, 'Criminal Justice' in Robert E Goodin, Philip Pettit, and Thomas W Pogge (eds), *A Companion to Contemporary Political Philosophy* (2nd edn, Wiley-Blackwell 2012). See, in particular, 513–14 'Criminal "Justice?"'

among scholars and practitioners on the issue of how best to cultivate respect in practice. The issue is complicated yet further since current practices would prove difficult to correct, sustained as they are by superficial understandings, convenient fictions, and a preoccupation with outcomes. These caveats aside, the second section proposes and evaluates three strategies for cultivating respect in policing and imprisonment in England and Wales. They are proposed on the assumption, of course, that policing and criminal justice practices are amenable to intentional design and redesign.[9]

When an institution fails to accomplish its stated purpose—in this case, respect—we might charge that failure to one of two causes, namely, the flawed design of the institution for that purpose or the inability of the individuals within that institution to fulfil that purpose.[10] The strategies proposed in this chapter embrace both possibilities. Two of the strategies would involve changes at the *institutional* level and are prospectively—if not immediately—realisable. The other would involve changes at the *individual* level and would require a more patient approach to cultivating respect, built up over time through dialogue, experience, habituation, and strong relationships.

At the institutional level, then, there is scope for a revised approach to respect in official discourse, especially where definitional clarity is concerned. There is scope too to promote respect strictly as an ethical standard and not—as has been the case in some contexts—as a rule.[11] At the individual level,

[9] Robert E Goodin, 'Institutions and their Design' in Robert E Goodin (ed), *The Theory of Institutional Design* (CUP 1996) (hereafter Goodin (ed), *Institutional Design*). In prioritising questions of institutional design, see Nicola Lacey and Hanna Pickard, 'To Blame or to Forgive? Reconciling Punishment and Forgiveness in Criminal Justice' (2015) 35(4) Oxford Journal of Legal Studies 665. See also Margalit's exacting account of why and how social institutions might aspire to 'decent' practices that are free of humiliation: Avishai Margalit, *The Decent Society* (Harvard University Press 1996) (hereafter Margalit, *Decent Society*).

[10] Russell Hardin, 'Institutional Morality' in Goodin (ed), *Institutional Design*, ibid.

[11] See ch 5 on respect as a matter of rule-following. See, in particular, Prison Rules 1999; National Offender Management Service, *Catering: Meals for Prisoners* (PSI 44/2010, National Offender Management Service 2010) (hereafter National Offender Management Service, *Catering: Meals for Prisoners*); National Offender Management Service, *Faith and Pastoral Care of Prisoners* (PSI 05/2016, National Offender Management Service 2016); National Offender Management Service, *Catering Operating Manual: Meals for Prisoners in Custody at Annex B of PSI 44/2010 on Catering: Meals for Prisoners* (National Offender Management

respect might be clarified from the ground-up through dialogue and consensus between state actors and citizens.[12] With a sense of modest realism, the chapter anticipates the challenges—as well as the advances that could be made—in implementing each proposal and inscribing respectful relations between state and subject.

A. The Elusive Promise

This book has offered the first sustained treatment of respect in policing and imprisonment, on the assumption that the value exerts a strong but insufficiently elaborated influence on both institutions. It has been driven by a conviction and a problem. The conviction is that reflecting on the ethical foundations and assumptions of policing and imprisonment in England and Wales is a worthwhile intellectual and practical endeavour.[13] The problem is that respect—an ethical guideline of both institutions and defined by some scholars as a 'fundamental moral right'—has been treated reductively in practice as a weak side-constraint on the pursuit of instrumental outcomes.[14]

It swiftly emerged that respect has a striking capacity to sharpen our critique of a diverse range of policies and practices—general

Service 2010); and National Offender Management Service, *Ensuring Equality* (PSI 31/2011, National Offender Management Service 2011).

[12] See the papers presented at The Jubilee Centre for Character and Virtues at the University of Birmingham, *Cultivating Virtues: Interdisciplinary Approaches*. 4th Annual Conference held at Oriel College, Oxford (2016) <http://www.jubileecentre.ac.uk/1643/conferences/cultivating-virtues> accessed 1 August 2019. See also The Jubilee Centre for Character and Virtues at the University of Birmingham, *Character and Public Policy: Educating for an Ethical Life*. 1st Annual Conference held at the University of Birmingham (2012) <http://www.jubileecentre.ac.uk/484/conferences/character-and-public-policy> accessed 1 August 2019.

[13] See further Jonathan Jacobs and Jonathan Jackson, 'Editors' Preface' in Jonathan Jacobs and Jonathan Jackson (eds), *The Routledge Handbook of Criminal Justice Ethics* (Routledge 2016) (hereafter Jacobs and Jackson (eds), *Criminal Justice Ethics*). On the practical relevance of theorising about the nature and status of moral values, see Jacobs, 'Criminal Justice and the Liberal Polity' (n 8).

[14] On respect as a fundamental moral right, see, eg, Dillon, 'Respect' (n 16) s 2 and Thomas E Hill Jr, *Respect, Pluralism, and Justice: Kantian Perspectives* (OUP 2000) (hereafter Hill, *Respect, Pluralism, and Justice*).

and specific—in this book, with reference to procedural justice (chapter 2), stop and search (chapter 3), penal policies and institutional sociologies (chapter 4), and prison mealtime (chapter 5). It has been possible to expose—in the spirit of immanent critique—a series of discrepancies between respect as it is endorsed at the level of official discourse and respect as it is realised in practice.[15] These discrepancies have yet to be acknowledged by either institution, let alone justified.

1. Competing forms of respect

A recurring theme of this book has been the complex relationship between competing forms of respect. The police and HM Prison Service endorse only a general—and thus indeterminate—category of respect. On this basis, it was hypothesised that respectful relations in practice would be similarly indeterminate and that there would be no attempt to understand—let alone realise—respect in its full complexity. Moreover, it was hypothesised that there would be a tendency to drift between two potentially competing forms of respect, namely, a *generalised* form of Kantian respect—offered on the grounds of personhood alone—and an *individualised* form of respect that values diversity and difference.[16]

A sceptical reader might have remained unconvinced by this hypothesis in light of the sociological truism that deficiencies in official discourse do not necessarily imply effects on the ground.[17] Of course, there is a natural impulse to look beyond a poorly expressed idea in official discourse to what we take to be the more fundamental causes of the respect deficit in practice, such

[15] For an appraisal and defence of immanent critique, see Dan Sabia, 'Defending Immanent Critique' (2010) 38(5) Political Theory 684.

[16] For an overview of the distinction, see Robin S Dillon, 'Respect' in Edward N Zalta (ed), *The Stanford Encyclopedia of Philosophy* (Stanford University 2018) <http://plato.stanford.edu/entries/respect/> accessed 1 August 2019 (hereafter Dillon, 'Respect'). On Kantian respect, see Mary J Gregor and Jens Timmermann (eds), Immanuel Kant, *Groundwork of the Metaphysics of Morals* (CUP 2012) published originally as Immanuel Kant, *Grundlegung zur Metaphysik der Sitten* (Johann Friedrich Hartknoch 1785) and Mary J Gregor (ed), Immanuel Kant, *The Metaphysics of Morals* (CUP 2017) published originally as Immanuel Kant, *Die Metaphysik der Sitten* (Friedrich Nicolovius 1798–1803).

[17] See, eg, Michael Hallsworth with Simon Parker and Jill Rutter, *Policy Making in the Real World: Evidence and Analysis* (Institute for Government 2011) ch 4, 'The Gap between Theory and Practice'.

as economic constraints, political constraints, or group values and affinities. However, a good deal of evidence has accumulated to suggest that a vague institutional commitment to respect is of practical—rather than merely conceptual—significance. In some cases, for example, the utterance of the word in official discourse appeared to be the leading reason for the 'performance' of the respectful act.[18]

In practice, respect comes in a plurality of forms. It is extended arbitrarily and we must often rely on contextual clues as to whether it is in evidence at all. It is unclear, for example, as to why there is a strong commitment to *respect of difference* at prison mealtime but a much weaker commitment to *respect of difference* in the everyday policing of citizens.[19] It is similarly unclear as to why there are so many attempts to 'perform'—even feign—a form of Kantian respect, from experimentation with procedural justice scripts to the attempts of prison managers to 'enforce' respect by demanding civility and good manners.[20] In these contexts, respect

[18] See further JO Urmson and Marina Sbisà (eds), John L Austin, *How to Do Things with Words* (2nd edn, Harvard University Press 1975) (hereafter Austin, *How to Do Things with Words*) and Sara Ahmed, *On Being Included: Racism and Diversity in Institutional Life* (Duke University Press 2012) (hereafter Ahmed, *On Being Included*). On discourse and communication as constitutive of organisations, see Timothy R Kuhn and Linda L Putnam, 'Discourse and Communication' in Paul S Adler, Paul du Gay, Glenn Morgan, and Michael Reed (eds), *The Oxford Handbook of Sociology, Social Theory, and Organization Studies: Contemporary Currents* (OUP 2014).

[19] See chs 3 and 5 and Sune Lægaard 'What Does "Respect for Difference" Mean?' in Peter Balint and Sophie Guérard de Latour (eds), *Liberal Multiculturalism and the Fair Terms of Integration* (Palgrave Macmillan 2013).

[20] See chs 2 and 4. See, in particular, Lorraine Mazerolle, Sarah Bennett, Emma Antrobus, and Elizabeth Eggins, 'Procedural Justice, Routine Encounters and Perceptions of Police: Main Findings from the Queensland Community Engagement Trial (QCET)' (2012) 8(4) Journal of Experimental Criminology 343; Dennis Rosenbaum and Daniel Lawrence, *Teaching Respectful Police-Citizen Encounters and Good Decision-Making: Results of a Randomized Control Trial with Police Recruits* (Institute for Public Policy and Social Research, Michigan State University 2011); Levin Wheller, Paul Quinton, Alistair Fildes, and Andy Mills, *The Greater Manchester Police Procedural Justice Training Experiment: The Impact of Communication Skills Training on Officers and Victims of Crime* (College of Policing 2013); and Jamie Bennett, *The Working Lives of Prison Managers: Global Change, Local Culture and Individual Agency in the Late Modern Prison* (Palgrave Macmillan 2015) (hereafter Bennett, *Prison Managers*).

comes to be associated not with the intrinsic valuing of others but with social indifference and instrumental action.

It is clear, then, that while respect has the potential to flourish in some contexts, it remains the remotest possibility in others. This might be attributed to a lack of clarity at the institutional level—for example, as to when and on what grounds respect of difference and diversity should override the more basic form of Kantian respect—which means that neither form of respect is fully realised. The consensus among a subset of philosophers that these forms of respect are incompatible complicates the situation yet further. Central to their concerns is the idea that a commitment to respect for difference and diversity inevitably introduces an element of hierarchical discrimination that is antithetical to the equality among persons that the Kantian idea of respect for personhood is supposed to express.[21] No wonder, then, that multicultural claims for equal respect—notably, those made in relation to the 'disproportionate and discriminatory' practice of stop and search—are routinely dismissed.[22]

A general category of respect is a tremendous rhetorical gift that can be used to justify all kinds of action by the state, including more strident policies that are patently unjust to some. A striking example of this tendency was found in a recent Supreme Court ruling—discussed in detail in chapter 3—in which the court backed the continued use of suspicionless stop and search powers on the grounds that they 'benefit' young black men.[23] In this context,

[21] Dillon, 'Respect' (n 16) and Colin Bird, 'Status, Identity, and Respect' (2004) 32(2) Political Theory 207 (hereafter Bird, 'Status, Identity, and Respect').

[22] See ch 3. See, in particular, Ben Bowling and Coretta Phillips, *Racism, Crime and Justice* (Longman 2002); Ben Bowling and Coretta Phillips, 'Disproportionate and Discriminatory: Reviewing the Evidence on Police Stop and Search' (2007) 70(6) The Modern Law Review 936; Rebekah Delsol and Michael Shiner, 'Regulating Stop and Search: A Challenge for Police and Community Relations in England and Wales' (2006) 14(3) Critical Criminology 241; Rebekah Delsol and Michael Shiner (eds), *Stop and Search: The Anatomy of a Police Power* (Palgrave Macmillan 2015) (hereafter Delsol and Shiner (eds), *Anatomy of a Police Power*); and Joel Miller, Nick Bland, and Paul Quinton, *The Impact of Stops and Searches on Crime and the Community*. Police Research Series Paper 127 (Home Office 2000).

[23] *R (Roberts) v Comr of Police of the Metropolis* [2015] UKSC 79, para 41. See also Adam Barnett, 'Britain's Supreme Court says targeting young black men for stop-and-search "benefits them"' *The Independent* (17 December 2015) <www.independent.co.uk/news/uk/crime/britain-s-supreme-court-says-targeting-young-black-men-for-stop-and-search-benefits-them-a6777651.html> accessed 1 August 2019.

something more is at stake than simply the truth or falsity of such a claim. An entire demographic is narrowly stereotyped and held out as the justification for a police power that has corrosive effects but nonetheless claims to 'respect' them. In reality, the state's treatment of young black men comes closer to paternalistic attention than respect.[24]

The development of a clear and systematic response to the respect claims of ethnic minority and other disadvantaged populations—which does not resort to a purely case-by-case solution—is a matter of some urgency. Ideally, both the police and HM Prison Service would routinely confront the question of how best to relate to these groups, such that it becomes institutionally embedded in their working cultures.[25] Galeotti's philosophical account—in prioritising Kantian respect without bracketing off individualised concerns about difference and diversity—presents one way forward for criminal justice.[26] She draws a distinction between strong and weak forms of recognition, where the former involves the intrinsic valuing of difference and the latter admits the difference and accepts it as valid, without going so far as to respect it. According to Galeotti, a weak form of recognition—rather than respect—for individual difference would facilitate the 'full inclusion' of the bearers of those differences, while ensuring that they continue to be respected strictly as persons neither despite nor in virtue of their association with particular characteristics.[27]

Galeotti's account provides some welcome clarity and appears to have the capacity to remedy the current situation whereby the police and HM Prison Service—intentionally or otherwise—appeal to two conflicting forms of respect. In recognising—but not respecting—difference, Galeotti's account resists any kind of 'moral sorting' or grading of attributes that could act as a disincentive for widespread systemic reform.[28] However, any serious

[24] Anna E Galeotti, 'Multicultural Claims and Equal Respect' (2010) 36(3/4) Philosophy & Social Criticism 441 (hereafter Galeotti, 'Multicultural Claims and Equal Respect').

[25] Ian Loader, 'Policing, Recognition, and Belonging' (2006) 605(1) The ANNALS of the American Academy of Political and Social Science 201.

[26] Galeotti, 'Multicultural Claims and Equal Respect' (n 24).

[27] ibid 443.

[28] Galeotti, 'Multicultural Claims and Equal Respect' (n 24). See also Mattias Iser, 'Recognition' in Edward N Zalta (ed), *The Stanford Encyclopedia of Philosophy*

strategy for cultivating respect must be as concerned with its implementation as with its logical coherence. The challenge is to integrate these ideas into criminal justice practice, and I consider the practical challenges of so doing in due course.

2. Respect, status, and power

It was hypothesised in chapter 1 that respect would be achievable—ideal-typically, at least—in both policing and imprisonment despite the structured status inequalities between the actors concerned. Following Sennett, it was envisaged that respect would have the effect of 'levelling out' any status inequalities or else rendering them inconsequential.[29] It was also mooted that—in contrast to status inequalities—power relations would be less open to challenge.[30] While both claims appear to hold true in the context of policing and imprisonment, there is no doubt that respect is infinitely more difficult to secure and sustain in such contexts—where status and power are especially pronounced—than in the everyday social relations with which Sennett is concerned.[31] It is worth reappraising the similarities and differences between status and power at this stage and considering why, in practice, respect is more likely to flourish when only status—and not power—is at stake.

Status is routinely associated with social standing. It has a dual dimension, consisting either of individuals conferring status on others or claiming status for themselves in an attempt to extract recognition, prestige, honour, privilege, or some other social benefit.[32] In chapter 3, the practice of stop and search was reimagined as a dialogue of claims and counter-claims to status and, in chapter 4, prisoners valued respect because of the

(Stanford University 2019) <http://plato.stanford.edu/entries/recognition/> accessed 1 August 2019; Bird, 'Status, Identity, and Respect' (n 21); James Johnson, 'Why Respect Culture?' (2000) 44(3) American Journal of Political Science 405; and Margalit, *The Decent Society* (n 9) ch 2, 'The Grounds of Respect' 62.

[29] Richard Sennett, *Respect: The Formation of Character in an Age of Inequality* (Penguin 2004) (hereafter Sennett, *Respect*).

[30] Jeffrey W Lucas and Amy R Baxter, 'Power, Influence, and Diversity in Organisations' (2012) 639(1) The ANNALS of the American Academy of Political and Social Science 49.

[31] Sennett, *Respect* (n 29).

[32] See, eg, Theodore D Kemper, *Status, Power and Ritual Interaction: A Relational Reading of Durkheim, Goffman and Collins* (Routledge 2011)

implicit acceptance it signalled not only for their intrinsic worth but also for their status, both of which were widely regarded as scarce goods.

While power cannot always be sharply demarcated from status—for example, it too might be used to obtain certain social benefits—its use is distinctive in that it is almost universally accompanied by acts of resistance. An individual is said to have power when he secures the submission of others, often against their will and despite their resistance.[33] When power is exercised in the penal context, it valorises the position of the marginal and removes the possibility that two individuals might genuinely come to accept and relate to each other as if they were of equal standing. It is notable too that power is exercised not only through individuals but also through institutions. Chapter 4 examined how managerialism facilitates the effective flow of power at the top of the organisation and has, by implication, come to be associated not only with target-setting but also with the social management of prisoners.[34] Chapter 5 explored how the ritualised preparation and provision of prison food was understood as yet another means by which to exercise institutional power over prisoners, thus discrediting official visions of penal liberalism in a fundamental way.[35]

It would appear, then, that when status is at stake, it is possible to achieve a level of mutuality that is conducive to genuinely respectful relations.[36] By contrast, power—especially when exercised without restraint—can dehumanise others and initiate a degree of

(hereafter Kemper, *Status, Power and Ritual Interaction*); Herbert Goldhamer and Edward A Shils, 'Types of Power and Status' (1939) *American Journal of Sociology* 45(2) 171; and Joseph Berger and Morris Zelditch Jr (eds), *Status, Power and Legitimacy: Strategies and Theories* (Transaction Publishers 1998).

[33] Kemper, *Status, Power and Ritual Interaction,* ibid. See also Richard M Emerson, 'Power-Dependence Relations' (1962) 27(1) American Sociological Review 31.

[34] See, eg, Alison Liebling, 'Prisons in Transition' (2006) 29(5) International Journal of Law and Psychiatry 422.

[35] See, eg, Rod Earle and Coretta Phillips, 'Digesting Men? Ethnicity, Gender and Food: Perspectives from a "Prison Ethnography"' (2012) 16(2) Theoretical Criminology 141 and Rebecca Godderis, 'Dining in: The Symbolic Power of Food in Prison' (2006) 45(3) The Howard Journal of Criminal Justice 255.

[36] Sennett, *Respect* (n 29). See also Peter Somerville, '"The Feeling's Mutual:" Respect as the Basis for Cooperative Interaction' in Millie (ed), *Securing Respect* (n 6).

conflict that inhibits mutuality and, by extension, respect.[37] This view is consistent with Miller's claim that social order or 'conditions of social calm' are necessary in order to uphold moral rights such as respect.[38]

3. *Instrumentalism*

Instrumentalism—as it relates to policing and imprisonment—was an explicit recurring theme of the book. While it is inevitable that such institutions will be driven, at least in part, by a means-end mentality, it is important that such commitments are held in their proper place. Otherwise, both institutions risk distorting or undermining those commitments that are better viewed as intrinsic, foundational, or non-instrumental.[39] This claim certainly holds true where respect is concerned. In practice, a lasting preoccupation with instrumental outcomes of various kinds—crime control, order maintenance, social management, and managerialism—has resulted in a considerable degree of ambivalence—even apathy—on the part of the police and HM Prison Service towards the non-instrumental issue of how best to cultivate respect and incorporate the value into their respective rationales.[40]

Just as Dzur claims that a social institution 'works on us even as we work within it and through it', it is usually possible to treat the actions of staff as deriving from the overall purpose or vision of the institution.[41] An obvious risk of instrumentalism is that it encourages an apathetic attitude among staff, who tend

[37] On the challenge of exercising power with restraint in policing, see Howard S Cohen and Michael Feldberg, *Power and Restraint: The Moral Dimension of Police Work* (Praeger 1991).

[38] Seumas Miller, *The Moral Foundations of Social Institutions* (CUP 2010) ch 9, 'The Police' 161 (hereafter Miller, *The Moral Foundations of Social Institutions*).

[39] See further Andrew Ashworth, *Principles of Criminal Law* (3rd edn, OUP 1999) 58–60. See also John Gardner, 'Ashworth on Principles' in Lucia Zedner and Julian V Roberts (eds), *Principles and Values in Criminal Law and Criminal Justice: Essays in Honour of Andrew Ashworth* (OUP 2012) and Arie Freiberg, 'Affective Versus Effective Justice: Instrumentalism and Emotionalism in Criminal Justice' (2001) 3(2) Punishment & Society 265.

[40] See, eg, Her Majesty's Chief Inspector of Prisons for England and Wales, *Annual Report 2017–18* (n 2).

[41] Albert W Dzur, 'Participatory Innovation in Criminal Justice: Why, How, and How Far?' in Stephen Farrall, Barry Goldson, Ian Loader, and Anita Dockley

not to feel that they are making a co-ordinated contribution to a shared non-instrumental aim—such as respect—and instead come to see themselves as bearing a merely expendable relation to their work.[42] We need only look to the previous chapter for a stark illustration of this point. According to one prison officer, all prisoners had surrendered their right to respect by virtue of having become convicted criminals.[43] While this view does not sit easily with the inclusive understanding of respect developed in this book, we can make sense of it by referring to the context in which it was uttered, namely, a prison that treats respect as a weak side-constraint on the pursuit of managerialist outcomes. It remains an open question as to how best to design penal institutions where instrumental and non-instrumental concerns are simultaneously—and productively—at play.

4. *Institutional respect*

In natural speech, we tend to attribute moral values not only to individuals but also to groups or institutions.[44] While it is well established that respect regulates social relations between individuals, another recurring theme of the book has been the role and value of respect at the institutional level. Might it be possible to treat respect as an attribute of an institution itself, such that we can describe it as institutionally respectful—or disrespectful—in the same manner that the Metropolitan Police has been described as institutionally racist?[45]

When we attribute a moral value such as respect to an institution, we are automatically committed to a particular standpoint

(eds), *Justice and Penal Reform: Re-shaping the Penal Landscape* (Routledge 2016) 181.

[42] Christopher Bennett, 'Review Essay: Actions, Institutions, and the Common Good' (2011) 30(2) Criminal Justice Ethics 205.

[43] See ch 5. See, in particular, David Jenkins, 'Respect in Prison' in Robert Hardy (convenor), *Respect in Prison.* Transcript of a conference held at Bishop Grossteste College, Lincoln (Bishop of Lincoln (Robert Hardy) 1991) and Butler and Drake, 'Reconsidering Respect' (n 6).

[44] Miranda Fricker, 'Can There Be Institutional Virtues?' in Tamar Szabó Gendler and John Hawthorne (eds), *Oxford Studies in Epistemology: Volume 3* (OUP 2010) (hereafter Fricker, 'Institutional Virtues').

[45] ibid. See also John Lea, 'The Macpherson Report and the Question of Institutional Racism' (2000) 39(3) The Howard Journal of Criminal Justice 219 and Anna Souhami, 'Understanding Institutional Racism: The Stephen Lawrence

on the nature of groups. The default position is to understand a group as nothing more than a sum of individuals. But when we describe the police or HM Prison Service as institutionally respectful or disrespectful, we add to our repertoire a concept of a group as a collective which, though composed of individuals, cannot be reduced to the sum of its parts. A sceptical reader is likely to maintain that it is simply not possible to treat respect as an attribute of an institution, since institutions do not possess any of the features we would usually associate with a respectful exchange: they are not agents and lack humanity on the basis of which to claim or extend respect.[46] We might compromise by saying that it is only *in combination* with the individuals and groups whose work realises an institution's priorities that an institution might be said to exhibit respect.[47]

5. Reconciling respect with other purposes, values, and rationales

Another recurring theme of the book has been the precise role that respect might play in the practice of criminal justice more generally.[48] Unless respect is the sole ideal in terms of which we should design criminal justice institutions, how is it to be reconciled with other purposes, values, and rationales? Must there be a process of weighing or even specification of some values as strong side-constraints under certain circumstances? These questions were particularly pertinent in chapter 2, which finely differentiated between the pursuit of respect and recognition in procedural justice, as well as in chapters 4 and 5, which explored the ways in which HM Prison Service has committed—at the level of official

Inquiry and the Police Service Reaction' in Michael Rowe (ed), *Policing Beyond Macpherson: Issues in Policing, Race and Society* (Routledge 2007).

[46] See, however, Fricker, 'Institutional Virtues' (n 44).

[47] ibid and Christian List and Philip Pettit, *Group Agency: The Possibility, Design, and Status of Corporate Agents* (OUP 2011) ch 3, 'The Structure of Group Agents'.

[48] cf the debate, conducted in relation to Hart's theory of punishment, about whether it is possible to combine quasi-utilitarian and quasi-retributive considerations when they come into conflict: Alan W Norrie, *Law, Ideology and Punishment: Retrieval and Critique of the Liberal Ideal of Criminal Justice* (Kluwer Academic 1991) and HLA Hart, *Punishment and Responsibility: Essays in the Philosophy of Law* (Clarendon Press 1968).

discourse, at least—to treating offenders with both decency and respect.[49]

While there is no doubt that respect has a contribution of its own to make, in matters of criminal justice, at least, it is but one consideration among others. While attractive in theory, any attempt to initiate a process of ranking would prove challenging and perhaps even futile in practice. Criminal justice practice is better understood as being defined by a plurality of values, which are not fixed or ordered in a definite way and are not derivable from a single fundamental value.[50] These values are irreducibly diverse, incommensurable, incalculable, fragmented—and perhaps even in conflict with each other—and, by implication, are not amenable to a process of ranking. An alternative strategy for criminal justice institutions, then, might be to balance the numerous values at stake—notably, respect, recognition, decency, and dignity—and view them as alternative foundations for criminal justice practice on which the pluralist can rely selectively.[51]

6. *The liberal credentials of criminal justice*

As we have seen, both institutions promise that their practices will preserve and value respect, but too often default on that promise by treating respect as a weak side-constraint on the pursuit of instrumental outcomes. When respect is devalued in this way, it

[49] On the relevance of recognition to procedural justice, see Karen A Hegtvedt, 'Justice Frameworks' in Peter J Burke (ed), *Contemporary Social Psychological Theories* (2nd edn, Stanford University Press 2006) 50. On the priority of decency and respect in Her Majesty's Prison Service, see National Offender Management Service, *Annual Report and Accounts 2015–2016* (National Offender Management Service 2016) (hereafter National Offender Management Service, *Annual Report 2015–2016*) and National Offender Management Service, *Business Plan 2014–2015* (National Offender Management Service 2014).

[50] Jacobs, 'Criminal Justice and the Liberal Polity' (n 8) and Lucia Zedner, 'Reparation and Retribution: Are They Reconcilable?' (1994) 57(2) The Modern Law Review 228. For Garland's manifesto for a pluralist sociology of punishment, see David Garland, *Punishment and Modern Society* (Clarendon Press 1990).

[51] See, eg, Michael T Cahill, 'Punishment Pluralism' in Mark D White (ed), *Retributivism: Essays on Theory and Policy* (OUP 2011). On the multiple meanings of 'pluralism' in Kantian ethics, see Hill, *Respect, Pluralism, and Justice* (n 14) ch 1, 'Kantian Pluralism'.

undermines the liberal credentials of criminal justice and weakens its claim to delivering 'justice'.[52]

Since Kant placed respect for persons at the centre of moral theory and insisted that all individuals are owed respect by virtue of their humanity, respect has been a core ideal of political liberalism. Political liberalism is also associated with extending the same freedoms to all citizens and attempting to enlarge those freedoms to the greatest extent compatible with according equal freedoms to all.[53] These ideals were subsequently inscribed into liberal practices of criminal justice. If criminal justice institutions are genuine in their commitment to liberalism, they will treat citizens as the primary unit of concern and acknowledge them as agents accountable for their own wrongdoing.[54] These institutions will also be concerned to preserve and protect the 'jurisdiction' of citizens—to borrow Thorburn's term—and demonstrate restraint in criminalising and sanctioning them.[55] This is not to say that, in practice, all professional actors demonstrate a principled commitment to political liberalism. Nor is it to say that liberal practices of criminal justice will always be consistent with the core ideal of respect.[56] Nonetheless, when individuals regard and treat each other as rational agents and are provided with opportunities to assume responsibility for their actions, there is great potential for respect to be cultivated.[57]

[52] On liberalism and criminal justice, see n 8.

[53] Dillon, 'Respect' (n 16); Victor J Seidler, *Kant, Respect and Injustice: The Limits of Liberal Moral Theory* (Routledge & Kegan Paul 1986); Martha C Nussbaum, 'Political Liberalism and Respect: A Response to Linda Barclay' (2003) 4(2) SATS: Northern European Journal of Philosophy 25; and Blain Neufeld, 'Civic Respect, Political Liberalism, and Non-Liberal Societies' (2005) 4(3) Politics, Philosophy & Economics 275. Political liberalism also gives expression to a certain conception of the equality of all human beings with respect to state power: Matthias Katzer, 'The Basis of Universal Liberal Principles in Nussbaum's Political Philosophy' (2010) 2(2) Public Reason 60.

[54] Jacobs, 'Criminal Justice and the Liberal Polity' (n 8) and RA Duff, 'Responsibility, Citizenship, and Criminal Law' in RA Duff and Stuart P Green (eds), *Philosophical Foundations of Criminal Law* (OUP 2011).

[55] Malcolm Thorburn, 'Criminal Law as Public Law' in RA Duff and Stuart P Green (eds), *Philosophical Foundations of Criminal Law* (OUP 2011) 32. See also Jonathan Jacobs, 'The Liberal Polity, Criminal Sanction, and Civil Society' (2013) 32(3) Criminal Justice Ethics 231.

[56] Jacobs, 'Criminal Justice and the Liberal Polity' (n 8).

[57] ibid.

It follows that when respect is treated as secondary to core police activity, it will become increasingly difficult for criminal justice to protect its liberal credentials.[58] We found a striking illustration of this point in chapter 2, which critiqued the instrumental preoccupations of scholars and practitioners of procedural justice.[59] Tyler claims that, by treating citizens with fairness and respect, the police can increase their legitimacy as well as citizens' compliance with the law.[60] By marketing procedural justice primarily on pragmatic 'law and order' grounds—and not as a practice to be valued for its own sake—Tyler makes a strategic attempt, we might assume, to engage police officers and persuade them to modify their behaviour for instrumental gain.[61] It is ironic, then, that procedural justice should prove so popular among the liberal left. On closer examination, the relevance of respect to procedural justice is thinly substantiated. Procedural justice scholars and practitioners appear to be concerned with the value only insofar as it supports the pursuit of instrumental outcomes, thus undermining the liberal project of criminal justice.[62]

B. Institutional Design

There is much to be gained by engaging in a form of ethical thought that is grounded in the complex realities of policing and imprisonment and by a willingness to articulate the ethical significance of those realities. While respect is a promising intellectual resource for these purposes, analytic work of this kind can only detain us so long. Respect is also a matter of material significance with immediate implications for policing and imprisonment reform. But what, exactly, is to be done about the severe respect deficit in both institutions? The next task is to

[58] See n 8.

[59] See ch 2. See, in particular, Mike Hough, Jonathan Jackson, Ben Bradford, Andy Myhill, and Paul Quinton, 'Procedural Justice, Trust, and Institutional Legitimacy' (2010) 4(3) Policing 203 and Lyn Hynds and Kristina Murphy, 'Public Satisfaction with Police: Using Procedural Justice to Improve Police Legitimacy' (2007) 40(1) Australian & New Zealand Journal of Criminology 27.

[60] Tom R Tyler, 'Enhancing Police Legitimacy' (2004) 593(1) The ANNALS of the American Academy of Political and Social Science 84.

[61] ibid.

[62] See ch 2.

confront questions of institutional design and propose alternative ways ahead.

In formulating three key strategies for embedding respect in policing and imprisonment, the discussion that follows is necessarily in sharp contrast to the sustained critique of respect developed in preceding chapters. It will be essential, for example, to offer some criteria for determining what these institutional practices might look like. Between whom can respect flourish and under what conditions? Without overstating the reformative potential of respect or inflating expectations of what criminal justice institutions can realistically accomplish, there is scope to prioritise respect in policy-making in addition to the standard diet of instrumental and utilitarian concerns. The aim would be to create and sustain policing and imprisonment practices that are *characterised*—rather than merely *constrained*—by respect, which would no doubt lead to more nuanced policy prescriptions.

1. Strategies of amelioration, accommodation, and transformation

It will be helpful to preface the discussion of criminal justice reform with a broader reflection on reform processes in criminal justice institutions. Seidman's strategies for effecting change—amelioration, accommodation, and transformation—are instructive here.[63] While the strategies differ in their directness, scope, and time frame, they are not mutually exclusive and there is inevitably some overlap between them.[64]

In Seidman's taxonomy, an ameliorative strategy is pragmatic, requiring the institution to realise short-term improvements while it develops a permanent solution. The obvious risk of this strategy is that the institution resorts to weak or superficial attempts at reform.[65] A strategy of accommodation is subtler. It requires the

[63] Louis M Seidman, 'Hyper-Incarceration and Strategies of Disruption: Is There a Way Out?' (2011) 9(1) Ohio State Journal of Criminal Law 109 (hereafter Seidman, 'Hyper-Incarceration'). See also Hannah Graham and Rob White, 'The Ethics of Innovation in Criminal Justice' in Jacobs and Jackson (eds), *Criminal Justice Ethics* (n 13).

[64] Seidman, 'Hyper-Incarceration' (n 63).

[65] ibid.

institution to accept existing penal cultures and practices while seeking to adapt in a piecemeal fashion. While this strategy does not promise immediate transformation, it prioritises incremental change from the inside by realigning interests and softening harsh policies from the margins.[66] Meanwhile, a transformative strategy is evidently bolder. It requires the institution to disrupt the status quo by relinquishing existing orders of penal power and social stratification altogether. The results are less predictable in their impact. While the strategy could spark wide-ranging reform, it could also amount to inchoate and utopian visions, which do little to mobilise the actions needed to realise them, either in part or in their totality.[67]

This chapter now directs its attention to the issue of how best to embed respect in policing and imprisonment. The changes proposed at the *institutional* level would involve immediate change in a manner that is suggestive of Seidman's strategy of amelioration. Meanwhile, the change proposed at the *individual* level would require incremental change in a manner that alludes to his strategy of accommodation. Throughout, the aim is to ensure that respect is considered *as important* as the institution's instrumental concerns, in sharp contrast to current practice whereby respect almost always concedes space to those concerns.

(a) Institutional commitments to respect

In matters of institutional design and redesign, Dryzek suggests we attend closely to the ways in which the dominant discourses of the institution need to be reinforced, reshaped, or undermined.[68] His claim is especially relevant to policing and imprisonment, where—as we have seen—there is scope to revise the manner in which respect is endorsed in the official discourse of both institutions. At present, respect is akin to an official word, a keyword—or even a slogan—and is presented with all the brevity, intensity, and urgency that we associate with the best marketing:[69]

[66] ibid.

[67] ibid.

[68] John S Dryzek, 'The Informal Logic of Institutional Design' in Goodin (ed), *Institutional Design* (n 9).

[69] Raymond Williams, *Keywords: A Vocabulary of Culture and Society* (Fontana 1976). On slogans, see Ira Sharkansky, 'Slogan as Policy' (2002) 4(1) Journal of Comparative Policy Analysis: Research and Practice 75 and Robert E Denton Jr, 'The Rhetorical Functions of Slogans: Classifications and Characteristics' (1980)

Standards of professional behaviour

I will act with self-control and tolerance, treating members of the public and colleagues with respect and courtesy.[70]

Met values

Treats others consistently, fairly and with respect.[71]

Working culture

Develop a workforce and working culture that demonstrates respect.[72]

Our proud values

Respect for all.[73]

Our values

In delivering offender management services, we will … treat offenders with respect.[74]

National Offender Management Service commissioning intentions

All prisons will be safe and decent … where people treat each other with respect and courtesy.[75]

Three discrete issues require bearing in mind here. First, it is not immediately clear whether both institutions proceed on the basis that they already exhibit respect or whether it is a value to which they

28(2) Communication Quarterly 10. Respect arguably sits alongside other established slogans of criminal justice, such as 'doing the right thing in the right way' in policing and 'decency' in imprisonment: College of Policing, *Code of Ethics: A Code of Practice for the Principles and Standards of Professional Behaviour for the Policing Profession of England and Wales* (College of Policing 2014). See policing principles, s 2.1 'Doing the right thing in the right way' (hereafter College of Policing, *Code of Ethics*) and National Offender Management Service, *Annual Report 2015–2016* (n 49) 17 'Decency'.

[70] College of Policing, *Code of Ethics* (n 69) s 3.1.

[71] Metropolitan Police, *Information Pack: Chief Superintendent Selection Process* (Metropolitan Police 2017) 19 (hereafter Metropolitan Police, *Chief Superintendent Selection Process*).

[72] Metropolitan Police, *Communities, Equalities and People Committee* (Metropolitan Police 2 September 2010) Priority 1: Our People.

[73] Nottinghamshire Police, *Our Code of Ethics, Vision and Values* (Nottinghamshire Police 2016) <http://www.nottinghamshire.police.uk/visionandvalues> accessed 1 August 2019 (hereafter Nottinghamshire Police, *Code of Ethics*).

[74] National Offender Management Service, *Annual Report 2015–2016* (n 49) 3.

[75] National Offender Management Service, *National Framework: Agreement for Services Commissioned from Public Sector Prisons in England from 2015* (National Offender Management Service 2015) 8.

aspire. The Metropolitan Police portrays respect as a characteristic of the organisation ('treats others consistently, fairly and with respect'), while the other statements commit the institution to a future course of action ('develop a workforce and working culture that demonstrates respect'). Second, in all six statements, the commitment to respect is simply announced, and not explained. That a word is open-textured and contestable is no reason to deflect from specifying its meaning. We need to be alert to the tendency of both institutions to appeal to a vague and indeterminate category of respect since, as we have seen, this indeterminacy can filter through institutions, with implications for interpersonal relations on the ground.[76] Third, there is an exclusive focus on regulating respect in vertical relations between the institution and the individual. There are no commitments to regulate horizontal relations between individuals—either in public spaces or in conditions of confinement—in which respect is often the core value at stake. The commitment of Nottinghamshire Police to 'respect for all' is especially ambiguous where vertical and horizontal relations are concerned.[77]

If respect is to become more than progressive rhetoric, there must be a concerted effort to address the prior question of *what it is* to respect and be respected in the complex moral contexts of policing and imprisonment. At present, police and prison officers are expected to act respectfully without having been supplied with a sufficient explanation of what respect actually involves.[78] Only in exceptional cases do the authors of these documents elaborate—if only superficially—on respect:

> *Authority, respect and courtesy*
> Examples of meeting this standard:
>
> Remain composed and respectful, even in the face of provocation.
> Retain proportionate self-restraint in volatile situations.
> Recognise the particular needs of victims and witnesses for policing support.
> Use your authority only in ways that are proportionate, lawful, accountable, necessary and ethical.[79]

[76] See further Ahmed, *On Being Included* (n 18).
[77] Nottinghamshire Police, *Code of Ethics* (n 73).
[78] See, eg, Butler and Drake, 'Reconsidering Respect' (n 6).
[79] College of Policing, *Code of Ethics* (n 69) s 2.3.

> *Integrity*
>
> We act ethically … respecting and valuing individuals for the diversity they bring.[80]
>
> *Working professionally*
>
> Respecting others
>
> Promotes equality of opportunity; treating all people with … respect. Challenges discriminatory behaviour, and upholds and fosters diversity.[81]

These statements give practical effect to two key issues raised earlier in abstract terms. Encouragingly, the College of Policing emphasises conditions of 'social calm' and restraint as necessary for the cultivation of respect.[82] Meanwhile, the Competency and Qualities Framework published by HM Prison Service—somewhat problematically—posits *respect of difference* as an ethical guideline having elsewhere endorsed only a Kantian form of respect.[83] The additional commentary lacks precision and bears little relevance to the rich and varied conditions in which respect is negotiated in practice. As such, the publication could be viewed as an act which, in itself, lacks respect.[84] An alternative commitment to respect might read:

> *The priority of respect*
>
> HM Prison Service is committed to extending respect to all prisoners and to regulating relations between prisoners where respect is often the core value at stake. Respect—as the only suitable acknowledgement of a person's humanity—is understood by all as a value that need not be negotiated and cannot be forfeited. We recognise the individual and group identities of all prisoners and aim to provide an environment in which prisoners can express those identities freely.

[80] Metropolitan Police, *Chief Superintendent Selection Process* (n 71) 19.

[81] Her Majesty's Prison Service, *Competency and Qualities Framework* (Her Majesty's Prison Service undated) 15 (hereafter Her Majesty's Prison Service, *Competency and Qualities Framework*).

[82] On 'social calm', see Miller, *The Moral Foundations of Social Institutions* (n 38) ch 9, 'The Police' 161.

[83] Her Majesty's Prison Service, *Competency and Qualities Framework* (n 81) and on forms of respect, see Dillon, 'Respect' (n 16).

[84] Mark Halsey, 'Risking Desistance: Respect and Responsibility in Custodial and Post-Release Contexts' in Pat Carlen (ed), *Imaginary Penalities* (Willan 2008). On language, what it represents, and its capacity to offend, see Judith Butler, *Excitable Speech: A Politics of the Performative* (Routledge 1997).

Should there be limited resources to develop more detailed publications or should the task of clarifying respect prove too arduous, both institutions could commit to cultivating respect in practice without necessarily publicising their adherence to the value. In a world where the policed and imprisoned are too often rendered vulnerable to the sharp end of official action, it would be better to make no public commitment to respect than a vague commitment that fails to serve as a guide to respectful relations in practice.[85] After all, an appeal to the word 'respect' in official discourse is not strictly necessary if respect is deemed to have been cultivated and saying 'respect' does not make it so.[86]

Ahmed adopts a sceptical view of the mission statement, reorienting our understanding of what is fundamentally at stake when institutions subscribe to certain keywords. For Ahmed, the publication of a mission statement amounts to little more than an institutional performance. The statement presents an opportunity for image management in which the institution inevitably markets itself in positive terms and confirms that it is performing well. The risk of image management is that it becomes a substitute for action, since the statements tend to conceal the ongoing challenges of the institution, for example, in upholding respect. On Ahmed's reasoning, it should come as no surprise that respect is presented in a diluted form, since the medium itself relies on a degree of superficiality.[87]

(b) Respect as an ethical standard

A common—but misguided—assumption appears to be that the best way to give effect to an ethical standard as complex as respect is to posit it as a rule. Chapter 1 drew attention to respect as it is firmly embedded in the *Standard Minimum Rules for the Treatment of Prisoners,* which require prison officers in 193 member states to 'command the respect of prisoners' and reaffirm

[85] See, eg, Ahmed, *On Being Included* (n 18) and Ian Loader, 'In Search of Civic Policing: Recasting the "Peelian" Principles' (2016) 10(3) Criminal Law and Philosophy 427.

[86] Austin, *How to Do Things with Words* (n 18). See, in particular, 7–11 'Can Saying Make It So?'

[87] Sara Ahmed, '"You End up Doing the Document Rather than Doing the Doing": Diversity, Race Equality and the Politics of Documentation' (2007) 30(4) Ethnic and Racial Studies 590. See also Ahmed, *On Being Included* (n 18) and Sara Ahmed, 'The Language of Diversity' (2007) 30(2) Ethnic and Racial Studies 235.

their self-respect.[88] Chapter 2 reflected on recent experimentation with procedural justice scripts. In an attempt to *enact* respect, police officers recited a particular form of words and adhered to a strict set of rules for ethical action.[89] Chapter 3 considered and subsequently rejected the proposal that stop and search might be rendered more respectful through tighter legal regulation.[90] In chapter 4, prison managers reduced respect to a matter of civility and good manners. And, as we know, civility is a virtue of external conformity with socially established rules and is much less concerned with social relations and sincere dispositions.[91] Chapter 5 drew attention to the PSI on *Catering: Meals for Prisoners,* which requires catering staff in public sector prisons to *show*, through strict rule-adherence, that standards of meal preparation—and, by extension, respectful relations—are being actively sustained.[92]

It is important that both institutions make a concerted effort to resist 'proceduralising' respect or implementing a rule-based approach of this kind. Respect is only likely to become fully embedded in practice if both institutions abandon their formal adherence to legalism and approach respect strictly as an ethical standard.[93] However, to dismiss rule-based forms of respect in this context is not to dismiss the importance of rule-following more generally, which lies at the core of the activities of the criminal justice state and its agents. As Loader and Zedner observe, were it not for the centrality of rules, it would not be possible to talk of 'injustice' or other forms of maltreatment by the state.[94] And as Braithwaite observes, the most promising means by which

[88] United Nations Office on Drugs and Crime, *The United Nations Standard Minimum Rules for the Treatment of Prisoners (The Nelson Mandela Rules)* (UNODC 2015).

[89] See n 20.

[90] Michael Shiner, 'Regulation and Reform' in Delsol and Shiner (eds), *Anatomy of a Police Power* (n 22).

[91] Bennett, *Prison Managers* (n 20).

[92] National Offender Management Service, *Catering: Meals for Prisoners* (n 11).

[93] Judith N Shklar, *Legalism: Law, Morals, and Political Trials* (Harvard University Press 1964); John Braithwaite, 'Rules and Principles: A Theory of Legal Certainty' (2002) 27 Australian Journal of Legal Philosophy 47 (hereafter Braithwaite, 'Rules and Principles'); and Robert Baldwin, 'Why Rules Don't Work' (1990) 53(3) The Modern Law Review 321.

[94] Ian Loader and Lucia Zedner, 'Review Essay: Police Beyond Law?' (2007) 10(1) New Criminal Law Review 142.

to achieve consistency in complex domains is through an 'appropriate mix' of rules and standards.[95]

However, when respect is reduced to a matter of formal rule-following, and respectful relationships to a series of duties and rights determined by rules, it leads all too quickly to caricature. Rules formally bind state actors in such a way that inhibits free-flowing dialogue and spontaneous action, producing behaviour that is only superficially respectful. As we know, a respectful action must be accompanied by the appropriate intent, namely, an expression of genuine concern for—and willingness to value—another.[96] Yet there is no need for respectful intent when the respectful action itself is prescribed by a rule. State actors who remain unconvinced of the merits of respect need only rehearse a set of actions in order to give the appearance that respectful relations are in place.[97]

By contrast, were institutions to understand respect as an ethical standard, their attention would be redirected towards the nature and potential of the value itself. Unlike rule-following, an ethical standard does not specify the precise means by which to cultivate respect. This flexibility would prompt a degree of ethical reflection among police and prison officers that rule-following does not. They would be obliged, for example, to identify common challenges and evaluate whether their responses to them are genuinely respectful. And although they are not unrestricted free agents, they would be encouraged to think imaginatively about respect and take steps to ensure that their future actions better exemplify the value. For police and prison officers who are genuinely invested in criminal justice reform, this would be a challenging and exciting—even exhilarating—responsibility.[98]

(c) Dialogue and consensus

This leads to a related suggestion. There is scope to clarify and embed respect from the ground-up, not only through quiet introspection—as described above—but through dialogue and consensus. A working

[95] Braithwaite, 'Rules and Principles' (n 93) 47.

[96] See, eg, Dillon, 'Respect' (n 16).

[97] See, eg, National Offender Management Service, *Catering: Meals for Prisoners* (n 11).

[98] See further Jeremy Waldron, '*The Coxford Lecture*. Inhuman and Degrading Treatment: The Words Themselves' (2010) 23(2) Canadian Journal of Law & Jurisprudence 269.

group of state actors and citizens could be oriented around the question of how best to give practical effect to respect in practice. There is an obvious benefit to harnessing the potential of a group and conferring greater responsibility on a subset of individuals who are heavily invested in criminal justice practice. They might—in the manner envisaged by Marks and Sklansky—have the opportunity to become participants in—and not merely objects of—reform activity.[99] And being part of a group comes with a number of freedoms, such as the leeway to think through the merits and limits of respect coupled with the agency to choose when, if ever, to enter the discussion with a point worth raising. A less obvious benefit is that the deliberative process itself would help to build mutual respect, civic engagement, and feelings of secure belonging among group members.[100] In particular, the act of inviting traditionally excluded groups into a process of deciding what respectful practice should look like in policing and imprisonment might itself cultivate respect in ways that generate a virtuous circle.

That said, the process of clarifying respect from the ground-up would require both institutions to adopt an optimistic view of the possibilities and benefits of ethical disagreement. Respect, as we know, is flexible, elusive, and likely to invite diverse interpretations by members of the working group. As a result, the group may not necessarily demonstrate shared sensibilities or have a collective 'voice'. It is a common misconception, however, that ethical disagreement can prevent us from confronting and resolving complex problems. In reality, disagreement does not necessarily have to be overcome, and instead can become an important and constitutive feature of the group's relations.[101] It might encourage individual members to reflect, for example, on the coherence and consistency of their beliefs. They might even modify their outlook on respect, having had the opportunity to critique and contest the

[99] Monique Marks and David Sklansky (eds), *Police Reform from the Bottom Up: Officers and their Unions as Agents of Change* (Routledge 2011).

[100] See, eg, Dillon, 'Respect' (n 16) and Ian Loader and Neil Walker, *Civilizing Security* (CUP 2007). See, in particular, ch 8, 'The Democratic Governance of Security'.

[101] Bernard Williams, *Ethics and the Limits of Philosophy* (Fontana 1985) ch 8, 'Knowledge, Science, Convergence'. See also Charles L Stevenson, 'The Nature of Ethical Disagreement' in Steven M Cahn (ed), *Exploring Ethics: An Introductory Anthology* (4th edn, OUP 2016) (hereafter Stevenson, 'Ethical Disagreement'). On respecting others' freedom to disagree, see Lawrence K Schmidt, 'Respecting Others: The Hermeneutic Virtue' (2000) 33 Continental Philosophy Review 359 (hereafter Schmidt, 'Respecting Others').

value. Although potentially complex and messy, a ground-up approach to cultivating respect would be far superior to promoting a pre-constituted idea of respect that stands above popular sentiment and purports to limit it.[102]

While the principal aim would be to approach respect in a manner that is grounded and pragmatic, the group would also—ideally, at least—become a platform for creative thought and experimentation where respect is concerned. Ultimately, the working group might arrive at a rich working definition of respect and might even be commissioned to develop a set of illustrative examples of good practice in a variety of policing and penal contexts. These examples could be distributed to all practitioners, to be read alongside general institutional commitments to respect.

In stop and search, for example, a police officer might exhibit respect by enquiring with the suspect as to whether he feels comfortable with the prospect of a physical search in a public space, providing the option of a search in private instead. The police officer must relate to the suspect in a manner that has not been rehearsed and is motivated instead by genuine concern for his privacy and bodily integrity.[103] As we have seen, at prison mealtime, many prisoners do not have access to a communal dining space and must instead consume meals in the confines of their cells. Subject to security constraints, prison officers might exhibit respect by unlocking the cells of these prisoners and inviting them to associate on the wing during these periods. More generally, both police and prison officers might begin to embed respect by addressing all suspects and prisoners by name, engaging in meaningful exchanges with them, and directing them to welfare or medical support services where necessary.[104]

***

[102] Stevenson, 'Ethical Disagreement' (n 101) and Schmidt, 'Respecting Others' (n 101).

[103] See ch 3 and, in particular, Leanne Weber and Ben Bowling, 'Introduction: Stop and Search in Global Context' (2011) 21(4) Policing and Society 353; Ben Bowling and Leanne Weber, 'Stop and Search in Global Context: An Overview' (2011) 21(4) Policing and Society 480; and Cécile Fabre, *Whose Body is it Anyway? Justice and the Integrity of the Person* (OUP 2006).

[104] This is standard practice at HMP Grendon. See, eg, Her Majesty's Chief Inspector of Prisons for England and Wales, *Report on an Unannounced Inspection of HMP Grendon* (Her Majesty's Inspectorate of Prisons for England and Wales 2013).

One of the most striking—and underappreciated—features of criminal justice scholarship and practice is that certain timeless ideas—such as respect—underpin almost all topical ones. Yet an extended preoccupation with achieving criminal 'justice' in instrumental terms has meant that our understanding of respect has been, at best, incomplete and fragmentary. Respect matters, and so too does conceptual precision. Greater sensitivity to respect—and other values—is crucial if we are to make sense of the complex realities of policing and imprisonment. In cultivating that sensitivity, I can only hope that scholars and practitioners alike might find some inspiration within these pages.

Bibliography

Ahmed Sara, 'The Language of Diversity' (2007) 30(2) Ethnic and Racial Studies 235

Ahmed Sara, '"You End Up Doing the Document Rather than Doing the Doing": Diversity, Race Equality and the Politics of Documentation' (2007) 30(4) Ethnic and Racial Studies 590

Ahmed Sara, *On Being Included: Racism and Diversity in Institutional Life* (Duke University Press 2012)

Allen Rob, Ashworth Andrew, Cotterrell Roger, Coyle Andrew, Duff RA, Lacey Nicola, Liebling Alison, and Morgan Rod, *A Presumption Against Imprisonment: Social Order and Social Values* (British Academy 2014)

Anderson Elijah, 'The Iconic Ghetto' (2002) 642(1) The ANNALS of the American Academy of Political and Social Science 8

Appiah Kwame Anthony, *The State and the Shaping of Identity*, The Tanner Lectures on Human Values delivered at Clare Hall, University of Cambridge (Tanner Humanities Center, University of Utah 2001)

Arendt Hannah, *The Human Condition* (University of Chicago Press 1958)

Arrington Robert L, 'On Respect' (1978) 12(1) The Journal of Value Inquiry 1

Ashworth Andrew, *Principles of Criminal Law* (3rd edn, OUP 1999)

Ashworth Andrew, 'Criminal Justice, Not Criminology?' in Mary Bosworth and Carolyn Hoyle (eds), *What Is Criminology?* (OUP 2011)

Bagnoli Carla, 'Respect and Membership in the Moral Community' (2007) 10(2) Ethical Theory and Moral Practice 113

Baldwin Robert, 'Why Rules Don't Work' (1990) 53(3) The Modern Law Review 321

Balint Peter, 'Respect Relationships in Diverse Societies' (2006) 12(1) Res Publica 35

Banks Cyndi, *Criminal Justice Ethics: Theory and Practice* (5th edn, SAGE 2019)

Bannister Jon and Kearns Ade, 'Tolerance, Respect and Civility amid Changing Cities' in Andrew Millie (ed), *Securing Respect: Behavioural Expectations and Anti-social behaviour in the UK* (Policy Press 2009)

Bannister Jon, Fyfe Nick, and Kearns Ade, 'Respectable or Respectful? (In)civility and the City' (2006) 43(5/6) Urban Studies 919

Barnett Adam, 'Britain's Supreme Court says targeting young black men for stop-and-search "benefits them"' *The Independent* (17 December 2015) <www.independent.co.uk/news/uk/crime/britain-s-supreme-court-says-targeting-young-black-men-for-stop-and-search-benefits-them-a6777651.html> accessed 1 August 2019

Bastow Simon, 'Payment by Results in the Prison System: Challenges of Calibrating Success and Failure' (London School of Economics and Political Science, British Politics and Policy Blog 2013) <http://blogs.lse.ac.uk/politicsandpolicy/payment-by-results-in-the-prison-system-challenges-of-calibrating-success-and-failure/> accessed 1 August 2019

BBC News, 'Stop and Search: Police Code of Conduct Launched' (BBC News 26 August 2014) <www.bbc.co.uk/news/uk-28923242> accessed 1 August 2019

Bejan Teresa M, *Mere Civility: Disagreement and the Limits of Toleration* (Harvard University Press 2017)

Benditt Theodore M, 'Why Respect Matters' (2008) 42(4) The Journal of Value Inquiry 487

Bennett Christopher, 'Review Essay: Actions, Institutions, and the Common Good' (2011) 30(2) Criminal Justice Ethics 205

Bennett Jamie, 'Review of Coretta Phillips, *The Multicultural Prison: Ethnicity, Masculinity, and Social Relations among Prisoners* (2009)' (2013) 17(3) Theoretical Criminology 422

Bennett Jamie, *The Working Lives of Prison Managers: Global Change, Local Culture and Individual Agency in the Late Modern Prison* (Palgrave Macmillan 2015)

Bennett Steven C, 'The Privacy and Procedural Due Process Rights of Hunger Striking Prisoners' (1983) 58(5) New York University Law Review 1157

Bennett Tony, Grossberg Lawrence, and Morris Meaghan (eds), *New Keywords: A Revised Vocabulary of Culture and Society* (Blackwell 2005)

Berg Mark T and DeLisi Matt, 'The Correctional Melting Pot: Race, Ethnicity, Citizenship, and Prison Violence' (2006) 34(6) Journal of Criminal Justice 631

Berger Joseph and Zelditch Jr Morris (eds), *Status, Power and Legitimacy: Strategies and Theories* (Transaction Publishers 1998)

Bird Colin, 'Status, Identity, and Respect' (2004) 32(2) Political Theory 207

Black Julia, 'Decentring Regulation: Understanding the Role of Regulation and Self-regulation in a "Post-Regulatory" World' (2001) 54(1) Current Legal Problems 103

Bodansky Eva and Conee Earl, 'Isolating Intrinsic Value' (1981) 41(1) Analysis 51

Boettcher James W, 'Respect, Recognition, and Public Reason' (2007) 33(2) Social Theory and Practice 223

Bosworth Mary, *Engendering Resistance: Agency and Power in Women's Prisons* (Ashgate 1999)

Bosworth Mary, 'Gender, Race, and Sexuality in Prison' in Barbara H Zaitzow and Jim Thomas (eds), *Women in Prison: Gender and Social Control* (Lynne Rienner Publishers 2003)

Bosworth Mary and Carrabine Eamonn, 'Reassessing Resistance: Race, Gender and Sexuality in Prison' (2001) 3(4) Punishment & Society 501

Bosworth Mary and Kaufman Emma, 'Gender and Punishment' in Jonathan Simon and Richard Sparks (eds), *The SAGE Handbook of Punishment and Society* (SAGE 2013)

Bottoms Anthony E, 'Interpersonal Violence and Social Order in Prisons' (1999) 26 Crime and Justice 205

Bottoms Anthony E, 'Theoretical Reflections on the Evaluations of a Penal Policy Initiative' in Lucia Zedner and Andrew Ashworth (eds), *Criminological Foundations of Penal Policy: Essays in Honour of Roger Hood* (OUP 2003)

Bottoms Anthony, 'The Relationship Between Theory and Empirical Observations in Criminology' in Roy D King and Emma Wincup (eds), *Doing Research on Crime and Justice* (2nd edn, OUP 2007)

Bottoms Anthony and Tankebe Justice, 'Beyond Procedural Justice: A Dialogic Approach to Legitimacy in Criminal Justice' (2012) 102(1) The Journal of Criminal Law and Criminology 119

Bourgois Philippe, *In Search of Respect: Selling Crack in El Barrio* (CUP 1995)

Bourgois Philippe, 'In Search of Masculinity: Violence, Respect and Sexuality among Puerto Rican Crack Dealers in East Harlem' (1996) 36(3) The British Journal of Criminology 412

Bowling Ben, 'There is Still Much to Do on Stop and Search' *Centre for Crime and Justice Studies* (7 May 2014) <www.crimeandjustice.org.uk/resources/there-much-still-do-stop-and-search> accessed 1 August 2019

Bowling Ben and Marks Estelle, 'The Rise and Fall of Suspicionless Searches' (2017) 28(1) King's Law Journal 62

Bowling Ben and Phillips Coretta, *Racism, Crime and Justice* (Longman 2002)

Bowling Ben and Phillips Coretta, 'Disproportionate and Discriminatory: Reviewing the Evidence on Police Stop and Search' (2007) 70(6) The Modern Law Review 936

Bowling Ben and Weber Leanne, 'Stop and Search in Global Context: An Overview' (2011) 21(4) Policing and Society 480

Boyd Richard, 'The Value of Civility?' (2006) 43(5–6) Urban Studies 863

Božovič Miran (ed), Jeremy Bentham, *The Panopticon Writings* (Verso 1995)

Bradford Ben, 'Voice, Neutrality and Respect: Use of Victim Support Services, Procedural Fairness and Confidence in the Criminal Justice System' (2011) 11(4) Criminology & Criminal Justice 345

Bradford Ben, 'Police and Social Identity: Procedural Justice, Inclusion and Cooperation between Police and Public' (2014) 24(1) Policing and Society 22

Bradford Ben, 'Unintended Consequences' in Rebekah Delsol and Michael Shiner (eds), *Stop and Search: The Anatomy of a Police Power* (Palgrave Macmillan 2015)

Bradford Ben, *Stop and Search and Police Legitimacy* (Routledge 2016)

Bradford Ben and Jackson Jonathan, 'Enabling and Constraining Police Power: On the Moral Regulation of Policing' Jonathan Jacobs and Jonathan Jackson (eds), *The Routledge Handbook of Criminal Justice Ethics* (Routledge 2016)

Bradford Ben and Loader Ian, 'Police, Crime and Order: The Case of Stop and Search' in Ben Bradford, Beatrice Jauregui, Ian Loader, and Jonny Steinberg (eds), *The SAGE Handbook of Global Policing* (SAGE 2016)

Bradford Ben, Jackson Jonathan, and Hough Mike, 'Police Futures and Legitimacy: Redefining Good Policing' in Jennifer M Brown (ed), *The Future of Policing* (Routledge 2014)

Bradford Ben, Jackson Jonathan, and Stanko Elizabeth A, 'Contact and Confidence: Revisiting the Impact of Public Encounters with the Police' (2009) 19(1) Policing and Society 20

Bradley Ben, 'Extrinsic Value' (1998) 91(2) Philosophical Studies 109

Braithwaite John, 'Rules and Principles: A Theory of Legal Certainty' (2002) 27 Australian Journal of Legal Philosophy 47

Braithwaite John and Pettit Philip, *Not Just Deserts: A Republican Theory of Criminal Justice* (Clarendon Press 1990)

Brangan Louise, 'Review of Jamie Bennett, *The Working Lives of Prison Managers: Global Change, Local Culture and Individual Agency in the Late Modern Prison* (2015)' (2017) 17(2) Criminology & Criminal Justice 226

Brison Susan J, 'The Theoretical Importance of Practice' in Ian Shapiro and Judith Wagner DeCew (eds), *Theory and Practice: NOMOS XXXVII*. Yearbook of The American Society for Political and Legal Philosophy (New York University Press 1995)

Brown Alyson, *English Society and the Prison: Time, Culture and Politics in the Development of the Modern Prison 1850–1920* (Boydell 2003)

Brown Linda Keller and Mussell Kay (eds), *Ethnic and Regional Foodways in the United States: The Performance of Group Identity* (University of Tennessee Press 1984)

Bruner Jerome S, *Acts of Meaning* (Harvard University Press 1990)

Burnett John, *Plenty and Want: A Social History of Food in England from 1815 to the Present Day* (Routledge 1989)

Burney Elizabeth, *Making People Behave: Anti-Social Behaviour, Politics and Policy* (Willan 2005)

Burns Robert P, *A Theory of the Trial* (Princeton University Press 1999)

Burns Robert P, 'The Distinctiveness of Trial Narrative' in RA Duff, Lindsay Farmer, Sandra Marshall, and Victor Tadros (eds), *The Trial on Trial (Volume 1): Truth and Due Process* (Hart 2004)

Bushe Gervase, 'Appreciative Inquiry: Theory and Critique' in David M Boje, Bernard Burnes, and John Hassard (eds), *The Routledge Companion to Organizational Change* (Routledge 2011)

Buss Sarah, 'Respect for Persons' (1999) 29(4) Canadian Journal of Philosophy 517

Butler Judith, *Excitable Speech: A Politics of the Performative* (Routledge 1997)

Butler Judith, *Undoing Gender* (Routledge 2004)

Butler Michelle, 'What are you Looking at? Prisoner Confrontations and the Search for Respect' (2008) 48(6) The British Journal of Criminology 856

Butler Michelle and Drake Deborah H, 'Reconsidering Respect: Its Role in Her Majesty's Prison Service' (2007) 46(2) The Howard Journal of Criminal Justice 115

Buttny Richard and Williams Princess L, 'Demanding Respect: The Uses of Reported Speech in Discursive Constructions of Interracial Contact' (2000) 11(1) Discourse & Society 109

Bybee Keith J, *How Civility Works* (Stanford University Press 2016)

Cahill Michael T, 'Punishment Pluralism' in Mark D White (ed), *Retributivism: Essays on Theory and Policy* (OUP 2011)

Calhoun Cheshire, 'The Virtue of Civility' (2000) 29(3) Philosophy & Public Affairs 251

Campbell Liz, Ashworth Andrew, and Redmayne Mike, *The Criminal Process* (5th edn, OUP 2019)

Carrabine Eamonn and Longhurst Brian, 'Gender and Prison Organisation: Some Comments on Masculinities and Prison Management' (1998) 37(2) The Howard Journal of Criminal Justice 161

Choongh Satnam, *Policing as Social Discipline* (Clarendon Press 1997)

Choongh Satnam, 'Policing the Dross: A Social Disciplinary Model of Policing' (1998) 38(4) The British Journal of Criminology 623

Clemmer Donald, *The Prison Community* (Christopher Publishing House 1940)

Coghlan Anne T, Preskill Hallie, and Catsambas Tessie Tzavaras, 'An Overview of Appreciative Inquiry in Evaluation' (2003) 100 New Directions for Evaluation 5

Cohen Howard S and Feldberg Michael, *Power and Restraint: The Moral Dimension of Police Work* (Praeger 1991)

Cohen Stanley, *Against Criminology* (Transaction Publishers 1988)

Cohen Stanley and Taylor Laurie, *Psychological Survival: The Experience of Long-Term Imprisonment* (Penguin 1972)

College of Policing, *Code of Ethics: A Code of Practice for the Principles and Standards of Professional Behaviour for the Policing Profession of England and Wales* (College of Policing 2014)

College of Policing, *Definition of a Fair and Effective Stop and Search Encounter* (College of Policing 2016)

College of Policing, *Stop and Search: Legal Basis* (College of Policing 2018) <www.app.college.police.uk/app-content/stop-and-search/legal/legal-basis> accessed 1 August 2019

Cooper Robert Alan, 'Ideas and their Execution: English Prison Reform' (1976) 10(1) Eighteenth-Century Studies 73

Coyle Andrew, *Understanding Prisons: Key Issues in Policy and Practice* (Open University Press 2005)

Coyle Andrew, *Humanity in Prison: Questions of Definition and Audit* (International Centre for Prison Studies 2014)

Coyle Michael J, *Talking Criminal Justice: Language and the Just Society* (Routledge 2013)

Cresswell Tim, *Place: A Short Introduction* (Blackwell 2004)

Crewe Ben, *The Prisoner Society: Power, Adaptation, and Social Life in an English Prison* (OUP 2009)

Crewe Ben, 'Depth, Weight, Tightness: Revisiting the Pains of Imprisonment' (2011) 13(5) Punishment & Society 509

Crewe Ben and Liebling Alison, 'Are Liberal-Humanitarian Penal Values and Practices Exceptional?' in Thomas Ugelvik and Jane Dullum (eds), *Penal Exceptionalism? Nordic Prison Policy and Practice* (Routledge 2011)

Crewe Ben, Liebling Alison, and Hulley Susie, 'Staff Culture, Use of Authority and Prisoner Quality of Life in Public and Private Sector Prisons' (2011) 44(1) Australian & New Zealand Journal of Criminology 94

Cross Maria, 'Prisons' in Maria Cross and Barbara MacDonald (eds), *Nutrition in Institutions* (Wiley-Blackwell 2009)

Dallmayr Fred R and McCarthy Thomas A (eds), *Understanding and Social Inquiry* (University of Notre Dame Press 1977)

Darwall Stephen L, 'Two Kinds of Respect' (1977) 88(1) Ethics 36

Darwall Stephen L, 'Respect and the Second-Person Standpoint' (2004) 78(2) Proceedings and Addresses of the American Philosophical Association 43

Darwall Stephen L, *The Second-Person Standpoint: Morality, Respect, and Accountability* (Harvard University Press 2006)

Davies Margaret, 'Exclusion and the Identity of Law' (2005) 5 Macquarie Law Journal 5

Davis Robert C, Mateu-Gelabert Pedro, and Miller Joel, 'Can Effective Policing Also Be Respectful? Two Examples in the South Bronx' (2005) 8(2) Police Quarterly 229

Day Mark, Hewson Alex, and Spiropoulos Charles, *Strangeways 25 Years' On: Achieving Fairness and Justice in our Prisons* (Prison Reform Trust 2015)

de Cremer David and Blader Steven L, 'Why do People Care About Procedural Fairness? The Importance of Belongingness in Responding and Attending to Procedures' (2006) 36(2) European Journal of Social Psychology 211

de Graaf Kaitlyn and Kilty Jennifer M, 'You Are What You Eat: Exploring the Relationship Between Women, Food, and Incarceration' (2016) 18(1) Punishment & Society 27 de Sousa Ronald, *The Rationality of Emotion* (MIT Press 1987)

Delsol Rebekah, 'Effectiveness' in Rebekah Delsol and Michael Shiner (eds), *Stop and Search: The Anatomy of a Police Power* (Palgrave Macmillan 2015)

Delsol Rebekah and Shiner Michael, 'Regulating Stop and Search: A Challenge for Police and Community Relations in England and Wales' (2006) 14(3) Critical Criminology 241

Delsol Rebekah and Shiner Michael (eds), *Stop and Search: The Anatomy of a Police Power* (Palgrave Macmillan 2015)

Denton Jr Robert E, 'The Rhetorical Functions of Slogans: Classifications and Characteristics' (1980) 28(2) Communication Quarterly 10

Department of Health in collaboration with Stroud Mike, *Guidelines for the Clinical Management of People Refusing Food in Immigration Removal Centres and Prisons* (Department of Health 2009)

Dillon Robin S, 'Respect and Care: Toward Moral Integration' (1992) 22(1) Canadian Journal of Philosophy 105

Dillon Robin S, 'Respect: A Philosophical Perspective' (2007) 38(2) Gruppendynamik und Organisationsberatung 201

Dillon Robin S, 'Respect' in Edward N Zalta (ed), *The Stanford Encyclopedia of Philosophy* (Stanford University 2018) <http://plato.stanford.edu/entries/respect/> accessed 1 August 2019

Dixon David, *Law in Policing: Legal Regulation and Police Practices* (OUP 1997)

Douglas Mary, *Purity and Danger: An Analysis of the Concepts of Pollution and Taboo* (Routledge and Kegan Paul 1966)

Douglas Mary, 'Deciphering a Meal' (1972) 101(1) Dædalus 61

Douglas Mary, *Implicit Meanings: Selected Essays in Anthropology* (Routledge 1975)

Drummond John J, 'Respect as a Moral Emotion: A Phenomenological Approach' (2006) 22(1) Husserl Studies 1

Dryzek John S, 'The Informal Logic of Institutional Design' in Robert E Goodin (ed), *The Theory of Institutional Design* (CUP 1996)

Du Cane Edmund F, *The Punishment and Prevention of Crime* (Macmillan 1885)

Dubber Markus, *The Police Power: Patriarchy and the Foundations of American Government* (Columbia University Press 2005)

Duff RA, 'Punishment, Dignity and Degradation' (2005) 25(1) Oxford Journal of Legal Studies 141

Duff RA, 'A Criminal Law for Citizens' (2010) 14(3) Theoretical Criminology 293

Duff RA, 'Responsibility, Citizenship, and Criminal Law' in RA Duff and Stuart P Green (eds), *Philosophical Foundations of Criminal Law* (OUP 2011)

Duff RA, 'Citizens (Even) in Prison' (2014) 43(1) Netherlands Journal of Legal Philosophy 3

Duff RA and Marshall Sandra, 'Benefits, Burdens and Responsibilities: Some Ethical Dimensions of Situational Crime Prevention' in Andrew von Hirsch, David Garland, and Alison Wakefield (eds), *Ethical and Social Perspectives on Situational Crime Prevention* (Hart 2000)

Durkheim Émile, *The Rules of Sociological Method* (1st American edn, Free Press 1982)

Dworkin Ronald, *Taking Rights Seriously* (Duckworth 1977)

Dzur Albert W, 'Participatory Innovation in Criminal Justice: Why, How, and How Far?' in Stephen Farrall, Barry Goldson, Ian Loader, and Anita Dockley (eds), *Justice and Penal Reform: Re-shaping the Penal Landscape* (Routledge 2016)

Dzur Albert W, Loader Ian, and Sparks Richard (eds), *Democratic Theory and Mass Incarceration* (OUP 2016)

Dzur Albert W, Loader Ian, and Sparks Richard, 'Punishment and Democratic Theory: Resources for a Better Penal Politics' in Albert W Dzur, Ian Loader, and Richard Sparks (eds), *Democratic Theory and Mass Incarceration* (OUP 2016)

Earle Rod and Phillips Coretta, 'Digesting Men? Ethnicity, Gender and Food: Perspectives from a "Prison Ethnography"' (2012) 16(2) Theoretical Criminology 141

Edwards John SA, Hartwell Heather J, and Schafheitle Joachim, 'Prison Foodservice in England' (2009) 20(4) Journal of Foodservice 157

Ellemers Naomi, Doosje Bertjan, and Spears Russell, 'Sources of Respect: The Effects of Being Liked by Ingroups and Outgroups' (2004) 34(2) European Journal of Social Psychology 155

Elliot Charles, *Locating the Energy for Change: An Introduction to Appreciative Inquiry* (International Institute for Sustainable Development 1999)

Emerson Richard M, 'Power-Dependence Relations' (1962) 27(1) American Sociological Review 31

Enggist Stefan, Møller Lars, Galea Gauden, and Udesen Caroline (eds), *Prisons and Health* (World Health Organization 2014)

Equality and Human Rights Commission, *Stop and Think: A Critical Review of Stop and Search Powers in England and Wales* (Equality and Human Rights Commission 2016)

Eskridge Jr William N, 'Gadamer/Statutory Interpretation' (1990) 90(3) Columbia Law Review 609

Espeland Wendy Nelson and Sauder Michael, 'Rankings and Reactivity: How Public Measures Recreate Social Worlds' (2007) 113(1) American Journal of Sociology 1

Espeland Wendy Nelson and Stevens Mitchell L, 'Commensuration as a Social Process' (1998) 24 Annual Review of Sociology 313

Fabre Cécile, *Whose Body is it Anyway? Justice and the Integrity of the Person* (OUP 2006)

Fabre Cécile and Miller David, 'Justice and Culture: Rawls, Sen, Nussbaum and O'Neill' (2003) 1(1) Political Studies Review 4

Farmer Lindsay, 'Disgust, Respect, and the Criminalization of the Offence' in Rowan Cruft, Matthew H Kramer, and Mark R Reiff (eds), *Crime, Punishment, and Responsibility: The Jurisprudence of Antony Duff* (OUP 2011)

Faulkner David, *Criminal Justice and Government at a Time of Austerity* (Criminal Justice Alliance 2010)

Feeley Malcolm M and Simon Jonathan, 'The New Penology: Notes on the Emerging Strategy of Corrections and its Implications' (1992) 30(4) Criminology 449

Fitzalan Howard Flora and Wakeling Helen, *Analytical Summary 2019: Prisoner and Staff Perceptions of Procedural Justice in English and Welsh Prisons* (Her Majesty's Prison & Probation Service 2019)

Fjellström Christina, 'Mealtime and Meal Patterns from a Cultural Perspective' (2004) 48(4) Scandinavian Journal of Nutrition 161

Flam Helena and King Debra (eds), *Emotions and Social Movements* (Routledge 2005)

Fraser Nancy, 'Rethinking Recognition' (2000) 3 New Left Review 107

Freeden Michael, *Liberal Languages: Ideological Imaginations and Twentieth-Century Progressive Thought* (Princeton University Press 2005)

Freiberg Arie, 'Affective Versus Effective Justice: Instrumentalism and Emotionalism in Criminal Justice' (2001) 3(2) Punishment & Society 265

Fricker Miranda, 'Can There Be Institutional Virtues?' in Tamar Szabó Gendler and John Hawthorne (eds), *Oxford Studies in Epistemology: Volume 3* (OUP 2010)

Gadamer Hans-Georg, *Truth and Method* (2nd rev edn, Continuum 2004)

Galeotti Anna E, 'Multicultural Claims and Equal Respect' (2010) 36(3/4) Philosophy & Social Criticism 441

Gardner John, 'Ashworth on Principles' in Lucia Zedner and Julian V Roberts (eds), *Principles and Values in Criminal Law and Criminal Justice: Essays in Honour of Andrew Ashworth* (OUP 2012)

Garfinkel Harold, 'Conditions of Successful Degradation Ceremonies' (1956) 61(5) American Journal of Sociology 420

Garland David, *Punishment and Modern Society* (Clarendon Press 1990)

Garland David, 'The Limits of the Sovereign State: Strategies of Crime Control in Contemporary Society' (1996) 36(4) The British Journal of Criminology 445

Garland David, *The Culture of Control: Crime and Social Order in Contemporary Society* (OUP 2001)

Garland David and Sparks Richard, 'Criminology, Social Theory and the Challenge of our Times' in David Garland and Richard Sparks (eds), *Criminology and Social Theory* (Clarendon Press 2000)

Garner Bryan A, *The Oxford Dictionary of American Usage and Style* (OUP 2000)

Garside Richard and Mills Helen, *UK Justice Policy Review: Volume 1, 6 May 2010 to 5 May 2011* (Centre for Crime and Justice Studies 2011)

Geertz Clifford, *The Interpretation of Cultures* (Basic Books 1973)

Gibson-Light Michael, 'Ramen Politics: Informal Money and Logics of Resistance in the Contemporary American Prison' (2018) 41(2) Qualitative Sociology 199

Gilroy Paul, *After Empire: Melancholia or Convivial Culture?* (Routledge 2004)

Godderis Rebecca, 'Dining in: The Symbolic Power of Food in Prison' (2006) 45(3) The Howard Journal of Criminal Justice 255

Goffman Erving, *The Presentation of Self in Everyday Life* (Social Sciences Research Centre, University of Edinburgh 1956)

Goffman Erving, *Asylums: Essays on the Social Situation of Mental Patients and Other Inmates* (Doubleday & Co 1961)

Goldhamer Herbert and Shils Edward A, 'Types of Power and Status' (1939) 45(2) American Journal of Sociology 171

Goldsmith Andrew, 'Taking Police Culture Seriously: Police Discretion and the Limits of Law' (1990) 1(2) Policing and Society 91

Goodin Robert E, 'Institutions and their Design' in Robert E Goodin (ed), *The Theory of Institutional Design* (CUP 1996)

Graham Hannah and White Rob, 'The Ethics of Innovation in Criminal Justice' in Jonathan Jacobs and Jonathan Jackson (eds), *The Routledge Handbook of Criminal Justice Ethics* (Routledge 2016)

Green Leslie, 'Two Worries about Respect for Persons' (2010) 120(2) Ethics 212

Green OH, 'Introduction' Special Issue on Respect for Persons (1982) 31 Tulane Studies in Philosophy 1

Gregor Mary J (ed), Immanuel Kant, *The Metaphysics of Morals* (CUP 2017)

Gregor Mary J and Timmermann Jens (eds), Immanuel Kant, *Groundwork of the Metaphysics of Morals* (CUP 2012)

Grill Kalle, 'Respect for What? Choices, Actual Preferences, and True Preferences' (2015) 41(4) Social Theory and Practice 692

Haggerty Kevin D, 'Displaced Expertise: Three Constraints on the Policy-relevance of Criminological Thought' (2004) 8(2) Theoretical Criminology 211

Hall Stuart, Critcher Charles, Jefferson Tony, Clarke John, and Roberts Brian, *Policing the Crisis: Mugging, the State and Law and Order* (2nd edn, Palgrave Macmillan 2013)

Hallsworth Michael, with Parker Simon and Rutter Jill, *Policy Making in the Real World: Evidence and Analysis* (Institute for Government 2011)

Halsey Mark, 'Risking Desistance: Respect and Responsibility in Custodial and Post-Release Contexts' in Pat Carlen (ed), *Imaginary Penalities* (Willan 2008)

Hardin Russell, 'Institutional Morality' in Robert E Goodin (ed), *The Theory of Institutional Design* (CUP 1996)

Hardin Russell, *Trust* (Polity 2006)

Hardy Robert (convenor), *Respect in Prison.* Transcript of a Conference held at Bishop Grossteste College, Lincoln (Bishop of Lincoln (Robert Hardy) 1991)

Hargreaves Jodie, Husband Hannah, and Linehan Chris, *Police Powers and Procedures in England and Wales*, year ending 31st March 2017 (2nd edn, Home Office 2017)

Hart HLA, *Punishment and Responsibility: Essays in the Philosophy of Law* (Clarendon Press 1968)

Haslanger Sally, *Good Food: Ethics and Politics of Food* (24.03, Massachusetts Institute of Technology: OpenCourseWare 2017) <http://ocw.mit.edu> accessed 1 August 2019

Hegtvedt Karen A, 'Justice Frameworks' in Peter J Burke (ed), *Contemporary Social Psychological Theories* (2nd edn, Stanford University Press 2006)

Helm Bennett W, *Communities of Respect: Grounding Responsibility, Authority, and Dignity* (OUP 2017)

Henry Alistair, 'Policing and Ethnic Minorities' in Alistair Henry and David J Smith (eds), *Transformations of Policing* (Ashgate 2007)

Her Majesty's Chief Inspector of Prisons for England and Wales, *Annual Report 2011–12* (The Stationery Office 2012)

Her Majesty's Chief Inspector of Prisons for England and Wales, *Annual Report 2012–13* (The Stationery Office 2013)

Her Majesty's Chief Inspector of Prisons for England and Wales, *Annual Report 2015–16* (The Stationery Office 2016)

Her Majesty's Chief Inspector of Prisons for England and Wales, *Annual Report 2017–18* (The Stationery Office 2018)

Her Majesty's Chief Inspector of Prisons for England and Wales, *Report on an Unannounced Inspection of HMP Grendon* (Her Majesty's Inspectorate of Prisons for England and Wales 2013)

Her Majesty's Chief Inspector of Prisons for England and Wales, *Report on an Unannounced Inspection of HMP Birmingham* (Her Majesty's Inspectorate of Prisons for England and Wales 2014)

Her Majesty's Chief Inspector of Prisons for England and Wales, *Report on an Unannounced Inspection of HMP Northumberland* (Her Majesty's Inspectorate of Prisons for England and Wales 2014)

Her Majesty's Chief Inspector of Prisons for England and Wales, *Report on an Announced Inspection of HMP Oakwood* (Her Majesty's Inspectorate of Prisons for England and Wales 2014)

Her Majesty's Chief Inspector of Prisons for England and Wales, *Report on an Announced Inspection of HMP Elmley* (Her Majesty's Inspectorate of Prisons for England and Wales 2015)

Her Majesty's Chief Inspector of Prisons for England and Wales, *Report on an Unannounced Inspection of HMP Lowdham Grange* (Her Majesty's Inspectorate of Prisons for England and Wales 2015)

Her Majesty's Chief Inspector of Prisons for England and Wales, *Report on an Unannounced Inspection of HMP and YOI Bronzefield* (Her Majesty's Inspectorate of Prisons for England and Wales 2015)

Her Majesty's Chief Inspector of Prisons for England and Wales, *Report on an Unannounced Inspection of HMP Swaleside* (Her Majesty's Inspectorate of Prisons for England and Wales 2016)

Her Majesty's Chief Inspector of Prisons for England and Wales, *Report on an Unannounced Inspection of HMP Birmingham* (Her Majesty's Inspectorate of Prisons for England and Wales 2017)

Her Majesty's Chief Inspector of Prisons for England and Wales, *Report on an Unannounced Inspection of HMP Liverpool* (Her Majesty's Inspectorate of Prisons for England and Wales 2017)

Her Majesty's Inspectorate of Constabulary, *Stop and Search Powers: Are the Police Using Them Effectively and Fairly?* (Her Majesty's Inspectorate of Constabulary 2013)

Her Majesty's Inspectorate of Constabulary, *2017 PEEL Assessment* (Her Majesty's Inspectorate of Constabulary 2017)

Her Majesty's Inspectorate of Constabulary, *PEEL: Police Legitimacy 2017. A National Overview* (Her Majesty's Inspectorate of Constabulary 2017)

Her Majesty's Inspectorate of Prisons for England and Wales and Her Majesty's Inspectorate of Constabulary, *Expectations for Police Custody: Criteria for Assessing the Treatment of and Conditions for Detainees in Police Custody* (Her Majesty's Inspectorate of Prisons for England and Wales and Her Majesty's Inspectorate of Constabulary 2016)

Her Majesty's Inspectorate of Prisons for England and Wales, *Parallel Worlds: A Thematic Review of Race Relations in Prisons* (Her Majesty's Inspectorate of Prisons for England and Wales 2005)

Her Majesty's Inspectorate of Prisons for England and Wales, *Changing Patterns of Substance Misuse in Adult Prisons and Service Responses* (Her Majesty's Inspectorate of Prisons for England and Wales 2015)

Her Majesty's Inspectorate of Prisons for England and Wales, *Life in Prison: Food* (Her Majesty's Inspectorate of Prisons for England and Wales 2016)

Her Majesty's Inspectorate of Prisons for England and Wales, *Urgent Notification: HMP Birmingham* (Her Majesty's Inspectorate of Prisons for England and Wales 16 August 2018)

Her Majesty's Prison and Probation Service, *Annual Report and Accounts 2017–18* (HC 1175, The Stationery Office 2018)

Her Majesty's Prison and Probation Service, *Equality Objectives* <https://www.gov.uk/government/organisations/her-majestys-prison-and-probation-service/about/equality-and-diversity> accessed 1 August 2019

Her Majesty's Prison and Probation Service, *Prison Service Instructions (PSIs)* <https://www.justice.gov.uk/offenders/psis> accessed 1 August 2019

Her Majesty's Prison and Probation Service, *Prison Service Orders (PSOs)* <http://www.justice.gov.uk/offenders/psos> accessed 1 August 2019

Her Majesty's Prison Service, *Competency and Qualities Framework* (Her Majesty's Prison Service undated)

Herman Barbara, *Moral Literacy* (Harvard University Press 2007)

Heyd David, 'Supererogation' in Edward N Zalta (ed), *The Stanford Encyclopedia of Philosophy* (Stanford University 2016) <http://plato.stanford.edu/entries/supererogation/> accessed 1 August 2019

Higginbotham Peter, *The Prison Cookbook* (The History Press 2010)

Hildreth John Angus D, Moore Don A, and Blader Steven L, 'Revisiting the Instrumentality of Voice: Having Voice in the Process Makes People Think They Will Get What They Want' (2014) 27(2) Social Justice Research 209

Hill Jr Thomas E, *Respect, Pluralism, and Justice: Kantian Perspectives* (OUP 2000)

Hinde RSE, *The British Penal System 1773–1950* (Duckworth 1951)

Hinton Timothy, 'Must Egalitarians Choose Between Fairness and Respect?' (2001) 30(1) Philosophy & Public Affairs 72

Home Office, *Regulations for Prisons in England and Wales issued by the Secretary of State for the Home Department* (Shaw and Sons 1840)

Home Office, *Prison Disturbances April 1990: Report of an Inquiry by The Rt Hon Lord Justice Woolf (Parts I and II) and His Honour Judge Stephen Tumim (Part II)* (Cm 1456, The Stationery Office 1991)

Home Office (Respect Task Force), *Respect Action Plan* (Home Office/The National Archives 2006)

Home Office, *A Consultation on Police Powers of Stop and Search* (Home Office 2013)

Home Office, *Best Use of Stop and Search Scheme* (Home Office 2014)

Home Office, *Police Powers of Stop and Search: Summary of Consultation Responses and Conclusions* (Home Office 2014)

Home Office, *Code of Practice for the Exercise by Police Officers of Statutory Powers of Stop and Search and Police Officers and Police Staff of Requirements to Record Public Encounters: Police and Criminal Evidence Act 1984* Code A (The Stationery Office 2009)

Home Office, *Revised Code of Practice for the Exercise by Police Officers of Statutory Powers of Stop and Search and Police Officers and Police Staff of Requirements to Record Public Encounters: Police and Criminal Evidence Act 1984 Code A* (The Stationery Office 2014)

Home Office, *Revised Code of Practice for the Detention, Treatment and Questioning of Persons by Police Officers: Police and Criminal Evidence Act 1984 Code C* (The Stationery Office 2018)

Honneth Axel, *The Struggle for Recognition: The Moral Grammar of Social Conflicts* (Polity 1995)

Honneth Axel, *Disrespect: The Normative Foundations of Critical Theory* (Polity 2007)

Hood Roger, 'Criminology and Penal Change: A Case Study of the Nature and Impact of Some Recent Advice to Governments' in Roger Hood (ed), *Crime, Criminology and Public Policy: Essays in Honour of Sir Leon Radzinowicz* (Heinemann Educational 1974)

Hough Mike, 'Procedural Justice and Professional Policing in Times of Austerity' (2013) 13(2) Criminology & Criminal Justice 181

Hough Mike, Jackson Jonathan, Bradford Ben, Myhill Andy, and Quinton Paul, 'Procedural Justice, Trust, and Institutional Legitimacy' (2010) 4(3) Policing 203

House of Commons Home Affairs Committee, *The Macpherson Report—Ten Years On*. Twelfth Report of Session 2008–09 (HC 427, The Stationery Office 2009)

House of Commons Justice Committee, *Written Evidence: Role of the Prison Officer.* Memorandum submitted by the Institute of Criminology, University of Cambridge (Justice Committee Publications 2009)

House of Commons Justice Committee, *Written Evidence: Role of the Prison Officer.* Memorandum submitted by Helen Arnold, Institute of Criminology, University of Cambridge (Justice Committee Publications 2009)

House of Commons Justice Committee, *Written Evidence: Role of the Prison Officer.* Memorandum submitted by the Ministry of Justice (Justice Committee Publications 2009)

House of Commons Justice Committee, *Cutting Crime: The Case for Justice Reinvestment*. First Report of Session 2009–10, Volume 1 (HC 94-I, The Stationery Office 2010)

House of Commons Justice Committee, *Prisons: Planning and Policies.* Ninth Report of Session 2014–15 (HC 309, The Stationery Office 2015)

House of Commons, *BAME Communities: Stop and Search* (HC Deb 23 May 2018, vol 641, col 357WH)

Howard John, *The State of the Prisons in England and Wales, with Preliminary Observations, and an Account of Some Foreign Prisons* (Thoemmes Press 1777)

Howard Michael, *Speech to the Conservative Party Conference* (Bodleian Library: Conservative Party Archive 6 October 1993)

Hudson Barbara, 'Review of Mary Bosworth, *Engendering Resistance: Agency and Power in Women's Prisons* (1999)' (2002) 11(1) Critical Criminology 83

Hudson Richard A, *Language Networks: The New Word Grammar* (OUP 2007)

Hudson Stephen D, 'The Nature of Respect' (1980) 6(1) Social Theory and Practice 69

Hulley Susie, Liebling Alison, and Crewe Ben, 'Respect in Prisons: Prisoners' Experiences of Respect in Public and Private Sector Prisons' (2012) 12(1) Criminology & Criminal Justice 3

Hynds Lyn and Murphy Kristina, 'Public Satisfaction with Police: Using Procedural Justice to Improve Police Legitimacy' (2007) 40(1) Australian & New Zealand Journal of Criminology 27

Ignatieff Michael, 'State, Civil Society, and Total Institutions: A Critique of Recent Social Histories of Punishment' (1981) 3 Crime and Justice 153

Independent Monitoring Board, *Annual Report of the Independent Monitoring Board at HMP Leicester 2015–2016* (Independent Monitoring Board 2016)

Independent Police Commission, *Policing for a Better Britain* (Independent Police Commission 2013)

Iser Mattias, 'Recognition' in Edward N Zalta (ed), *The Stanford Encyclopedia of Philosophy* (Stanford University 2019) <http://plato.stanford.edu/entries/recognition/> accessed 1 August 2019

Jackson Jonathan and Bradford Ben, *Police Legitimacy: A Conceptual Review* (National Policing Improvement Agency 2010)

Jackson Jonathan, Bradford Ben, Hough Mike, Myhill Andy, Quinton Paul, and Tyler Tom R, 'Why do People Comply with the Law? Legitimacy and the Influence of Legal Institutions' (2012) 52(6) The British Journal of Criminology 1051

Jacobs Jonathan, 'Criminal Justice and the Liberal Polity' (2011) 30(2) Criminal Justice Ethics 173

Jacobs Jonathan, 'The Liberal Polity, Criminal Sanction, and Civil Society' (2013) 32(3) Criminal Justice Ethics 231

Jacobs Jonathan and Jackson Jonathan (eds), *The Routledge Handbook of Criminal Justice Ethics* (Routledge 2016)

Jacobs Jonathan and Jackson Jonathan, 'Editors' Preface' in Jonathan Jacobs and Jonathan Jackson (eds), *The Routledge Handbook of Criminal Justice Ethics* (Routledge 2016)

Jameson Nicki and Allison Eric, *Strangeways 1990: A Serious Disturbance* (Larkin Publications 1995)

Jenkins David, 'Respect in Prison' in Robert Hardy (convenor), *Respect in Prison.* Transcript of a conference held at Bishop Grosseteste College, Lincoln (Bishop of Lincoln (Robert Hardy) 1991)

Johnsen Berit, Granheim Per Kristian, and Helgesen Janne, 'Exceptional Prison Conditions and the Quality of Prison Life: Prison Size and Prison Culture in Norwegian Closed Prisons' (2011) 8(6) European Journal of Criminology 515

Johnson James, 'Why Respect Culture?' (2000) 44(3) American Journal of Political Science 405

Johnson Martyn, as told to Sam Rowe, 'No One has Any Respect for Police Officers Anymore' *The Telegraph* (19 November 2014)

Johnson Valerie J, *Diet in Workhouses and Prisons 1835–1895* (Garland 1985)

Kagan Shelly, 'Rethinking Intrinsic Value' (1998) 2(4) The Journal of Ethics 277

Kant Immanuel, *Grundlegung zur Metaphysik der Sitten* (Johann Friedrich Hartknoch 1785)

Kant Immanuel, *Die Metaphysik der Sitten* (Friedrich Nicolovius 1798–1803)

Katzer Matthias, 'The Basis of Universal Liberal Principles in Nussbaum's Political Philosophy' (2010) 2(2) Public Reason 60

Kaufman Emma, *Punish and Expel: Border Control, Nationalism, and the New Purpose of the Prison* (OUP 2015)

Keane John, *Violence and Democracy* (CUP 2004)

Keeling Peter, *No Respect: Young BAME Men, The Police and Stop and Search* (Criminal Justice Alliance 2017)

Kemper Theodore D, *Status, Power and Ritual Interaction: A Relational Reading of Durkheim, Goffman and Collins* (Routledge 2011)

Klikauer Thomas, *Managerialism: A Critique of an Ideology* (Palgrave Macmillan 2013)

Klikauer Thomas, 'What is Managerialism?' (2015) 41(7–8) Critical Sociology 1103

Kuhn Timothy R and Putnam Linda L, 'Discourse and Communication' in Paul S Adler, Paul du Gay, Glenn Morgan, and Michael Reed (eds), *The Oxford Handbook of Sociology, Social Theory, and Organization Studies: Contemporary Currents* (OUP 2014)

Kymlicka Will, *Multicultural Citizenship: A Liberal Theory of Minority Rights* (Clarendon Press 1995)

Lacey Nicola, 'Introduction: Making Sense of Criminal Justice' in Nicola Lacey (ed), *A Reader on Criminal Justice* (OUP 1994)

Lacey Nicola, 'Criminalization as Regulation: The Role of Criminal Law' in Christine Parker, Colin Scott, Nicola Lacey, and John Braithwaite (eds), *Regulating Law* (OUP 2004)

Lacey Nicola, *The Prisoners' Dilemma: Political Economy and Punishment in Contemporary Democracies* (CUP 2008)

Lacey Nicola, 'Criminal Justice' in Robert E Goodin, Philip Pettit, and Thomas W Pogge (eds), *A Companion to Contemporary Political Philosophy* (2nd edn, Wiley-Blackwell 2012)

Lacey Nicola and Pickard Hanna, 'To Blame or to Forgive? Reconciling Punishment and Forgiveness in Criminal Justice' (2015) 35(4) Oxford Journal of Legal Studies 665

Lægaard Sune, 'What Does "Respect for Difference" Mean?' in Peter Balint and Sophie Guérard de Latour (eds), *Liberal Multiculturalism and the Fair Terms of Integration* (Palgrave Macmillan 2013)

Lægaard Sune, 'Attitudinal Analyses of Toleration and Respect and the Problem of Institutional Applicability' (2015) 23(4) European Journal of Philosophy 1064

Lammy David, *Open Letter to the Prime Minister* (7 September 2017) <https://assets.publishing.service.gov.uk/government/uploads/system/uploads/attachment_data/file/643002/david-lammy-open-letter-to-prime-minister.pdf> accessed 1 August 2019

Lammy David, *The Lammy Review: An Independent Review into the Treatment of, and Outcomes for, Black, Asian and Minority Ethnic Individuals in the Criminal Justice System* (Ministry of Justice 2017)

Laursen Julie and Laws Ben, 'Honour and Respect in Danish Prisons: Contesting "Cognitive Distortions" in Cognitive-Behavioural Programmes' (2017) 19(1) Punishment & Society 74

Layder Derek, *New Strategies in Social Research: An Introduction and Guide* (Polity 1993)

Layder Derek, *Sociological Practice: Linking Theory and Social Research* (SAGE 1998)

Lea John, 'The Macpherson Report and the Question of Institutional Racism' (2000) 39(3) The Howard Journal of Criminal Justice 219

Leishman Frank, Loveday Barry, and Savage Stephen P, *Core Issues in Policing* (2nd edn, Longman 2000)

Lempert Lora Bex, *Women Doing Life: Gender, Punishment and the Struggle for Identity* (New York University Press 2016)

Lennon Genevieve and Murray Kath, 'Under-regulated and Unaccountable? Explaining Variation in Stop and Search Rates in Scotland, England and Wales' (2018) 28(2) Policing and Society 157

Lerman Amy E and Weaver Vesla, 'Staying Out of Sight? Concentrated Policing and Local Political Action' (2014) 651(1) The ANNALS of the American Academy of Political and Social Science 202

Liebling Alison, *Prisons and their Moral Performance: A Study of Values, Quality, and Prison Life* (OUP 2004)

Liebling Alison, 'Prisons in Transition' (2006) 29(5) International Journal of Law and Psychiatry 422

Liebling Alison, 'Perrie Lecture: The Cost to Prison Legitimacy of Cuts' (2011) 198 Prison Service Journal 3

Liebling Alison, 'Why Prison Culture Matters' in James M Byrne, Donald Hummer, and Faye S Taxman (eds), *The Culture of Prison Violence* (Pearson 2008)

Liebling Alison, *Prisons Research: Measuring the Quality of Prison Life*. Impact Case Study prepared for the Research Excellence Framework (Research Excellence Framework 2014)

Liebling Alison and Crewe Ben, 'Prisons Beyond the New Penology: The Shifting Moral Foundations of Prison Management' in Jonathan Simon and Richard Sparks (eds), *The SAGE Handbook of Punishment and Society* (SAGE 2013)

Liebling Alison, Crewe Ben, and Hulley Susie, 'Values and Practices in Public and Private Sector Prisons: A Summary of Key Findings from an Evaluation' (2011) 196 Prison Service Journal 55

Liebling Alison, Hulley Susie, and Crewe Ben, 'Conceptualising and Measuring the Quality of Prison Life' in David Gadd, Susanne Karstedt, and Steven F Messner (eds), *The SAGE Handbook of Criminological Research Methods* (SAGE 2011)

Lind E Allan and Tyler Tom R, *The Social Psychology of Procedural Justice* (Plenum 1988)

Lippert-Rasmussen Kasper, 'Against Self-Ownership: There Are No Fact-Insensitive Ownership Rights over One's Body' (2008) 36(1) Philosophy & Public Affairs 86

Lippke Richard L, *Rethinking Imprisonment* (OUP 2007)

List Christian and Pettit Philip, *Group Agency: The Possibility, Design, and Status of Corporate Agents* (OUP 2011)

Loader Ian, 'Policing and the Social: Questions of Symbolic Power' (1997) 48(1) The British Journal of Sociology 1

Loader Ian, 'Policing, Recognition, and Belonging' (2006) 605(1) The ANNALS of the American Academy of Political and Social Science 201

Loader Ian, 'Fall of the "Platonic Guardians": Liberalism, Criminology and Political Responses to Crime in England and Wales' (2006) 46(4) The British Journal of Criminology 561

Loader Ian, 'For Penal Moderation: Notes Towards a Public Philosophy of Punishment' (2010) 14(3) Theoretical Criminology 349

Loader Ian, 'Why Do the Police Matter? Beyond the Myth of Crime-Fighting' in Jennifer M Brown (ed), *The Future of Policing* (Routledge 2014)

Loader Ian, 'In Search of Civic Policing: Recasting the "Peelian" Principles' (2016) 10(3) Criminal Law and Philosophy 427

Loader Ian and Sparks Richard, *Public Criminology?* (Routledge 2010)

Loader Ian and Walker Neil, *Civilizing Security* (CUP 2007)

Loader Ian and Zedner Lucia, 'Review Essay: Police Beyond Law?' (2007) 10(1) New Criminal Law Review 142

Loftus Bethan, *Police Culture in a Changing World* (OUP 2009)

Lopez Theresa, Zamzow Jennifer, Gill Michael, and Nichols Shaun, 'Side Constraints and the Structure of Commonsense Ethics' (2009) 23(1) Philosophical Perspectives 305

Loucks Nancy, *Prison Rules: A Working Guide* (4th ed, Prison Reform Trust 2000)

Lucas Jeffrey W and Baxter Amy R, 'Power, Influence, and Diversity in Organisations' (2012) 639(1) The ANNALS of the American Academy of Political and Social Science 49

Lupton Deborah, *Food, the Body and the Self* (SAGE 1996)

Lustgarten Laurence, 'The Future of Stop and Search' [2002] Criminal Law Review 603

Lynch Mona, *Sunbelt Justice: Arizona and the Transformation of American Punishment* (Stanford University Press 2009)

Macpherson Sir William, *Report of the Stephen Lawrence Inquiry* (Cm 4262-I, Home Office 1999)

Malpas Jeff, 'Hans-Georg Gadamer' in Edward N Zalta (ed), *The Stanford Encyclopedia of Philosophy* (Stanford University 2018) <http://plato.stanford.edu/entries/gadamer/> accessed 1 August 2019

Margalit Avishai, *The Decent Society* (Harvard University Press 1996)

Marks Monique and Sklansky David (eds), *Police Reform from the Bottom Up: Officers and their Unions as Agents of Change* (Routledge 2011)

Marshall David, 'Food as Ritual, Routine or Convention' (2005) 8(1) Consumption, Markets & Culture 69

Marshall David and Bell Rick, 'Meal Construction: Exploring the Relationship Between Eating Occasion and Location' (2003) 14(1) Food Quality and Preference 53

Mastrofski Stephen D, Snipes Jeffrey B, and Supina Anne E, 'Compliance on Demand: The Public's Response to Specific Police Requests' (1996) 33(3) Journal of Research in Crime and Delinquency 269

Mathiesen Thomas, 'The Sociology of Prisons: Problems for Future Research' (1966) 17(4) The British Journal of Sociology 360

Mazerolle Lorraine, Bennett Sarah, Antrobus Emma, and Eggins Elizabeth, 'Procedural Justice, Routine Encounters and Perceptions of Police: Main Findings from the Queensland Community Engagement Trial (QCET)' (2012) 8(4) Journal of Experimental Criminology 343

Mazerolle Lorraine, Bennett Sarah, Davis Jacqueline, Sargeant Elise, and Manning Matthew, *Legitimacy in Policing: A Systematic Review* (The Campbell Collaboration 2013)

Mazerolle Lorraine, Sargeant Elise, Cherney Adrian, Bennett Sarah, Murphy Kristina, Antrobus Emma, and Martin Peter, *Procedural Justice and Legitimacy in Policing* (Springer 2014)

Mazerolle Lorraine and Terrill William, 'Making Every Police-Citizen Interaction Count: The Challenges of Building a Better Cop' (2018) 17(1) Criminology & Public Policy 89

McBarnett Doreen J, *Conviction: Law, the State and the Construction of Justice* (Macmillan 1981)

McCandless Rhydian, Feist Andy, Allan James, and Morgan Nick, *Do Initiatives Involving Substantial Increases in Stop and Search Reduce Crime? Assessing the Impact of Operation BLUNT 2* (Home Office 2016)

McDermott Kathleen and King Roy D, 'A Fresh Start: The Enhancement of Prison Regimes' (1989) 28(3) The Howard Journal of Criminal Justice 161

Mennicken Andrea, '"Too Big to Fail and Too Big to Succeed:" Accounting and Privatisation in the Prison Service of England and Wales' (2013) 29(2) Financial Accountability & Management 206

Mennicken Andrea, 'Accounting for Values in Prison Privatization' in Susanna Alexius and Kristina Tamm Hallström (eds), *Configuring Value Conflicts in Markets* (Edward Elgar 2014)

Mennicken Andrea, 'The Quantification of Decency' transcript of presentation at *Moral Economies, Economic Moralities*, University of California, Berkeley (Society for the Advancement of Socio-Economics 2016)

Metropolitan Police, *Communities, Equalities and People Committee* (Metropolitan Police 2 September 2010)

Metropolitan Police, *Stop and Search of People of Different Gender to the Searching Officer* (Metropolitan Police 2016)

Metropolitan Police, *Information Pack: Chief Superintendent Selection Process* (Metropolitan Police 2017)

Middleton David, 'Introduction' Special Issue on Respect (2006) 12(1) Res Publica 1

Mill John Stuart, *On Liberty* (JW Parker and Son 1859)

Miller Joel, Bland Nick, and Quinton Paul, *The Impact of Stops and Searches on Crime and the Community.* Police Research Series Paper 127 (Home Office 2000)

Miller Peter, 'Accounting and Objectivity: The Invention of Calculating Selves and Calculable Spaces' (1992) 9(1/2) Annals of Scholarship 61

Miller Peter, 'Governing by Numbers: Why Calculative Practices Matter' (2001) 68(2) Social Research 379

Miller Seumas, 'Moral Rights and the Institution of the Police' in Tom Campbell and Seumas Miller (eds), *Human Rights and the Moral Responsibilities of Corporate and Public Sector Organisations* (Kluwer Academic 2004)

Miller Seumas, *The Moral Foundations of Social Institutions* (CUP 2010)

Miller Seumas, 'Political Theory, Institutional Purpose and Policing' in Ben Bradford, Beatrice Jauregui, Ian Loader, and Jonny Steinberg (eds), *The SAGE Handbook of Global Policing* (SAGE 2016)

Millie Andrew (ed), *Securing Respect: Behavioural Expectations and Anti-Social Behaviour in the UK* (Policy Press 2009)

Millie Andrew, *Philosophical Criminology* (Policy Press 2016)

Millie Andrew and Bullock Karen, 'Policing in a Time of Contraction and Constraint: Re-imagining the Role and Function of Contemporary Policing' (2013) 13(2) Criminology & Criminal Justice 133
Mills Sara, *Discourse: The New Critical Idiom* (Routledge 2004)
Ministry of Justice, *Breaking the Cycle: Effective Punishment, Rehabilitation and Sentencing of Offenders* (Cm 7972, The Stationery Office 2010)
Ministry of Justice, *Green Paper Evidence Report. Breaking the Cycle: Effective Punishment, Rehabilitation and Sentencing of Offenders* (Ministry of Justice 2010)
Ministry of Justice, *Her Majesty's Prison and Probation Service Annual Digest 2017–18* (Ministry of Justice 2018)
Ministry of Justice and Her Majesty's Prison and Probation Service, *Women's Policy Framework* (Ministry of Justice and Her Majesty's Prison & Probation Service 2018)
Ministry of Justice, Her Majesty's Prison and Probation Service, and Her Majesty's Prison Service, 'Birmingham Prison Contract Ended' (Ministry of Justice, Her Majesty's Prison and Probation Service, and Her Majesty's Prison Service 1 April 2018) <https://www.gov.uk/government/news/birmingham-prison-contract-ended> accessed 1 August 2019
Mintz Sidney W and du Bois Christine M, 'The Anthropology of Food and Eating' (2002) 31 Annual Review of Anthropology 99
Monaghan Jake, 'The Special Moral Obligations of Law Enforcement' (2017) 25(2) The Journal of Political Philosophy 218
Moore George E, *Principia Ethica* (CUP 1903)
Moran Dominique, '"Doing time" in Carceral Space: Timespace and Carceral Geography' (2012) 94(4) Geografiska Annaler: Series B, Human Geography 305
Moran Dominique, *Carceral Geography: Spaces and Practices of Incarceration* (Ashgate 2015)
Moran Dominique and Jewkes Yvonne, 'Linking the Carceral and the Punitive State: A Review of Research on Prison Architecture, Design, Technology and the Lived Experience of Carceral Space' (2015/2) no 702–703 Annals de géographie 163
Morgan Rod, 'Imprisonment: Current Concerns and a Brief History Since 1945' in Mike Maguire, Rod Morgan, and Robert Reiner (eds), *The Oxford Handbook of Criminology* (2nd edn, OUP 1997)
Morris Mark, 'The UK Prison Service Close Supervision Centres' in David Jones (ed), *Humane Prisons* (Radcliffe 2006)
Murcott Anne, 'The Cultural Significance of Food and Eating' (1982) 41(2) Proceedings of the Nutrition Society 203
Murray Kath and Harkin Diarmaid, 'Policing in Cool and Hot Climates: Legitimacy, Power and the Rise and Fall of Mass Stop and Search in Scotland' (2017) 57(4) The British Journal of Criminology 885

Narveson Jan (ed), *Respecting Persons in Theory and Practice: Essays on Moral and Political Philosophy* (Rowman & Littlefield 2002)

Narveson Jan, 'Race, Social Identity, Human Dignity: Respect for Individuals' (2000) 16 Social Philosophy Today 159

National Audit Office, *Serving Time: Prisoner Diet and Exercise* (HC 939, The Stationery Office 2006)

National Offender Management Service, *Adult Safeguarding in Prison* (PSI 16/2015, National Offender Management Service 2015)

National Offender Management Service, *Annual Report and Accounts 2012–2013* (National Offender Management Service 2013)

National Offender Management Service, *Annual Report and Accounts 2015–2016* (National Offender Management Service 2016)

National Offender Management Service, *Annual Report and Accounts 2016–2017* (National Offender Management Service 2017)

National Offender Management Service, *Business Plan 2014–2015* (National Offender Management Service 2014)

National Offender Management Service, *Catering Operating Manual: Meals for Prisoners in Custody at Annex B of PSI 44/2010 on Catering: Meals for Prisoners* (National Offender Management Service 2010)

National Offender Management Service, *Catering: Meals for Prisoners* (PSI 44/2010, National Offender Management Service 2010)

National Offender Management Service, *Ensuring Equality* (PSI 32/2011, National Offender Management Service 2011)

National Offender Management Service, *Equality of Treatment for Employees* (PSI 33/2010, National Offender Management Service 2011)

National Offender Management Service, *Faith and Pastoral Care of Prisoners* (PSI 05/2016, National Offender Management Service 2016)

National Offender Management Service, *Freedom of Information Request, Reference 77329* (National Offender Management Service August 2012)

National Offender Management Service, *Freedom of Information Request, Reference 92064* (National Offender Management Service July 2014)

National Offender Management Service, *Freedom of Information Request, Reference 96015* (National Offender Management Service February 2015)

National Offender Management Service, *Incentives and Earned Privileges* (PSI 30/2013, National Offender Management Service 2013)

National Offender Management Service, *Management of Prisoners at Risk of Harm to Self, to Others or from Others (Safer Custody)* (PSI 64/2011 (revised 2013), National Offender Management Service 2013)

National Offender Management Service, *National Framework: Agreement for Services Commissioned from Public Sector Prisons in England from 2015* (National Offender Management Service 2015)

National Offender Management Service, *Race Review 2008. Implementing Race Equality in Prisons: Five Years On* (National Offender Management Service 2008)

National Offender Management Service, *Women Prisoners* (PSO No 4800, Issue No 297, National Offender Management Service 2008)

Nedelsky Jennifer, 'Reconceiving Autonomy: Sources, Thoughts and Possibilities' (1989) 1(1) Yale Journal of Law and Feminism 7

Neufeld Blain, 'Civic Respect, Political Liberalism, and Non-Liberal Societies' (2005) 4(3) Politics, Philosophy & Economics 275

Nolan Daniel, 'Consequentialism and Side Constraints' (2009) 6(1) Journal of Moral Philosophy 5

Norrie Alan W, *Law, Ideology and Punishment: Retrieval and Critique of the Liberal Ideal of Criminal Justice* (Kluwer Academic 1991)

Norwegian Ministry of Justice and the Police, *Punishment That Works – Less Crime – A Safer Society.* Report to the Storting on the Norwegian Correctional Services (Norwegian Ministry of Justice and the Police 2008)

Nottinghamshire Police, *Our Code of Ethics, Vision and Values* (Nottinghamshire Police 2016) <http://www.nottinghamshire.police.uk/visionandvalues> accessed 1 August 2019

Nozick Robert, *Anarchy, State, and Utopia* (Basic Books 1974)

Nussbaum Martha C, 'Political Liberalism and Respect: A Response to Linda Barclay' (2003) 4(2) SATS: Northern European Journal of Philosophy 25

Nussbaum Martha C, *Beyond the Social Contract: Toward Global Justice*, The Tanner Lectures on Human Values delivered at Australian National University and Clare Hall, University of Cambridge (Tanner Humanities Center, University of Utah 2002 and 2003)

O'Malley Pat, *Risk, Uncertainty and Government* (GlassHouse 2004)

Office of the United Nations High Commissioner for Human Rights, *Human Rights Standards and Practice for the Police (Expanded Pocket Book on Human Rights for the Police)* Professional Training Series No.5/Add.3 (United Nations 2004)

Oprisko Robert L, *Honor: A Phenomenology* (Routledge 2012)

Owen Barbara, Wells James, and Pollock Joycelyn, *In Search of Safety: Confronting Inequality in Women's Imprisonment* (University of California Press 2017)

Oyeniran Femi, 'Stop and Search: It's Time for the Police to Abolish this Ineffective and Damaging Procedure' *The Independent* (21 July 2013) <www.independent.co.uk/voices/comment/stop-and-search-its-time-for-the-police-to-abolish-this-ineffective-and-damaging-procedure-8724542.html> accessed 1 August 2019

Packer Herbert L, 'Two Models of the Criminal Process' (1964) 113(1) University of Pennsylvania Law Review 1

Palmiotto Michael J and Unnithan N Prabha, *Policing and Society: A Global Approach* (Delmar Cengage Learning 2011)

Parker Martin, *Against Management: Organization in the Age of Managerialism* (Polity 2002)

Pateman Carole, 'Self-Ownership and Property in the Person: Democratisation and a Tale of Two Concepts' (2002) 10(1) The Journal of Political Philosophy 20

Paternoster Raymond, Brame Robert, Bachman Ronet, and Sherman Lawrence W, 'Do Fair Procedures Matter? The Effect of Procedural Justice on Spouse Assault' (1997) 31(1) Law & Society Review 163

Pepin Sarah, *Effect of Police Stop and Search Powers on BAME Communities* (House of Commons Library 2018, no CDP-2018-0125)

Petersilia Joan, 'Review of Marie Gottschalk, *Caught: The Prison State and the Lockdown of American Politics* (2015)' (2017) 19(5) Punishment & Society 625

Phillips Anne, *Our Bodies, Whose Property?* (Princeton University Press 2013)

Phillips Coretta, *The Multicultural Prison: Ethnicity, Masculinity, and Social Relations among Prisoners* (OUP 2012)

Pickard Jim, 'G4S Stripped of Control over "Failed" Birmingham Jail' *Financial Times* (20 August 2018)

Player Elaine and Jenkins Michael (eds), *Prisons after Woolf: Reform through Riot* (Routledge 1994)

Player Elaine and Jenkins Michael, 'Introduction' in Elaine Player and Michael Jenkins (eds), *Prisons after Woolf: Reform through Riot* (Routledge 1994)

Polanyi Michael, *The Tacit Dimension* (Doubleday 1966)

Police Executive Research Forum, *Legitimacy and Procedural Justice: A New Element of Police Leadership* (Bureau of Justice Assistance, US Department of Justice 2014)

Pratt Alison and Garton Grimwood Gabrielle, *Prisoners: Incentives and Earned Privileges Scheme* (SN/HA/6942, House of Commons Library 2014)

Pratt John, 'Review of Richard Sparks, Anthony E Bottoms, and Will Hay, *Prisons and the Problem of Order* (1996)' (1998) 38(1) The British Journal of Criminology 179

Pratt John, 'Norbert Elias and the Civilised Prison' (1999) 50(2) The British Journal of Sociology 271

Pratt John, *Punishment and Civilization: Penal Tolerance and Intolerance in Modern Society* (SAGE 2002)

Priestley Philip, *Victorian Prison Lives* (Methuen 1985)

Prison Commission, *Report of Departmental Committee on Diets* (The Stationery Office 1925)

Prison Commission, *Report of the Commissioners of Prisons and the Directors of Convict Prisons for the Year 1924–25* (Cmd 2597, The Stationery Office 1926)

Prison Reform Trust, *Bromley Briefings: Prison Factfile* (Prison Reform Trust 2017)
Prison Reform Trust, *The Woolf Report: A Summary of the Main Findings and Recommendations of the Inquiry into Prison Disturbances* (Prison Reform Trust 1991)
Quinney Richard, 'Criminology as Moral Philosophy, Criminologist as Witness' in Darnell F Hawkins, Samuel L Myers Jr, and Randolph N Stone (eds), *Crime Control and Social Justice: The Delicate Balance* (Praeger 2003)
Quinton Paul, 'The Formation of Suspicions: Police Stop and Search Practices in England and Wales' (2011) 21(4) Policing and Society 357
Quinton Paul, 'Race Disproportionality and Officer Decision-Making' in Rebekah Delsol and Michael Shiner (eds), *Stop and Search: The Anatomy of a Police Power* (Palgrave Macmillan 2015)
Rabinow Paul and Sullivan William M (eds), *Interpretive Social Science: A Second Look* (University of California Press 1987)
Radzinowicz Leon and Hood Roger, *The Emergence of Penal Policy in Victorian and Edwardian England* (Clarendon Press 1990)
Rawls John, *A Theory of Justice* (Belknap Press of Harvard University Press 1971)
Rawls John, *Justice as Fairness: A Restatement* (Harvard University Press 2001)
Raz Joseph, *Value, Respect, and Attachment* (CUP 2001)
Raz Joseph, 'On Respect, Authority, and Neutrality: A Response' (2010) 120(2) Ethics 279
Ristroph Alice, 'The Thin Blue Line from Crime to Punishment' (2018) 108(2) The Journal of Criminal Law and Criminology 305
Robert Dominique, 'Managerialism' in Mary Bosworth (ed), *Encyclopedia of Prisons and Correctional Facilities* (SAGE 2005)
Rolls Edmund T, *Emotion and Decision-making Explained* (OUP 2013)
Rønnow-Rasmussen Toni and Zimmerman Michael J (eds), *Recent Work on Intrinsic Value* (Springer 2005)
Rosenbaum Dennis and Lawrence Daniel, *Teaching Respectful Police-Citizen Encounters and Good Decision-Making: Results of a Randomized Control Trial with Police Recruits* (Institute for Public Policy and Social Research, Michigan State University 2011)
Rowe Abigail, '"Tactics", Agency and Power in Women's Prisons' (2016) 56(2) The British Journal of Criminology 332
Royal Commission on the Police, *Report of the Royal Commission on Police Powers and Procedure* (The Stationery Office 1929)
Royal Commission on the Police, *Final Report* (The Stationery Office 1962)
Saarikkomäki Elsa, 'Perceptions of Procedural Justice Among Young People: Narratives of Fair Treatment in Young People's Stories of Police

and Security Guard Interventions' (2016) 56(6) The British Journal of Criminology 1253

Sabia Dan, 'Defending Immanent Critique' (2010) 38(5) Political Theory 684

Sanders Andrew, Young Richard, and Burton Mandy, *Criminal Justice* (4th edn, OUP 2010)

Sayer Andrew, 'Class, Moral Worth and Recognition' (2005) 39(4) Sociology 947

Scanlon Thomas M, *What We Owe to Each Other* (Belknap Press of Harvard University Press 1998)

Schinkel Marguerite, 'Review of Ben Crewe, *The Prisoner Society: Power, Adaptation, and Social Life in an English Prison* (2009)' (2010) 57(3) Probation Journal 343

Schmidt Lawrence K, 'Respecting Others: The Hermeneutic Virtue' (2000) 33 Continental Philosophy Review 359

Schwartz-Shea Peregrine and Yanow Dvora, *Interpretive Research Design: Concepts and Processes* (Routledge 2012)

Scraton Phil, Sim Joe, and Skidmore Paula, *Prisons under Protest* (Open University Press 1991)

Seidler Victor J, *Kant, Respect and Injustice: The Limits of Liberal Moral Theory* (Routledge & Kegan Paul 1986)

Seidman Louis M, 'Hyper-Incarceration and Strategies of Disruption: Is There a Way Out?' (2011) 9(1) Ohio State Journal of Criminal Law 109

Sennett Richard, *Respect: The Formation of Character in an Age of Inequality* (Penguin 2004)

Sennett Richard, 'Views on Respect' BBC News (9 January 2006) <http://news.bbc.co.uk/1/hi/uk/4589616.stm> accessed 1 August 2019

Sharkansky Ira, 'Slogan as Policy' (2002) 4(1) Journal of Comparative Policy Analysis: Research and Practice 75

Shiner Michael, 'Regulation and Reform' in Rebekah Delsol and Michael Shiner (eds), *Stop and Search: The Anatomy of a Police Power* (Palgrave Macmillan 2015)

Shiner Michael, 'The Politics of the Powers' in Rebekah Delsol and Michael Shiner (eds), *Stop and Search: The Anatomy of a Police Power* (Palgrave Macmillan 2015)

Shklar Judith N, *Legalism: Law, Morals, and Political Trials* (Harvard University Press 1964)

Sibley David and van Hoven Bettina, 'The Contamination of Personal Space: Boundary Construction in a Prison Environment' (2009) 41(2) Area 198

Sieh Edward W, 'Less Eligibility: The Upper Limits of Penal Policy' (1989) 3(2) Criminal Justice Policy Review 159

Sim Joe, *Punishment and Prisons: Power and the Carceral State* (SAGE 2009)

Simester AP, du Bois-Pedain Antje, and Neumann Ulfrid (eds), *Liberal Criminal Theory: Essays for Andreas von Hirsch* (Hart 2014)

Simon Jonathan, 'Punishment and the Political Technologies of the Body' in Jonathan Simon and Richard Sparks (eds), *The SAGE Handbook of Punishment and Society* (SAGE 2013)

Skinner Quentin, *Visions of Politics. Volume 1: Regarding Method* (CUP 2002)

Skogan Wesley G, 'Why Reforms Fail' (2008) 18(1) Policing and Society 23

Skolnick Jerome H, *Justice without Trial: Law Enforcement in a Democratic Society* (Wiley 1966)

Smith Catrin, 'Punishment and Pleasure: Women, Food and the Imprisoned Body' (2002) 50(2) The Sociological Review 197

Smoyer Amy B and Kjær Minke Linda, *Food Systems in Correctional Settings: A Literature Review and Case Study* (World Health Organization 2015)

Smoyer Amy B and Lopes Giza, 'Hungry on the Inside: Prison Food as Concrete and Symbolic Punishment in a Women's Prison' (2016) 19(2) Punishment & Society 240

Somerville Peter, '"The Feeling's Mutual:" Respect as the Basis for Cooperative Interaction' in Andrew Millie (ed), *Securing Respect: Behavioural Expectations and Anti-Social Behaviour in the UK* (Policy Press 2009)

Souhami Anna, 'Understanding Institutional Racism: The Stephen Lawrence Inquiry and the Police Service Reaction' in Michael Rowe (ed), *Policing Beyond Macpherson: Issues in Policing, Race and Society* (Routledge 2007)

Sparks Richard, 'Can Prisons Be Legitimate? Penal Politics, Privatization, and the Timeliness of an Old Idea' (1994) 34(S1) The British Journal of Criminology 14

Sparks Richard and Bottoms Anthony E, 'Legitimacy and Order in Prisons' (1995) 46(1) The British Journal of Sociology 45

Sparks Richard and Bottoms Anthony E, 'Legitimacy and Imprisonment Revisited: Some Notes on the Problem of Order Ten Years After' in James M Byrne, Donald Hummer, and Faye S Taxman (eds), *The Culture of Prison Violence* (Pearson 2008)

Sparks Richard, Bottoms Anthony E, and Hay Will, *Prisons and the Problem of Order* (Clarendon Press 1996)

Spurr Michael, 'Perrie Lecture: Reducing Costs and Maintaining Values' (2011) 198 Prison Service Journal 12

Squires Peter, '"You lookin' at me?" Discourses of Respect and Disrespect, Identity and Violence' in Andrew Millie (ed), *Securing Respect: Behavioural Expectations and Anti-Social Behaviour in the UK* (Policy Press 2009)

Stanford P Kyle, 'Instrumentalism' in Sahotra Sarkar and Jessica Pfeifer (eds), *The Philosophy of Science: An Encyclopedia* (Routledge 2005)

Steinhoff Uwe (ed), *Do All Persons Have Equal Moral Worth? On 'Basic Equality' and Equal Respect and Concern* (OUP 2015)

Stevenson Charles L, 'The Nature of Ethical Disagreement' in Steven M Cahn (ed), *Exploring Ethics: An Introductory Anthology* (4th edn, OUP 2016)

Stith Richard, 'The Priority of Respect: How Our Common Humanity Can Ground Our Individual Dignity' (2004) 44(2) International Philosophical Quarterly 165

Sunshine Jason and Tyler Tom R, 'The Role of Procedural Justice and Legitimacy in Shaping Public Support for Policing' (2003) 37(3) Law & Society Review 513

Sykes Gresham M, *The Society of Captives: A Study of a Maximum Security Prison* (Princeton University Press 1958)

Tankebe Justice, 'Police Legitimacy' in Michael D Reisig and Robert J Kane (eds), *The Oxford Handbook of Police and Policing* (OUP 2014).

Taylor Charles, 'The Politics of Recognition' in Amy Gutmann (ed), *Multiculturalism: Examining the Politics of Recognition* (Princeton University Press 1992)

The Jubilee Centre for Character and Virtues at the University of Birmingham, *Character and Public Policy: Educating for an Ethical Life*. 1st Annual Conference held at the University of Birmingham (2012) <http://www.jubileecentre.ac.uk/484/conferences/character-and-public-policy> accessed 1 August 2019

The Jubilee Centre for Character and Virtues at the University of Birmingham, *Cultivating Virtues: Interdisciplinary Approaches*. 4th Annual Conference held at Oriel College, Oxford (2016) <http://www.jubileecentre.ac.uk/1643/conferences/cultivating-virtues> accessed 1 August 2019

The Police Foundation, *The Briefing* (Series 2, edn 3, The Police Foundation 2012)

Thibaut John W and Walker Laurens, *Procedural Justice: A Psychological Analysis* (Wiley 1975)

Thomas Jim, 'Passing Time: The Ironies of Food in Prison Culture' in Lawrence C Rubin (ed), *Food for Thought: Essays on Eating and Culture* (McFarland 2008)

Thorburn Malcolm, 'Criminal Law as Public Law' in RA Duff and Stuart P Green (eds), *Philosophical Foundations of Criminal Law* (OUP 2011)

Tiratelli Matteo, Quinton Paul, and Bradford Ben, 'Does Stop and Search Deter Crime? Evidence from Ten Years of London-Wide Data' (2018) 58(5) The British Journal of Criminology 1212

Tomasi John, 'Kymlicka, Liberalism, and Respect for Cultural Minorities' (1995) 105(3) Ethics 580

Tomlinson M Heather, 'Not an Instrument of Punishment: Prison Diet in the Mid-Nineteenth Century' (1978) 2(1) Journal of Consumer Studies and Home Economics 15

Tyler Tom R, 'Conditions Leading to Value-Expressive Effects in Judgments of Procedural Justice: A Test of Four Models' (1987) 52(2) Journal of Personality and Social Psychology 333

Tyler Tom R, *Why People Obey the Law* (Yale University Press 1990)

Tyler Tom R, 'Governing amid Diversity: The Effect of Fair Decision-making Procedures on the Legitimacy of Government' (1994) 28(4) Law & Society Review 809

Tyler Tom R, 'Multiculturalism and the Willingness of Citizens to Defer to Law and Legal Authorities' (2000) 25(4) Law & Social Inquiry 983

Tyler Tom R, 'Enhancing Police Legitimacy' (2004) 593(1) The ANNALS of the American Academy of Political and Social Science 84

Tyler Tom R, 'Trust and Legitimacy: Policing in the USA and Europe' (2011) 8(4) European Journal of Criminology 254

Tyler Tom R and Bies Robert J, 'Beyond Formal Procedures: The Interpersonal Context of Procedural Justice' in John S Carroll (ed), *Applied Social Psychology and Organizational Settings* (Psychology Press 2015)

Tyler Tom R and Blader Steven L, *Cooperation in Groups: Procedural Justice, Social Identity, and Behavioral Engagement* (Psychology Press 2000)

Tyler Tom R, Fagan Jeffrey, and Geller Amanda, 'Street Stops and Police Legitimacy: Teachable Moments in Young Urban Men's Legal Socialization' (2014) 11(4) Journal of Empirical Legal Studies 751

Tyler Tom R and Huo Yuen J, *Trust in the Law: Encouraging Public Cooperation with the Police and Courts* (Russell Sage Foundation 2002)

Tyler Tom R and Lind E Allan, 'A Relational Model of Authority in Groups' (1992) 25 Advances in Experimental Social Psychology 115

Tyler Tom R and Smith Heather J, 'Justice, Social Identity, and Group Processes' in Tom R Tyler, Roderick M Kramer, and Oliver P John (eds), *The Psychology of the Social Self* (Erlbaum 1999)

Ugelvik Thomas, 'The Hidden Food: Mealtime Resistance and Identity Work in a Norwegian Prison' (2011) 13(1) Punishment & Society 47

Uglow Steve, *Policing Liberal Society* (OUP 1988)

United Nations Office on Drugs and Crime, *The United Nations Standard Minimum Rules for the Treatment of Prisoners (The Nelson Mandela Rules)* (UNODC 2015)

Urmson JO and Sbisà Marina (eds), John L Austin, *How to Do Things with Words* (2nd edn, Harvard University Press 1975)

van Stokkom Bas, 'Dealing with Defiant Citizens: Building Emotional Intelligence into Police Work' in Susanne Karstedt, Ian Loader, and Heather Strang (eds), *Emotions, Crime and Justice* (Hart 2011)

van Zyl Smit Dirk, 'Review of Alison Liebling, *Prisons and their Moral Performance: A Study of Values, Quality, and Prison Life* (2004)' (2005) 45(5) The British Journal of Criminology 765

Waddington PAJ, Stenson Kevin, and Don David, 'In Proportion: Race, and Police Stop and Search (2004) 44(6) The British Journal of Criminology 889

Waldron Jeremy, '*The Coxford Lecture*. Inhuman and Degrading Treatment: The Words Themselves' (2010) 23(2) Canadian Journal of Law & Jurisprudence 269

Walzer Michael, 'Civility and Civic Virtue in Contemporary America' (1974) 41(4) Social Research 593

Walzer Michael, *Interpretation and Social Criticism* (Harvard University Press 1993)

Weber Leanne and Bowling Ben, 'Valiant Beggars and Global Vagabonds: Select, Eject, Immobilise' (2008) 12(3) Theoretical Criminology 355

Weber Leanne and Bowling Ben, 'Introduction: Stop and Search in Global Context' (2011) 21(4) Policing and Society 353

Weber Max, *The Theory of Social and Economic Organization* (William Hodge & Co 1947)

Weber Max, *Economy and Society: An Outline of Interpretive Sociology* (Bedminster Press 1968)

Weinberger Barbara, *The Best Police in the World: An Oral History of English Policing from the 1930s to the 1960s* (Scolar Press 1995)

Wheller Levin, Quinton Paul, Fildes Alistair, and Mills Andy, *The Greater Manchester Police Procedural Justice Training Experiment: The Impact of Communication Skills Training on Officers and Victims of Crime* (College of Policing 2013)

White Jay D, *Taking Language Seriously: The Narrative Foundations of Public Administration Research* (Georgetown University Press 2001)

Williams Bernard, *Ethics and the Limits of Philosophy* (Fontana 1985)

Williams Raymond, *Keywords: A Vocabulary of Culture and Society* (Fontana 1976)

Winfree Jr L Thomas, Newbold Greg, and Tubb III S Houston, 'Prisoner Perspectives on Inmate Culture in New Mexico and New Zealand: A Descriptive Case Study' (2002) 82(2) The Prison Journal 213

Wolff Jonathan, 'Fairness, Respect, and the Egalitarian Ethos' (1998) 27(2) Philosophy & Public Affairs 97

Wood Allen W, 'Respect and Recognition' in John Skorupski (ed), *The Routledge Companion to Ethics* (Routledge 2010)

Woolf The Rt Hon Lord, 'Strangeways 25 Years' On: Achieving Fairness & Justice in Prison' transcript of speech delivered at The Honourable Society of the Inner Temple (Inner Temple 1 April 2015)

Young Iris Marion, *Intersecting Voices: Dilemmas of Gender, Political Philosophy, and Policy* (Princeton University Press 1997)

Young Jock, *Policing the Streets: Stops and Searches in North London* (Middlesex University 1994)

Yuval-Davis Nira, Kannabiran Kalpana, and Vieten Ulrike (eds), *The Situated Politics of Belonging* (SAGE 2006)

Zedner Lucia, *Women, Crime, and Custody in Victorian England* (OUP 1991)

Zedner Lucia, 'Reparation and Retribution: Are They Reconcilable?' (1994) 57(2) The Modern Law Review 228

Zedner Lucia, 'Useful Knowledge? Debating the Role of Criminology in Post-war Britain' in Lucia Zedner and Andrew Ashworth (eds), *The Criminological Foundations of Penal Policy: Essays in Honour of Roger Hood* (OUP 2003)

Zedner Lucia, *Criminal Justice* (OUP 2004)

Zedner Lucia, 'Pre-Crime or Post-Criminology?' (2007) 11(2) Theoretical Criminology 261

Zelinsky Wilbur, 'You Are Where You Eat' in Barbara G Shortridge and James R Shortridge (eds), *The Taste of American Place: A Reader on Regional and Ethnic Foods* (Rowman & Littlefield 1998)

Zimmerman Michael J, 'Intrinsic vs. Extrinsic Value' in Edward N Zalta (ed), *The Stanford Encyclopedia of Philosophy* (Stanford University 2019) <http://plato.stanford.edu/entries/value-intrinsic-extrinsic/> accessed 1 August 2019

Index

Note: *For the benefit of digital users, indexed terms that span two pages (e.g., 52–53) may, on occasion, appear on only one of those pages.*

Abolition
Of prisons 102–3
Of stop and search 69, 85, 89–90, 91
Abolitionism
As political movement 89–90, 91
As theoretical perspective 69, 89–90
Academic disciplines
Ambivalence towards respect 2–3, 10–26
Accountability
Of citizens for wrongdoing 180
Of Her Majesty's Prison Service 109–10, 119, 163
Of police 78–79, 91, 185
Actuarial justice - *see* justice models
Affect - *see also* emotions and respect, *affective basis of* 17, 24–25, 54–55, 60–61, 157
Austerity
Facilitating respect 134, 162–64
Undermining respect 134, 162–64
Autonomy
At prison mealtime 133–34, 150, 158, 159–60
Principle of 12–14, 18–19, 24, 25–26, 64–65, 82–83, 106–7, 113–14

Bagnoli, Carla 1, 10–11, 55, 64–65, 115–16
Balint, Peter 6, 8–9, 18–19, 59, 78, 84–85, 145, 171–72
Belonging 4–5, 34, 45–46, 54, 59, 61, 77, 78, 83–84, 173, 189–90
Black and minority ethnic 4–5, 18–19, 23–24, 28–29, 30, 34, 35, 54, 59–60, 68–69, 73, 74–77, 78–79, 84–85, 99–100, 101–2, 112, 123, 124–25, 132, 133–34, 138, 143–46, 147, 151–52, 172–73, 175, 187
Bottoms, Anthony 14, 39, 52, 60–61, 99–100, 101–2, 103–8, 111–12, 117, 157–58
Bourgois, Philippe 1, 4–5, 11, 12, 23–26, 28–29, 34, 54, 59, 77

Civility 93, 107–8, 127–28, 129–31, 137–38, 150, 171–72, 187–88
Lack thereof 8–9
Coercion
Of citizens by the state 33
College of Policing
Code of Ethics 2–3, 5–6, 7–8, 44–45, 63, 183, 184, 185
Community
In prisons 100, 102–3, 115–16, 120
Membership of 1, 10–11, 55, 90, 115–16
Police relations with the 56–57, 68, 71–72, 76, 171–72
Weakening of 8–9
Compliance
Theories of 47–48
With institutional policy 129–30, 144–46, 159
With the authorities 47–50, 51, 54–55, 120, 129–30, 131, 159–60
With the law 48–49, 51, 65, 181
Conceptual precision
Value of 32–33, 76–77, 91, 92–93, 164, 192
Contracting out - *see* imprisonment, *private sector*
Courtesy
And respect 2–3, 5–6, 7–8, 44–45, 47–48, 70–71, 74, 80, 116, 131, 184, 185
Crime
Control of 2, 12, 32–33, 43, 45–48, 50–51, 53, 60, 67, 68–69, 71–72, 83–84, 93, 99, 172, 176
Detection of 71–73, 74–75, 76–77

Crime (*cont.*)
Positive incentives to commit 136–37
Prevention of 2, 26–27, 71–73, 74–75, 76–77, 135–37
Criminal justice
Constrained but not *characterised* by respect 3–4, 39–40, 53–55, 119, 126, 129–31, 153, 182
In the applied domain 7–8, 167
'Utopian critique' of 167
Criminal Justice and Public Order Act 1994 75–76, 165
Criminal process, the
Defining stages of 2, 7–8, 33, 166–67
Models of 46, 47–48, 50–51
Custody - *see* imprisonment

Darwall, Stephen L
Crewe's adaptation of the Darwall model 121–22
Two kinds of respect 14–15, 17–18, 20, 64–65, 106–7
Decency
And dignity 109–10
And justice 100–1
And respect 2–3, 7–8, 11, 19–20, 22, 98–99, 125–26, 133, 178–79
As a slogan 183, 184
'Decent, but austere' 111–14
Minimal form of 21–22
Quantification of 118–19
The Decency Agenda 114–16, 120, 125–26
The Decent Society 5, 14, 18–19, 21–22, 30, 167–68, 173–74
Degradation
Instances of 34, 132–33, 135, 138
The word itself 34–35
Detention - *see* imprisonment
Dialogue
As a reform strategy 168–69, 189–91
Between criminal justice and related disciplines 10
Between state actors and citizens 56–58, 91–92, 158
Difference - *see* diversity; multiculturalism
Differential treatment - *see also* discrimination 120
Justified by respect 106–7, 144
Dignity - *see also* intrinsic worth; moral worth
And decency 109–10
And respect 2–3, 11, 13, 15, 19–20, 22, 24, 80
The concept of 12–13, 21–22, 23, 27, 179
Dillon, Robin S 1, 10–11, 12–15, 17–18, 20, 23, 26–28, 33, 34–35, 59, 81, 89, 99, 118–19, 129–30, 143, 153, 157, 169, 170, 172, 180, 186, 189–90
Discretion
In prisons 110, 122–23, 128–29, 139–40, 148–49, 155–56
Use and abuse by police officers 72–73, 87, 88–89, 90–91
Discrimination - *see also* differential treatment
Direct and indirect stereotyping 75–76, 78–79
In accounts of respect 13–14, 172
In policy documentation 186
Instances of 59, 68–69, 70, 71–79, 80, 172
Disrespect
Conceptual analysis of 17–18, 21
Instances of 9, 21, 24–25, 51, 59, 81, 89–90, 117, 155–56, 177–78
Slang term 'diss' 24–25
Diversity - *see also* multiculturalism
Acknowledgment of 18–19, 30, 59, 170, 172, 173
Ethnic 28–29, 30, 77, 123, 124–25
In institutions 29, 30, 59, 123, 124–25, 170–71, 172, 174, 186, 187
The word itself 30, 187
Due process - *see* models of policing
Duff, RA 2, 9–10, 14, 26–27, 33, 37, 101, 180
Dworkin, Ronald
Right to equal concern and respect 15–16, 17, 30, 75–76
Trump right 32–33

Effectiveness - *see also* instrumentalism
Of policing 45–47, 50, 52, 56–57, 60, 70–72, 83–84, 87–89, 91
Of prisons 109–10, 118, 122–23, 128, 148, 159, 163, 175
Of punishment 31–32

Efficiency - *see* effectiveness; instrumentalism
Egalitarianism 16, 19, 23, 62–63, 65, 86, 106–7
Emotions - *see also* affect
And recognition 65
And respect 17, 54–55, 65, 153, 157
'Emotional texture' of prisons 115
In police-public encounters 53, 54–55, 60–61
In prisons 128–29, 133–34, 140–41, 150, 157, 158, 160
Rationality of 17
Strategic expression of 54–55
Equality
Principle of 13–14, 15–16, 18–19, 20, 23, 64–65, 66, 106–7, 146, 172, 173–74, 175, 180, 186
Right to 15–16
Esteem 2–3, 11, 14–15, 19–20, 64, 121
Ethnic profiling
Evidence of 84
Ethnicity - *see* race and racism
Ethnography 11, 23–25, 120–22, 123–25, 127–31, 132, 175
'Every Contact Matters' 118, 133

Fairness
Distributive 32–33, 48, 62
Justice as 62–63
Principle of 8–9, 16, 43, 48, 51, 59, 60–61, 62–63, 66–67, 70–71, 75–76, 80, 86, 100–1, 106, 107–8, 111–12, 118, 125–27, 145, 171–72, 181, 184–85
Procedural 44–45, 61, 62, 63
Feigned respect 23, 27–28, 133, 142, 157, 170–72
As an insult 130–31
Femininity
Stereotypical forms of 112, 113–14
Food in prison 3–4, 117
As a mode of cultural exchange 124, 146–47
Breakfast packs 149–50
Consumption of 132–34, 137–38, 139, 148–52, 153–56, 160, 161–62, 163–64
Danish model 147
Ethnic and cultural meals 132, 133–34, 138, 143–47, 148, 150, 151–52, 155–56
Feedback procedure 152–53
Hunger strikes 132–33, 157, 158–59
In historical context 135–39
In women's prisons 132, 133–34, 136–37, 140–41, 153, 154–56
Kitchen work 143–44, 164
Menu design 138, 139–41, 143–44
Preparation of 132–34, 138, 139–50, 157, 160–61, 162
Punishment diet 135–36, 138
Resistance of, *see also* food in prison, *hunger strikes* 132–34, 139, 156–62
Ritual of 132, 148–50, 151, 153–54, 155–56, 157, 175
Self-catering 124, 146–48
Symbolic power of 132, 157–58, 175
Forfeiture
Of right to respect 1, 14, 142, 143, 186

Gadamer, Hans-Georg 35–36, 38, 39
Gender - *see* differential treatment; masculinity; femininity; women; intersectionality
Governance
Of crime 46–47

Hart, HLA 32–33, 178–79
Her Majesty's Inspectorate of Constabulary 44–45, 70–71, 86
Her Majesty's Inspectorate of Prisons for England and Wales 44–45, 123, 131, 146, 149, 151–53, 154–55, 161–62, 165–66, 191
Healthy prisons 153
Respect scores 39–40, 153–54
Her Majesty's Prison Grendon
Instances of respect 153, 191
Her Majesty's Prison and Probation Service 98–99, 125, 131, 133, 134, 140, 146, 153–54, 162
Hierarchy, concept of
In law 87–88
In post-Kantian accounts of respect 13–14, 172
In prison scholarship 101–2, 109, 110, 120, 131, 143
Hill Jr, Thomas E 1, 12–14, 18, 20, 21–22, 23, 25–26, 54–55, 86, 117, 169, 179

History
Of imprisonment 97–98, 103–4, 106–7, 126–27
Of policing 44–45, 68, 73
Of prison mealtime 132–33, 135–39
Home Office 8–9, 44–45, 69, 70–72, 74, 75–76, 83, 88–89, 91–92, 100–1, 103, 105–6, 127, 133, 136, 165, 172
Honneth, Axel
Disrespect 21
Tripartite model of 'love, respect, and esteem' 64–65
House of Commons Justice Committee 93, 98–99, 114, 147, 148
Howard, John
Minimalist vision for respect 135
Reformative penal project of 135
Human dignity - *see* dignity
Humanity 1, 8–9, 11, 14, 21, 25–26, 34–35, 64–65, 81, 84–85, 90, 98–99, 106–7, 115–16, 118–19, 121, 133, 164, 177–78, 180, 186
Humiliation 21–22, 24, 167–68

Ideal theory - *see* normative theory; criminal justice, *'utopian critique' of*
Identity
Attempts to undermine 59, 150
Conceptual analysis of 11, 13–14, 19, 22–23, 54, 66, 78, 112–13, 130–31, 145–46, 172, 173–74
'Identity work' 133–34, 157–58, 160
Performance of 112–13, 133–34, 146, 160–61
Respect for 49–50, 63, 64, 78, 81–82, 91, 159
Image management 187
Immanent critique 169–70
Imprisonment
And 'moral communities' 115–16
And reformation - *see also* 'Rehabilitation Revolution' 114, 129, 151–52,
'Changed texture' of 5
Conditions of 9, 33, 98–99, 100–1, 103–5, 114, 120, 123, 126–27, 135, 136–37, 145–46, 148, 151–52, 155–56, 158, 162, 165–66, 184–85
Control in 104–6, 108–9, 110, 111–12, 113–14, 122–23, 124–25, 128–30, 155, 158, 159–60
Fiscal matters in 134, 162–64
Gender - *see* differential treatment; masculinity; femininity; women; intersectionality
Liberal-humanitarian values in 31–32, 111, 130–31, 167–68
'Pains' of 150
Private sector 9–10, 97, 101, 115, 131, 134, 139, 140, 153, 154–55, 162, 166–67
Public sector 9–10, 97, 101, 115, 118, 131, 134, 139, 140, 153, 155, 162, 166–67, 184, 187–88
Respect as a core value of 4–5, 33, 34, 98–99, 133
Revised 'pains' of 5, 117
Security in 105–6, 108–9, 111–12, 113–14, 129, 140, 147, 151, 191
Spatial dynamics in 151–52
Incapacitation - *see* imprisonment
Incarceration - *see* imprisonment
Institutional sociology 99–103, 108–9, 112, 127
Institutions
Design of 1, 9, 110–11, 151–52, 163, 167–68, 176–77, 178–79, 181–91
Just and unjust 26–27
Instrumental outcomes *see* instrumentalism
Instrumentalism 176–77
Narrow form of 43, 53, 60, 68–69
Proper place of 2, 43, 55, 93, 164, 176
Interpretive approach - *see* interpretivism
Interpretivism
Description of 36–37
In theory and practice 37–40
Justification of 10, 35–36
Intersectionality 78–79
Intrinsic and extrinsic value 26–27, 31
Intrinsic worth - *see also* dignity; moral worth 1, 17–18, 107–8, 117, 174–75
Iser, Mattias 19, 20, 21, 64, 173–74

Joint construal
Of policing and imprisonment 3, 33–35, 166–67

Justice models - *see also* procedural justice; Kant, Immanuel; Pettit, Philip; Rawls, John
Actuarial 116, 118–19
Natural 60–61
Retributive 135–36, 178–79

Kant, Immanuel 1, 12–15, 17, 18–19, 20, 21–22, 23, 25–26, 31, 54–55, 86, 117, 121, 169, 170, 171–72, 173, 179, 180, 186

Lacey, Nicola 1, 5, 10–11, 33, 50, 53–54, 87–88, 93, 101, 142, 167–68
Law
And decency 21–22
As an object of respect 15
Compliance with 48–49, 51–52
Limited effectiveness of 87–89
'Law and order' 43, 181
Legalism - *see also* respect, *as a rule* 47–48, 87–88, 188–89
Legitimacy
And compliance in prisons 104–5, 106, 112, 117
Dialogic approach to 14, 52–53
Erosion of 98–99, 163
Exclusion of 103–4, 115
In policing and procedural justice 43, 44–45, 46–50, 51, 52–53, 56–57, 59, 65–66, 181
In stop and search 68–69, 70, 71, 78–81, 83, 85, 86, 87, 91–92
Of quantitative methods 118–19
Prioritisation of 46, 52–53, 113
Relational character of 52
Liberalism 13–14, 18–19, 78, 167–68, 175, 179–81
Liebling, Alison 9–10, 31–32, 33, 97, 98–102, 103–4, 108–10, 111–12, 114–19, 125–26, 128, 129, 130–31, 133, 139, 155, 162, 163, 166–67, 175
Loader, Ian 4–5, 6, 12, 15–16, 33, 45–46, 53, 59, 62, 65–66, 71–73, 78, 83–84, 88–90, 91–92, 93, 167–68, 173, 176–77, 187, 188–90

Managerialism
As an instrumental outcome 32–33, 50, 101–2, 108–9, 113–14, 116, 118, 120–22, 126, 127
In women's imprisonment 110–11
The rise of 100–1, 109–12
The shifting nature of 127–31
Manners - *see* civility
Masculinity
And prison design 110–11
Stereotypical forms of 23–24, 25–26, 112, 122, 124–25, 129
Measuring the Quality of Prison Life 101, 118–19, 128, 133
Mental Capacity Act 2005 159
Merchant of Venice, The 1
Method - *see* interpretivism; immanent critique
Metropolitan Police 74, 81–82, 177, 184–85, 186
Millie, Andrew 8–10, 20, 23, 62, 74–75, 166–67, 175–76
Ministry of Justice 28–29, 114, 122–23, 131, 134, 140–41, 162
Models of policing
Due process and crime control 46, 47–48, 50–51, 68–69
Moral performance 33, 99–102, 103–4, 108–10, 111–12, 114–19, 125–26, 130–31
Moral rights - *see also* respect, *as a moral right*
Of persons 82–83
Of policing 90
Moral standing - *see* intrinsic worth; moral worth; respect
Moral values - *see* values
Moral vocabulary 24–25
And the Decency Agenda 114–17, 125–26
Moral worth - *see also* dignity; intrinsic worth
Assigning of 8–9, 12–13, 15–16, 18–19, 20, 22, 89
Multiculturalism 8–9, 11, 18–19, 51, 59, 84–85, 99–100, 101–2, 123–25, 133–34, 145–47, 148, 160–61, 171–74

National Offender Management Service 2–3, 7–8, 28, 123, 125, 134–35, 139, 140–42, 143–44, 146, 147, 148–49, 151, 152–53, 158–59, 162, 163, 168–69, 178–79, 183, 184, 187–88, 189
New Penology, The 109, 125–26, 128

Normative theory 1, 12, 21, 27, 47–48, 52–53, 62–63, 64, 104–5, 109
Nozick, Robert 2, 26–27

Obligation
Moral 12–13, 21–22, 83–84
Social 121
Office of the United Nations High Commissioner for Human Rights 34–35
Official discourse - *see also* image management; respect, *symbolic investment in*; respect, *vague institutional commitments to* 2–3, 4–5, 19–20, 28, 30, 34, 38, 39–40, 44–45, 53, 66–67, 70–71, 83–84, 98–99, 103–4, 114, 125–26, 133, 138, 139, 140–41, 144, 148–49, 165–66, 168–71, 178–79, 183, 185–86, 187
Order
The problem of 99–100, 101–2, 103–8, 117, 157–58
The pursuit of 2, 32–33, 47–48, 49–50, 71, 72–73, 74–75, 118, 147, 175–76
Outcomes - *see* effectiveness; instrumentalism

Participant observation - *see* ethnography
Paternalism - *see* state, *paternalism*
Penal institutions - *see* institutions
Penal policy 6, 46–47, 97–98, 101, 111–12, 135–37
Performance measures - *see* managerialism
Personhood 18–19, 28, 170, 172
Pettit, Philip 2, 26–27, 32–33, 167–68, 177–78
Philosophy
Relevance to criminal justice 12
Study of respect in 1, 2–3, 10–11, 12–23, 26–28, 31, 55, 59, 62–63, 64, 81, 99, 107, 143, 170, 172–74, 180, 190–91
Pluralism - *see* values, *balancing of*
Police
Human Rights Standards and Practice for the Police 34–35
Organisational culture 87, 90–91
Police and Criminal Evidence Act 1984
Code A 70–71, 75–76, 83, 88–89, 165
Code C 44–45
Policing
Respect as a core value of 33, 34, 44–45, 184–85
Respect as a subsidiary concern of 43, 74–75
Political philosophy
On respect 15–16, 62–63
On self-ownership 82–83
Poor Law Amendment Act 1834 135–36
Power - *see also* state, *exercise of power*; status, *and power*; status, *inequality*
Inequality 29, 33, 155–56, 157–58
Pragmatism - *see* instrumentalism
Prevention - *see* crime, *prevention of*
Prison managers 99–100, 101–2, 109, 110, 127–31, 142, 171–72, 187–88
Prison mealtime - *see* food in prison
Prison Rules 1999, The 139–40, 141–42, 146, 168–69
Prison Service Instructions
Adult Safeguarding in Prison 159
Catering: Meals for Prisoners 28, 140, 143–44, 168–69, 187–88, 189
Catering Operating Manual 143–44, 168–69
Ensuring Equality 146, 168–69
Equality of Treatment for Employees 146
Faith and Pastoral Care of Prisoners 143–44, 168–69
Incentives and Earned Privileges 134–35
Management of Prisoners at Risk of Harm to Self, to Others or from Others 158–59
Prison Service Order
Women Prisoners 140–41, 153
Prison studies - *see* imprisonment; institutional sociology
Prisoners
Experience of 'weight' and 'pain' by 5, 117, 123
Rights of 134, 163

The United Nations Standard Minimum Rules for the Treatment of Prisoners 34–35, 187–88
Prisoners (Temporary Discharge for Ill-Health) Act 1913 137–38
Prisons - *see* imprisonment
Procedural justice
Indicators 60–66
Instrumental account of 46–60
Non-instrumental account of 43–44, 45–46, 60–66
Scripted approach to 56–60, 171–72, 187–88
Progressivism
Instance of 137–38
Resistance to 9, 99, 128, 129–30, 185
Punishment
Emotional dimension of 2, 31–32, 33, 115, 133–34, 140–41, 150, 153, 157, 160, 176
Institutions of - *see* imprisonment

Race and racism - *see also* differential treatment; discrimination; ethnic profiling; intersectionality
And respect 11, 28–29
In policing 28–29, 68, 70, 72–73, 74–75, 77, 78–79, 84, 89, 172, 177
In prisons 28–29, 30, 101–2, 113, 114, 123, 124–25, 151, 161, 170–71, 172, 187
Racial discrimination - *see* race and racism; ethnic profiling
Rationality
Of emotions 17
Of respect 17, 153
Rawls, John 34–35, 62–63, 98–99
Recognition
As a form of mutuality 20, 64, 116
Concept of 8–9, 11, 13–14, 18–19, 20, 21, 45–46, 59, 64–65, 66–67, 78, 83–84, 89, 173–75
In procedural justice - *see* procedural justice, *indicators*
Relationship to disrespect 21, 117
Relationship to respect 2–3, 11, 12–15, 17–18, 19–20, 66, 106–7, 116, 117, 121, 178–79
Strong and weak forms of 173
Reform, of criminal justice
At the individual level 168–69, 183, 189–91
At the institutional level 168–69, 172, 177, 183–89
Rehabilitation Revolution, The 122–25
Respect
Affective basis of 17, 24–25, 54–55, 65, 153, 157
As a concept of critical enquiry 3–4, 40, 69, 134–35
As a form of mutuality 6, 20, 23, 25–26, 33, 53, 116, 124, 129–30, 145–46, 151–52, 155–56, 161, 175–76, 189–90
As a keyword or slogan 1, 4–5, 30, 99, 132, 162, 183
As a mode of recognition - *see* recognition, *relationship to respect*
As a moral right 12–13, 18, 55, 90, 99, 169, 175–76
As a moral value 2, 31–32, 55, 101, 111, 116, 117, 118–19, 129–30, 153–54, 177–78
As a rhetorical gift 172–73
As a rule 87–88, 139–43, 159, 168–69, 187–89
As a weak side-constraint on instrumental outcomes - *see* side-constraint, *weak form of*
As an attitude 1, 12–13, 15, 17–18, 22, 27–28, 57, 84–85, 107, 121, 130–31, 145
As an ethical standard 146, 168–69, 187–89
As 'expressive work' 23, 142
As non-interference 17, 83, 107–8
As relational and dialogic 17–18, 23, 27–28, 51–52, 59, 116, 145–46
Assumed universality of 34–35, 97–98
At the individual and institutional level 30, 168–69, 172, 177, 183
Competing forms of 28, 170–74
Deficit 3–4, 26–27, 78, 83–85, 101, 170–71, 181–82
Definitional ambiguity of 4–5, 8–26, 45, 54, 87–88, 101–2, 120, 145–46, 168–69, 185, 191
Elusive promise of 169–81

Respect (*cont.*)
Entitlement to - *see also* forfeiture, *of right to respect* 1, 10–11, 13–14, 17–18, 27–28, 81, 98–99, 105–6, 164,
Etymology of 17–18, 64
For legal rights 5–6
For persons 12–14, 17, 35, 55, 82–83, 121, 172, 180
In practice, examples of 191
Intrinsic case for 45–46, 60–66
Intuitive appeal of 8–9, 86–87, 162
Limits of 2–3, 5, 6, 19–23, 40, 78, 81–82, 103, 112, 125, 189–91
Of similarities and of differences 8–9, 13–14, 18–19, 22–23, 28–29, 34–35, 59, 78, 84–85, 143–46, 148, 170, 171–74, 186
Outcomes 98–99, 153–54
Performance of - *see* feigned respect
Procedural form of 76–77, 142, 143, 144–45, 159, 162, 188–89
Quantification of 101–2, 115–16, 118–19, 153–54
Reconciliation with other purposes, values, and rationales 178–79
Subjective experience of 11, 59, 66, 76–77, 118–19, 153–54
Through physical intimidation and violence 9, 23–24, 25–26, 121, 122, 124–25
Timeless nature of 192
Vague institutional commitments to 4–5, 83–84, 93, 123, 162, 170–71, 184–85, 187
Respect Agenda, The 8–9
Rules -*see* legalism; Prison Rules 1999, The; prisoners, *United Nations Standard Minimum Rules for the Treatment of Prisoners*; respect, *as a rule*

Sanction - *see* imprisonment; punishment
Sennett, Richard 1, 6, 9, 11, 12, 23, 25–26, 27–28, 29, 59, 76, 86–87, 106–7, 116, 142, 155–56, 161, 174, 175–76
Side-constraint
Origins of the term 2, 26–27, 31–33
Weak form of 2, 4–5, 26–27, 31–33, 35–36, 43–44, 45, 53, 55, 59–60, 66–67, 68–69, 73–74, 76, 81, 89, 98–99, 108–9, 116, 120, 127, 129–30, 132–33, 138, 143, 148, 158, 166–67, 169, 176–77, 178–80
Social class - *see also* intersectionality 8–9, 78–79, 112, 135–36
Social management 74–75, 175, 176
Social sciences
Study of respect in 1, 2–3, 10, 23–26, 27–28
Subjective beliefs and experiences 11
Social standing - *see* status
Staff Quality of Life 101, 118
State
Authority 30, 68–69, 86–87, 88–89, 104–5, 115, 155–56, 185
Paternalism 172–73
Power, exercise of 27–28, 29, 33, 44–45, 52–54, 57–58, 68–93, 99–100, 101–3, 104–5, 110, 112, 120, 122, 138, 145–46, 155–56, 157–58, 165, 172–73, 174–76, 180, 182–83, 187–88
Responsibility for acting respectfully 6, 8–9, 30, 84–85, 122, 134–35, 168–69, 172–73, 189–90
Role of the 21–22, 47–48, 73, 91, 99, 106–7, 137–38, 167–68, 188–89
Statistics
Interpretation of 74–75, 78–79, 84
Status - *see also* power
And power 29, 120, 122, 155–56, 174–76
Claims and counter-claims to 85–86, 155–56, 174–75
Dual dimension of 174–75
Hierarchies 101–2, 120
Inequality 4–5, 18–19, 23, 25–26, 34, 54, 76, 78–79, 86, 155–56, 174
Relationship to respect 2–3, 11, 13–14, 17, 19–20, 22–23, 25–26, 29, 54, 66, 84–85, 112–13, 117, 122, 130–31, 172, 173–76
Sensitivity 53–54
Subordination 54, 155–56
Stop and search
Abolition 69, 85, 89–90, 91

As a discredited tactic 85
Code of Conduct 91
Cultural bias 78
Disproportionate and discriminatory use of 68–69, 70, 71–79, 80, 172
Erosion of police legitimacy 68–69, 70, 79–81
Extra-legal practices 72–73
Instrumental outcomes 68–69, 71–73, 81, 83–84, 89, 91, 93
Interpretation by the judiciary 75–77, 172–73
Invasion of privacy 68–69, 70, 81–83
Legal regulation of 69, 85, 87–89, 91–92, 187–88
'Legitimating fictions' of 71–72
Nature of search 81–82, 191
Procedural justice training for 69, 85–87
Strategic use of 91
Violation of bodily integrity 68–69, 70, 81–83

Tankebe, Justice 14, 52–53, 60–61
Time 149–51
Distorted sense of 149
'Total speech situation' 59
Trust in institutions 48–49, 51, 65–66, 80, 83, 109–10, 181
Decline in 144–45
Trustworthiness
Of institutions 51–52, 56–57
Tyler, Tom R 43, 48–50, 51–52, 53, 59, 60, 64, 65–66, 79–81, 83, 181

Utilitarianism 178–79, 182
In stop and search 75–76
Utopian thought - *see* normative theory; criminal justice, *'utopian critique' of*

Vagrancy Act 1824 73
Value pluralism - *see* values, *balancing of*
Values
At the individual and institutional level 177–78
Balancing of 31–32, 40, 170–74
Distinguishing, the task of 2–3, 19–23, 116, 169, 178–79, 184–86, 192
In prisons 98–99, 101, 108–9, 111, 114–16, 128–31, 133, 143, 150, 163–64
Of procedural justice 43, 45–46
Quantification of 116, 118–19

Welfare
As a subsidiary concern in prisons 118
Of prisoners 146, 148, 191
Women
As subjects of stop and search 78–79
Incarceration of 110–11, 112, 113–14, 133–34, 136–37, 140–41, 153, 154–56
Resisting institutional control 112, 113–14
Women's Policy Framework 140–41
Woolf Report, The
Prisons after *Woolf* 126–31
Strangeways prison riot 103–4

Zedner, Lucia 6, 12, 33, 40, 46–48, 67, 111–12, 136–37, 176, 179, 188–89
Zimmerman, Michael J 26–27, 31

Printed and bound by CPI Group (UK) Ltd, Croydon, CR0 4YY